Violent Persuasions

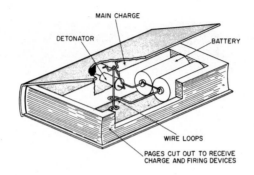

MAIN CHARGE

DETONATOR

BATTERY

WIRE LOOPS

PAGES CUT OUT TO RECEIVE
CHARGE AND FIRING DEVICES

c. The British also had a book boobytrap; but it was slightly
more complicated than the Soviet version, above.

Bay Press
115 West Denny Way
Seattle, Washington 98119

Designed by Philip Kovacevich
Set in Garamond #3, MetaFont, and Letter Gothic
Printed by Malloy Lithographing, Ann Arbor, Michigan

Library of Congress Cataloging-in-Publication Data
Violent Persuasions ; the politics and imagery of terrorism / edited by David J.
Brown and Robert Merrill.
p. cm.
ISBN 0-941920-25-9 (soft) : $18.95
1. Terrorism—Congresses. I. Brown, David J. II. Merrill, Robert. III. Title:
Politics and imagery of terrorism.
HV6430.V56 1993
303.6'25—dc20   93-26066
                                  CIP

Violent Persuasions:

The Politics and Imagery of Terrorism

Edited by

David J. Brown

Robert Merrill

BAY PRESS
SEATTLE

Contents

This book is dedicated to the memory of Gretchen Dater and Louise Ann Rogers, two students at the Maryland Institute, College of Art who lost their lives in the tragic crash of Pan Am Flight 103 over Lockerbie, Scotland; to all victims of political violence; and to the people and organizations whose struggle for truth, justice, and the well-being of all humans continues to be the only real solution to the crisis of violent persuasions.

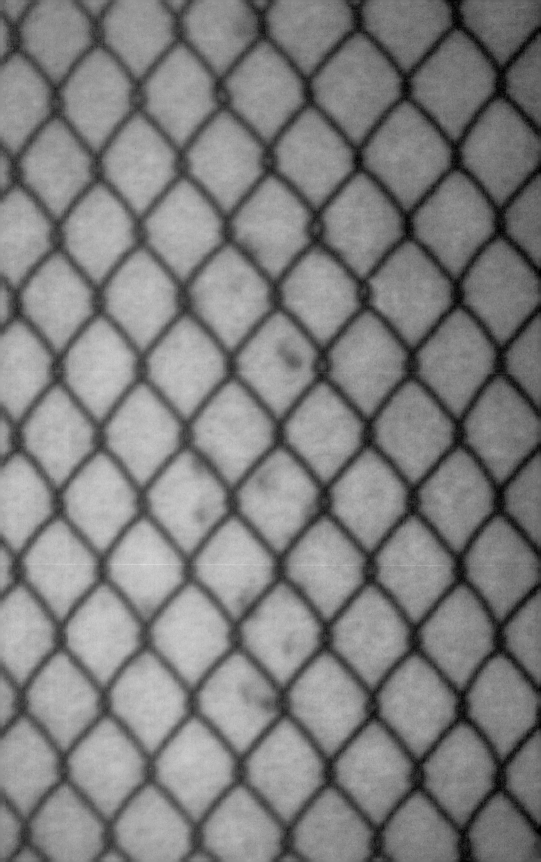

Preface and Acknowledgments

The term "terrorism" is widely misunderstood but nevertheless used. The images and texts in this book were the result of an exhibition at the Maryland Institute, College of Art in Baltimore called *Beyond Glory: Re-Presenting Terrorism*, co-curated by David J. Brown and Nina Felshin. The paintings, prints, sculptures, photographs, installations, films, and videos were exhibited from January to March of 1992. The exhibition was accompanied by a symposium, *The Politics and Imagery of Terrorism*, organized by David J. Brown, Robert Merrill, Mark Neustadt, and Lenora Foerstel. The unique twofold event posed some interesting questions: besides the obvious "what is terrorism and how does it affect us," we also considered other questions that had to do with the way terrorism is known. What if the iconic images of terrorism were suddenly not so easy to recognize; what if the categories and concepts taken for granted were somehow blurred? Would our understanding of terrorism still come out the same?

We sought to redefine terrorism in two ways: first, by re-presenting it in images other than those of the mainstream culture; and second, by investigating the reasons for its misrepresentation in popular culture. During the exhibition, visitors moved through chain-link-fenced rooms, camouflaged walls, and through plywood hallways where they were constantly monitored by surveillance cameras used in installations and placed strategically throughout the galleries. The exhibition featured the work of thirty-nine artists, and in the symposium thirteen scholars, authors, and artists discussed "other" images and "counter" arguments. Many of the works in the exhibition are included here in *Violent Persuasions* along with the symposium presentations. In order to keep the discussion current and to provide detail not possible in a symposium format, some of the texts published here have been revised and expanded. The volume concludes with Nina Felshin's extension of the theme of "re-presenting" terrorism to include artists not exhibited at *Beyond Glory* but whose concern is for what might be called the terrorism of everyday life.

The exhibition and symposium—and thus this book—became a reality with the gracious help of many people. Special appreciation and gratitude go to Nina Felshin, co-curator, for her research and devotion to the exhibition. She deserves credit for helping to focus the ideas and themes. Thanks to Maurice Berger for his essay and enthusiasm from the very start. Special thanks are also due to Fred Lazarus, President of the Maryland Institute, Barbara Price-Campolattaro, Vice-President and Dean of Academic Affairs, and Leslie King-Hammond, Dean of Graduate Studies. The Exhibitions Committee, Philip Koch, Ron Lang, Will Larson, Suzanne Garrigues, Art Benson, Howie Weiss, Libble Nead, Christine Neill, and Paul Kohl, provided hardy support, and thanks to the Symposium Committee, Lenora Foerstel and Mark Neustadt. Additional thanks go to Mark and his staff (Anita Klein and Mary Rayme) for symposium preparations and related headaches in scheduling. Doug Frost and Deborah Plutzik Briggs provided crucial help in grant research. Debra Rubino, Abegail Lattes, Brenda McElveen, and Laurel Durenberger worked tirelessly to being the exhibition and symposium to the attention of the media.

Our deepest respect goes to Kelly Shay, she of the cheerful attitude, for personally juggling the barrage of requests that were so administratively demanding, and Jerry Romanow whose leadership ensured proper installation and transportation of most of the works. We join him in applauding the contribution of students: Drew Schultz, Greg Clayton, Karl Franke, Anna Sobaski, Sarah Singh, Bonnie Lee Speigner, Ray Stein, Leah Taylor, and Amelia Young without whose help the vast scope of this project could not have been realized; David Bakker for his training manuals; Steve Ham, Jim Skipper, and Eric Cummings for video and audio recordings. Others who offered help and support unselfishly include Joe Lewis, Doug Ashford, Jo Tartt, Halley Harrisburg, Philip Brookman, Marilyn Zeitlin, Lynn McCary, Wendy Olsoff, Krystyna, Gravity, and AHC. Our thanks go to all these and to the participants of the symposium for their dedication to truth and justice.

The exhibition and symposium were supported in part by grants from the National Endowment for the Arts, the Amalie Rothschild Residency Program, the Rouse Company Program, and the Maryland State Arts Council. We are grateful for this support.

Foreword: Difficult Religion

David J. Brown

We bear witness to incredible times. With the push of a button, the flick of a switch, or the simple purchase of a magazine, millions of words and images become available to us. Japanese engineers have introduced a working motor that is only a fraction of an inch in length. A moral debate continues over the recent discovery of a DNA identification technique (more accurate than fingerprinting) and how it might be used to track individuals. Revolving satellites recognize objects on the earth's surface only a few meters in size. Information retrieval and processing provide us with up-to-the-second observation of worldly activities. We see the social, political, and cultural identities of many countries thrust into consciousness by full-page media coverage, overturning the protection of personal liberties while celebrating hands joined in independence. Some factors that have contributed to these events include the rising demand for nationalistic recognition, the decline of Soviet influence worldwide, the "official" end of the cold war, and the United States' assertion of the New World Order. The concept of democracy assumes the political equality of all individuals, including the rights to privacy, freedom, and the ability to petition authority for redress of grievances. There are, however, few places in the world where individuals enjoy such freedoms.

Edward Bernays, considered the father of public relations, stated that the great expansion in the twentieth century would be not outward but inward toward the human spirit and mind. We are way beyond Foucault, who marvelled at Jeremy Bentham's "Panopticon."[1] We now have the technology to penetrate, objectify, and discipline people on a truly mass scale. Bentham's crude nineteenth-century device was nonetheless a scientific and humanistic way of seeing, for man was still at the center of the panoptic structure. Man was looking at man. The "knowing eyes" of postmodern technology assume the perspective of God as a peeping tom.

As members of the world, we are born into a "difficult religion"—not in the spiritual sense of the word, but in the metaphori-
cal, describing the shaping of our identity by class and culture and
recognizing our inability as individuals to control or change our
circumstances. Mechanisms of power and systems of belief exist
which can prevent movement within these spheres, potentially
adding fuel to the fire of frustration for those of us seeking to initiate
those changes. This frustration can lead to the use of violence, seen
by many in our society as a viable solution to any problem. It can
certainly be argued that America has a preoccupation with violence.
It is abhorred by all of us, but we cannot seem to rid ourselves of its
twisted presence. But maybe we don't want to. Consider this: each
weekend 750,000 Americans participate in the game of "paintball."
Dressing "down" in battle fatigues, participants hunt another team's
members with guns that fire small pellets of paint to register a "hit."[2]
Weapons used in Operation Desert Storm were displayed on the mall
in Washington, D.C., which led to immense traffic jams for blocks
surrounding the immediate area. The Lockheed Missile and Space
Company advertised in the *Washington Post* its "Theater High-
Altitude Area Defense System," with an "onboard seeker" that "will
pinpoint the target for a kinetic kill."[3] In Independence, Missouri,
plans exist for American Park, an entertainment complex including a
museum, hotel, and shopping center featuring as a theme the
"Bomb" and its consequences.[4]

As Americans, we are fortunate to live in a country where the
Constitution insists that the multiple voices of the people be heard.
Yet a government ostensibly "of the people, by the people, and for
the people" continues to discourage the participation of the many.
Variances in opinion get brushed aside or diffused with sloganeering
and labeling. The level of intolerance has reached the upper register.
What could be more un-American or un-patriotic? It would seem
that the masses are best left in a naive state, for the political awaken-
ing of American society would create a "crisis of democracy." In *The
Culture of Terrorism*, Noam Chomsky mentions that Western leaders
would rather have the population in this passive, apathetic state.
"This is necessary if 'democracy' is to survive in the Orwellian sense
of proper discourse, where the term refers to the unhampered rule by
business-based sectors, a system of elite decisions with periodic

ratification, but, critically, no significant public role in the formation of state policy."[5]

The emphasis on social and political dis/content continues to be addressed by an ever-increasing number of artists who suggest that new realities must be faced and new solutions sought. An environment of neglect continues to breed a skewed reality. Art has always mirrored the realities of the world's mind and acted as a springboard to leave it, asking those of us who listen to seek those new solutions and redefine the boundaries of our existence. The artists in *Beyond Glory: Re-Presenting Terrorism* continue in this tradition. The works, some of which are reproduced here, are intended to critically explore the mis/understanding of terrorism and the widespread use of violence and other repressive means for political ends. The essays examine case histories of terrorism and the media's mis/representation of these activities.

While no definition of terrorism can be agreed upon by theorists (sometimes referred to as terrorologists), doesn't each of us harbor a firm conception of just what it is? Terrorism, as this book reveals, has many guises and forms, including repression, deception, racism, sexual exploitation, regulation, control of information, surveillance, the invasion of privacy, suspension of personal liberties, and the corruption of ideals—to name a few. In the installation *T/error*, Terry Berkowitz explores the notion of which came first: state terror and repression or the individual unlawful acts condemned by the world as "terrorism." She uses scattered debris, multi-channelled bilingual audio tracks, surveillance cameras, and video to achieve this effect. The room-sized three-dimensional rotating sculpture by Greg Barsamian, entitled *Putti*, uses motorized components and a programmable strobe light to transform a flying angel into a whirling helicopter and back again repeatedly, paying visual homage to Muybridge while toying with our notions of perception. Daniel Martinez's *Ignore Dominant Culture* is further evidence of his in-your-face-straight-ahead approach to social and political commentary. Northern Ireland artist Rita Duffy sarcastically captures the problems on her turf in *Freestate General* and *Off to War*. Martin Doblemeier's film *Grounds for Peace* chronicles the attempts of the Corrymeela community (also in Northern Ireland) toward peace by bringing together both Catholic and Protestant youth. Shu Lea Cheang coordinates videos from various groups in Korea, the Philippines, and Taiwan to tell their stories. Gregory Green's *Assault* uses twelve saw blades and working motors (the bottom four lifting the supporting base off the ground) to engage our imaginations in the possibilities of torture. Mary Lum's beautiful group of small drawings from the series *Accidents Happen* and *Historical Present* uses found images and texts in a process of "remembering" and "rediscovering."

Surrounded by all of these difficult images, Edward Herman extends his analysis of state terrorism to think tanks or para-academic institutions which give legitimacy to myths of terrorism. Ward Churchill, Native American and leader of the Colorado chapter of the American Indian Movement, and Angela Sanbrano, the Executive Director of the Citizens in Solidarity with the People of El Salvador, both proclaim that the FBI labelled their organizations as sponsors of terrorism. This sampling only begins to reflect the diversity of the exhibition and symposium. Only by firmly facing our reflections and understanding our culpability can the dialogue necessary for addressing our problems begin. It is our hope that you find out for yourself.

Part I:

Terrorism and the
Pleasures of Power

Visual Terrorism

Maurice Berger

. . . It is not I who seek it out . . . it is this element which rises from the scene, shoots out like an arrow, and pierces me. A Latin word exists to designate this wound, this prick, this mark made by a pointed instrument: the word suits me all the better in that it also refers to the notion of punctuation, and because the photographs I am speaking of are in effect punctuated, sometimes even speckled with these sensitive points; precisely, these marks, these wounds are so many points. This second element . . . I shall therefore call the *punctum*; for *punctum* is also: sting, speck, cut, little hole—and also a cast of the dice. The photograph's punctum is that accident which pricks me (but also bruises me, is poignant to me).

Roland Barthes, *Camera Lucida* (1981)

OPPOSITE
Terry Berkowitz
T/error, 1992
Room-sized
installation in
the Decker
Gallery, Maryland
Institute,
College of Art,
debris, video
cameras, TV
monitors, four
channels of
separate
audio texts.
Courtesy of
the artist.

Frantz Fanon argued in *The Wretched of the Earth*, his influential treatise on the status of colonialized peoples, that the social and cultural disposition of oppressed peoples might be changed most effectively through emancipating acts of violence. Fanon reasoned that the colonized subject could be liberated through instances of violence that both established personhood itself and created a new social order. Thus the author believed that violence could offer subjugated peoples a form of catharsis as it allowed them to realize their own power: "Violence alone, violence committed by the people, violence educated and organized by its leaders makes it possible for the masses to understand social truths and gives the key to them," observed Fanon. "At the level of individuals violence is a cleansing force, [it] frees the native from his inferiority complex and from his despair and inaction; it makes him fearless and restores his self respect."[1]

Fanon's ideas on the liberatory nature of political violence, shaped during his tenure as a psychiatrist in Algeria during the FLN uprising in the mid-1950s, have subsequently influenced many discourses on revolution. The intellectual, emotional, and moral complexity of Fanon's understanding of "violence," however, rarely informs the thinking of Western governments, news organizations, and universities—institutions governed by a codified "discourse of terrorism" that sees no moral justification for political violence. Ironically, while "counterterrorist" forces combat the threat of Terrorism (as if "terrorism" were one thing instead of a complex of possibilities), their vigilance can be equally virulent. In our own country, we need only think of the scourge of McCarthyism in the 1950s or the disruptive surveillance of the civil rights and antiwar movements in the 1960s and 1970s to understand the deadly effects of government-sanctioned intimidation.[2]

Despite attempts by the academic and political establishment to produce a coherent definition of terrorism, prevailing public attitudes toward political violence often vary. The social conditions that precipitate the terrorist act, for example, have often swayed popular opinion: deadly violence against states perceived as "democratic" may be less acceptable, say, than the violent rebellion of colonized or oppressed peoples in nations where free expression and dissent are prohibited. If autocratic regimes are also practicing genocide, the moral imperatives shift once again, as violent uprisings against state-sponsored murder may well be seen as liberatory rather than regressive. The intended (or even accidental) victims of the attack may also alter public opinion: the murder of an "innocent" child would most probably elicit outrage, that of a despotic politician, a sense of relief.

Ultimately, the most vexing issues surrounding the morality of terrorism center less on its political goals (e.g., the emancipation of oppressed peoples, the end of colonial rule, the collapse of an authoritarian regime, the survival of people marked for destruction) and more on its means—the strategies, conditions, and losses associated with violent political behavior.[3] Because almost all violent acts result in cruel and inhuman consequences, there exists an overarching moral imperative that mitigates against physical terrorism as a form of political speech. And in many instances of political violence, the

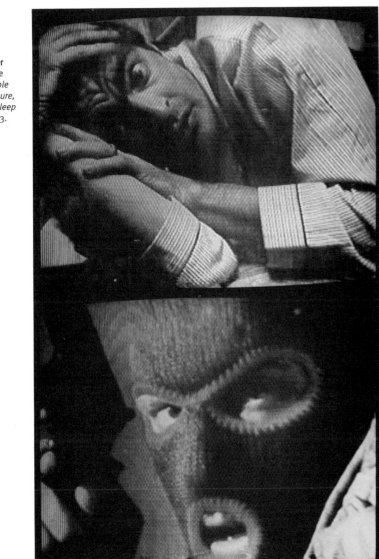

Martha Rosler stills from the video *A Simple Case for Torture, or, How to Sleep at Night*, 1983.

FRICTION
FUZE

EXPLOSIVE
LIQUID

From *Boobytraps*, a U.S. Department of the Army Training Manual from 1966 which outlines various explosive devices.

immediate victims are not directly responsible for the perceived injustices that are being avenged. These consequences lead one to ask whether terrorism must inflict physical devastation in order to achieve its ends or whether it might be possible in certain cases for "violence" to function through nonlethal, noninjuring symbolic gestures or representations. In other words, could an effective *visual* terrorism be constructed that elides the corporeal body, that spares physical victims?

The central question concerning the political effectiveness of terrorism hinges on the issue of representation itself, for such violent acts rely on the media, and its concomitant dissemination of information, to reach and ultimately manipulate the public. The literal goal of the terrorist is to produce not physical trauma but emotional trauma, to effectively "polarize the political attitudes of citizens regardless of personal threat."[4] Terrorism desires "to break the spirit of the opposition," writes Roland Gaucher. "A minister is assassinated; his successor takes warning. A policeman is killed; ten others tremble.... Terrorism seeks, above all, to create a sensation—within the ranks of the enemy, in the public opinion, and abroad."[5] Thus terrorism, whether it is perpetrated by or against the state, abhors neutrality; its *raison d'être* is to create conflict. Not the result of literally witnessing the actual violent act, the public's discomfort usually arises from its contact with media *re*-presentations of disruption, destruction, injury, and death. Terrorism, in other words, operates most effectively as a form of represented images and sounds:

Terrorist attacks are often choreographed to attract the attention of the electronic media and the international press. Taking and holding hostages increases the drama. If certain demands are not satisfied, the hostages may be killed. The hostages themselves mean nothing to the terrorists. Terrorism is aimed at the people watching, not the actual victims. Terrorism is theater. [6]

Depictions of terrorist devastation—through journalistic photographs, television news reports, and even in artistic or cinematic

20

recreations—are profoundly powerful. These images represent an important site for generating the fundamental political conflicts necessary to polarize and move the public. Within such visual representations, independent of the corporeal fact of the terrorist act, are contained that moment of extreme pain, that point of shock that arouses revulsion, the extreme example of that visual pin-prick Roland Barthes called the *punctum*. Glancing at a photograph of a child's corpse lying on the torn-up pavement of a Nicaraguan street, for example, Barthes isolates a mesmerizing detail of tragedy: "the corpse's one bare foot" as it pokes out from under a concealing white sheet.[7]

Such images, of course, often have a paradoxical effect: confronted with the reality of willful destruction and murder, the public often comes to fear or reject the political causes represented through violent acts. Yet such representations are always, in one sense or another, persuasive; they can help justify government-sponsored counterterrorist campaigns or move a people toward political change. The catalytic effect of disturbing imagery was dramatically evident in the Vietnam period. Public opinion began to turn against the war only after newspaper and television cameras began to focus on the bloody limbs, mutilated corpses, and maimed bodies that littered the killing fields of Southeast Asia. The effectiveness of these images was further intensified by the political context provided them by the antiwar movement. Until the fervor of this movement led to their rediscovery or recontextualization, such depictions, in fact, were relatively underrepresented in the media, presumably because they revealed too graphically the ugly side of the human spirit.[8]

The manipulative potential of visually terrifying imagery most often hinges on its ability to produce a form of trauma, to momentarily arrest speech through shock. Thierry de Duve, in an analysis of the unstaged snapshot (the material through which the media most often recapitulates the site of terrorism), for example, ascribes a "trauma effect" to the snapshot's instantaneous recording of an event. A special connection, he argues, exists between the snapshot and the temporal action it registers. Fundamentally, the camera collapses time, allowing an instant to represent an incident. Unlike the time-exposed, contrived photographic portrait, still life, or landscape, images that appeal to memory, history, cultural convention, and language itself, the snapshot, with its prerequisites of instantaneity, sharpness, and precision, initially inhibits speech:

Language fails to operate in front of the pinpointed
space of the photograph, and the onlooker is left momentarily aphasic. Speech, in turn, is reduced to the
sharpness of a hiccup. It is left unmoored, or better,
suspended between two moorings that are equally refused.
Either it grasps at the imaginary by connecting the
referential series, in order to develop the *formerly* into
a plausible chronology, only to realize that this attempt
will never leave the realm of fiction. Or it grasps at the
symbolic by connecting to the superficial series, in order
to construct upon the *here* a plausible scenography; and
in this case also the attempt is structurally doomed.
Such a shock, such a breakdown in the symbolic function,
such a failure of any secondary process—as Freud puts it—
bears a name. It is trauma.[9]

The breakdown in the symbolic function, the trauma induced by the snapshot (or its projection onto the television screen), is dependent not so much on the photo's content but on its representational structure. While certain photographs are incontestably traumatic—scenes of mutilation, death, or violence, for example—the trauma effect ultimately resides in the image's temporal disposition and the concomitant frustration of the viewer's sense of control. For example, de Duve recalls a famous (and politically effective) photograph from the Vietnam war in which a Saigon police chief executes a Vietcong soldier with a pistol shot in the head. The image's traumatic quality, de Duve argues, is generated not by the graphic depiction of the atrocities of war and assassination *per se*, but by the "paradoxical conjunction of the here and the formerly." In other words, the viewer will always be too late, in real life, to witness or prevent the death of the man and too early to see the actual events of this tragedy, "which at the surface of the photograph will never occur." Rather than the tragic content of the photograph, "even enhanced by the knowledge that it has really happened," concludes de Duve, "it is the sudden vanishing of the present tense, splitting into the contradiction of being simultaneously too late and too early, that is properly unbearable."[10]

Mel Chin
Jilavia Prison Bed
for Father Gheorghe
Calciu-Dumitreasa
1982
steel, cotton
70"x40"x36"
courtesy of the
Frumkin-Adams
Gallery, New York.

CANVAS

Thus, the contradiction of being simultaneously too late and too early and the resultant denial of speech can empower the image. Fixed in our minds is a visual catalog of such galvanizing moments: the corpses of passengers and the wreckage of Pan Am Flight 103 strewn on the charred ground of Lockerbie, Scotland; the soot-covered, horror-stricken faces of workers escaping the bombed World Trade Center towers in New York; the bullet-riddled teenager sprawled on a gravel-covered road in Northern Ireland. Their gruesomeness intensifying the snapshot's already innate traumatism, these instantaneous scenes of devastation render the viewer both speechless and helpless; they tempt an acceptance of the terrorist's demands—whether they be the end of colonial rule, the release of prisoners, or the obedient acceptance of the rules of the state—if only to diminish the climate of fear, the trauma that robs people of their sense of center.[11]

The fundamentally *visual*, representational channel of terrorist intimidation begs the central question posed at the outset of this essay: can such acts function without destruction, physical injury, and death? Indeed, the conditions that contribute to the "success" of the terrorist attack— fear, polarization, disorientation—can also be provoked by certain types of political speech, gestures, and visual representation. In this sense, the producers of our visual culture can play a significant role as political provocateurs through the production of socially conscious representations or protest and guerilla actions. Over the past few decades, artists and filmmakers have insightfully explored the emotional and intellectual economy of terrorism and counterterrorism as well as the oppression that engenders political violence—an observation supported by the work included in the recent Maryland Institute, College of Art exhibition *Beyond Glory: Re-Presenting Terrorism*. The most moving art objects in the exhibition critically represent bodies assaulted by terrorism and the various physical and intellectual instruments of political oppression. Such works—Leon Golub's *Mercenaries I* (1976), Pat Ward

Williams's *Day of the Dead—Little Angels* (1989), Alan Belcher's *Guns* (1988), Luis Cruz Azaceta's *Latin American Victims of Dictators* (1987), Mel Chin's *Jilavia Prison Bed* (1982), and Alison Saar's *Briar Patch* (1988)—build disturbing phenomenological relationships between the viewer's body and those of the victims of political assault. These works engender in the spectator a powerful sense of empathy and discomfort. Even more effective examples of cultural analysis occurred in the exhibition's video and film program—works that, for the most part, directly examined the ideology and political strategies of counterterrorism: Nina Rosenblum's documentary *Through the Wire* (1990), for example, investigates the extraordinary extent to which federal counterterrorist forces illegally incarcerated and demoralized radical leftist women; Martha Rosler's video *A Simple Case for Torture* (1983) explores the use of physical coercion to stifle dissent; and Chris Bratton and Annie Goldson's video *Framing the Panthers in Black and White* (from the *Counterterror* series, 1991) examines the destructive, even deadly consequences of government-sponsored counterterrorist operations against dissident groups in the United States.

Because high culture functions within a relatively limited sphere of influence, dependent as it is on the interests of its mostly upper-class patrons, other cultural figures have chosen more direct forms of cultural activism. Ultimately, it is through their actions that the possibility of a truly visual terrorism appears most viable. Ernst Friedrich, in his pioneering transnational publication *War against War* (*Krieg dem Krieg*, 1924), was one of the first to demonstrate how images, in their ability to produce trauma, could shock the public into political action. While Friedrich's compendium of photographs of horrifically disfigured faces of soldiers, maimed bodies, and violated and emaciated corpses did not prevent the outbreak of another world war, they served as a paradigm of visual guerilla tactics. Nearly half a century later, a brutal poster by the Art Workers' Coalition functioned as a dramatic backdrop for the antiwar movement in New York. As its central traumatizing device, *And Babies?/And Babies* (1970) employed a large-format color photograph of the blood-soaked corpses of the infant, female, and elderly victims of the infamous My Lai massacre in 1968. Over the past five years, the activist group ACT UP (the AIDS Coalition to Unleash Power) has utilized a number of theatrical, decentering tactics in an attempt to intimidate companies and institutions that continue to ignore or underestimate the tragedy of AIDS. Several years ago, a flurry of bookings, followed by mass cancellations, nearly bankrupted a major American airline. The carrier ultimately changed its discriminatory policy on passengers with AIDS. Other companies watched helplessly as their fax machines or phone systems were immobilized by AIDS activists protesting profiteering on AIDS drugs. More recently, Gran Fury, WAC (the Woman's Action Coalition), and other activist, culture-oriented coalitions have distributed graphic, often disturbing posters and statistical lists in an effort to disrupt the public's complacent assumptions about the continued oppression of gay men and lesbians, women, and people of color.

While there are no doubt many instances of political oppression that such forms of provocation cannot even begin to redress, it is important to consider the power of visual representation. The fearful, even hysterical response of the right-wing proponents of cultural censorship in America today attests to the innately threatening nature of certain images. While sticks and stones, bombs and bullets, can kill, maim, imprison, and even liberate, so might words and visual depictions. The decentering trauma that some of these representations and actions ultimately cause, independent or not of the injured or dead body, can itself function as an important political tool, a means of "violent" persuasion, at a time when the world continues to be plagued by the kinds of despair and inaction that provoked Fanon to embrace political violence in the first place.

Simulations and Terrors of Our Time

Robert Merrill

> We have about 50% of the world's wealth, but only 6.3% of
> its population. . . . In this situation, we cannot fail
> to be the object of envy and resentment. Our real task in
> the coming period is to devise a pattern of relationships
> which will permit us to maintain this position of dispar-
> ity without positive detriment to our national security.
> To do so, we will have to dispense with all sentimental-
> ity and day-dreaming; and our attention will have to be
> concentrated everywhere on our immediate national objec-
> tives. We need not deceive ourselves that we can afford
> the luxury of altruism and world benefaction. We should
> cease to talk about vague and . . . unreal objectives
> such as human rights, the raising of living standards,
> and democratization. The day is not far off when we are
> going to have to deal in straight power concepts. The
> less we are then hampered by idealistic slogans, the
> better.
>
> George Kennan, U.S. State Department, 1948

I. Imagining the Terror/The Terror of Imagining

George Kennan's thoughts were not intended for public consumption. In fact, such reports produced by the State Department's Policy
Planning Staff or the National Security Council on ways to deal with
the post-World War II decolonization of the Third World remain
within the purview of a secret government inside of or concealed
beneath the monumental government represented by the image of
the president and the "democratic" process. It is not that they are all
classified; it is rather that something else fills the imaginations of
typical Americans. Even though themes like "Kick their ass and steal
their gas" dominated right-wing talk radio during the Gulf war,
there never developed any public debate about U.S. foreign policy

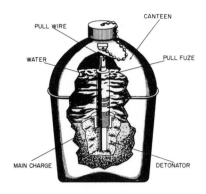

PULL WIRE

CANTEEN

WATER

PULL FUZE

MAIN CHARGE

DETONATOR

that took this bumper-sticker sloganeering right to its political foundations. Something else filled the pages of America's newspapers and journals or the radio and TV airwaves. In spite of what people seem to know, "straight power concepts" (or George Bush's "invincible force") are never the image of the U.S. government in its relations with the post-colonial world. Rather, the United States is more often imagined as severely disadvantaged by its democratic ideals and the deep benevolence of the American people when confronting towering "madmen" like Saddam Hussein, Ayatollah Khomeini, Abu Nidal, Muammar el-Qaddafi, and all the terrorist "icons" who, if we believe government spokespersons, are virtually holding the whole world hostage.

According to government and think-tank experts, the United States alone among nations of the world bears a special vulnerability to terrorism because of, to cite Robert Kupperman's *Final Warning: Averting Disaster in the New Age of Terrorism*, "who and what we are: an open society with an unfettered media." This analysis relies upon an understanding of terrorism more as spectacle or simulacrum than as a real event: "Terrorists rely on the reach of modern telecommunications to create a horrifying spectacle for an international audience, both to bolster their own perceived prowess and to make the victim government appear weak and incompetent."[1] The victim government is always the United States or its close allies. Kupperman does not mention the actual victims themselves because the kind of terrorism he is interested in at the Center for Strategic and International Studies concerns power relations between governments or social positioning. Terrorism is the way governments or insurrectionary groups send "messages" to each other.

This view is confirmed by a joint FBI/CIA report on terrorism which concludes, "The infrastructure of the United States, like that of its allies, is essentially open to terrorist attack; we continue to live as though we dwelled in the post-World War II world in which the United States is the undisputed master of all before it, a time in which no one would even dream of striking a major blow at our very

28

core."[2] In fact, the present infrastructure is nothing like it was in the 1950s, unless, of course, one means simply the images used to represent the nation: the family, the workplace, the soldier, etc. The appeal is to the image of the father in 1950s style sit-coms like *Father Knows Best*. This nostalgia is not simply idiocy; it represents a deep and almost always violent—pathological, that is—determination to return to a former state of being. In the face of global decolonization and a shrinking U.S. economy, America appears as an abused and humiliated father, only a shadow of his past glory. Kupperman's chapter on the media's complicity with international terrorism is called "Lights, Camera, Humiliation!" Reagan himself often seemed to embody that vulnerable father of the 1980s: the poorly informed, hen-pecked (by feminists), often confused old man obsessed with creating an image of strength and making the world respect him. If it took the death of 40,000 Nicaraguans, he was determined to make the upstart Daniel Ortega cry "uncle."

If it seems strange that so much of what is produced as "intelligence" by the CIA, FBI, NSC, other governmental agencies, and private research institutions is inordinately concerned with images, both of "America the vulnerable" and the terrorist monsters, we should be aware that the issue is not real occurrences of violence directed against civilians, as the contributors to this volume and the exhibition/symposium on *The Politics and Imagery of Terrorism* show, since violence against civilians is overwhelmingly committed by governments attempting to suppress liberation movements. Rather the issue for the power elite in the United States is the construction of what Cornelius Castoriadis has called the "radical imaginary." In *The Imaginary Institution of Society*, Castoriadis argues that no separation exists between the psychological and the social in the sense that the radical imaginary within each individual is the foundation of society.[3] Terrorism is about creating the individual psychological foundations for the kind of society that George Kennan describes in the passage I cited at the outset. Castoriadis uses the term "radical" in its literal Latin meaning, "root or foundation," not the ideological sense of someone who calls for root or foundational changes in political structures. But the relation of the two uses of the term is crucial. Radical political changes can really occur only after radical imaginary changes have occurred. For the power elite in the United States, such changes in the radical imaginary did begin to occur in the 1960s and were a threat to the military-industrial complex. The national security state relies for its legitimation on the intuitive recognition by ordinary people that "it is a dangerous world out there"—a refrain still heard in the Clinton administration (especially from Secretary of Defense Les Aspin and Secretary of State Warren Christopher) in spite of the withdrawal of the Soviet Union from the cold war and the public outcry for attention to domestic issues. I cannot discuss here the extent of the effort during the 1980s to rid America of the images of the 1960s, though it was worth noting that *Newsweek* devoted a special issue to defining the 1960s as a disease, something *Newsweek* thought Americans were finally recovering from.[4] The term "Vietnam Syndrome" denotes this disease-like weakness in the face of enemies, and following the Gulf war, President Bush announced that we had "kicked" the Vietnam syndrome.

Creating images of terrorism, then, is a process of stimulating and feeding the imaginations of Americans with certain kinds of images that will serve as the foundation for a certain kind of social structure and governmental policy. Any observer of public culture in the United States during the last dozen years well understands the complete inundation with scenes of terrorism. In 1987, Vice President George Bush wrote that informing the American people was the cornerstone of U.S. counterterrorism policy:

In February 1986, the Vice President's Task Force on Combatting Terrorism released its public report, which contained a number of policy recommendations. These recommendations became the cornerstone of US counterterrorism policy. One key proposal was to launch a public awareness effort to better inform the American people about the nature of terrorism and the threat it represents to our national security interests and to the freedoms we so deeply cherish.

I strongly favor providing the public with information because it sharpens awareness to the individual agendas of terrorist groups, the role of nations that support their depredations, and the necessity of tailoring multiple strategies to effectively combat this scourge.[5]

What follows Bush's remarks is the *Terrorist Group Profiles*, constructions of images of terrorists, a virtual pantheon of enemies of the Reagan/Bush administration that also just happen to be enemies of continued neocolonialism throughout the world. For those who can get beyond the imagery, who is included and who is excluded tells far more about the ideology of the construction of "terrorism" than it does about violence against innocent civilians. Nowhere does the Bush report mention Jonas Savimbi's UNITA, the contras, the Mujahadeen, Renamo, Pol Pot, Suharto in Indonesia, Mobutu in Zaire, the Israeli government, the Saudi royal family, and many more. The book literally has almost nothing to do with the massive violence and killing that plague the world. It is all a simulacrum.

It is no coincidence that just as the "discourse of terrorism" replaced any sensitivity to the real violence that was killing and torturing millions of people around the world each year, the French sociologist Jean Baudrillard published his famous declaration of hyperreal:

Simulation is no longer that of a territory, a referential being or a substance. It is the generation by models of a real without origin or reality: a hyperreal. The territory no longer precedes the map, nor survives it. Henceforth, it is the map that precedes the territory—*Precession of the Simulacra*—it is the map that engenders the territory.[6]

The study of terrorism takes us into the world of the hyperreal where "real" murder and violence occur on a huge scale but do not register even the slightest notice on the mediascape, public consciousness, or government policy. When the Marines decided they needed a "photo-op," we suddenly saw starving and warring people in Somalia. But even worse starvation and civil war have been occurring all along in the Sudan with no registration on the public consciousness. A careful reading of most terrorism experts shows that what they really mean when they say that Americans are more vulnerable to terrorism is that Americans, especially the government, are more susceptible to being simulated in media. What we look at shapes what we are or will become. For an American to appear in front of the world with a gun to his head turns out to be far more important than millions of

FIRING
DEVICE

people tortured in Brazil under direct supervision of U.S. State Department and Army advisors (see Joan Dassin, ed., *Torture in Brazil*). The U.S. government cannot afford to be represented as weak in the face of insurgency movements in the Third World. As representatives of the chief neocolonialist power behind the violent repressions occurring in the developing world, U.S. government leaders know that in reality they could not win an open war fought against a national liberation movement. Vietnam proved that. So instead, the United States has to take steps in advance to prevent such an occurrence from ever happening again. This is substantially the policy presented in the *National Security Strategy of the United States*, 1993, released by George Bush just before leaving office.[7] There is every indication that President Clinton will pursue the strategy of ensuring that no hostile powers emerge as a threat to U.S. domination. The role of terrorism in all this is to prepare ordinary Americans to support these policies, which in a sober analysis would be quite senseless.

II. The History of a Simulacrum

On January 28, 1981, the day the embassy hostages returned from Iran, Secretary of State Alexander Haig in a news conference announced the intention of the Reagan government to replace the Carter administration's human rights emphasis in U.S. foreign policy with a focus on counterterrorism. His words were "that international terrorism will take the place of human rights." He added that the Soviets "are involved in conscious policies, in programs, if you will, which foster, support and expand this activity."[8] What was wrong with Carter's emphasis on human rights was that it called forth a public discourse, public images, and a cast of players that did not serve the aggressive and militarist desires of the Reagan administration. The nature of the shift can be seen in a major policy address by George Shultz to the Anti-Defamation League on February 12, 1988, near the close of the Reagan administration. His said that he had always regarded Israel as the model for human rights enforcement: "times change and so does the challenge to human rights. . . . In this decade, an important part of the struggle for human rights is the struggle against terrorism. . . . We have to go on the offensive to disrupt terrorist networks, and bring them to justice."[9] In general, during the 1980s and 1990s, policing has been the model solution for all social problems. Two weeks later in East Jerusalem, Shultz turned to the Palestinian question. He did not speak *with* Palestinians, however; he spoke *at* them and *for* them. The opening line of his talk runs thus: "I have a statement for Palestinians." The tone of his "statement" is hostile and cold as he tells the world that Palestinians must negotiate with Israel: "Opportunity knocks loudly on your doors. Now is the time to get to work. We have a workable plan." The plan links the issue of Palestinian self-determination to a comprehensive peace agreement between all the Arab nations and Israel.[10] Unfortunately, the rights Shultz envisions for Palestinians amount to little more than the garrisoned enclaves they now inhabit on the West Bank and Gaza Strip.

The decision to focus on counterterrorism presented real problems for the Reagan administration because CIA annual reports on terrorism had for several years indicated that terrorism was declining from its highpoint in 1975 and that U.S. citizens and property were only rarely the principal targets of terrorism, with the exception of acts by the Ku Klux Klan, Puerto Rican independence groups, and Cuban exiles—none of which served the interests of the administration. Moreover, the CIA's most recent report compiled in 1980 concluded that the terrorism which did exist was the uncoordinated, random, and sporadic outburst of disaffected individuals or small groups like the Red Army Faction in Germany (who in 1979 attempted to blow up Haig's car) or the Red Brigades in Italy. William Casey, Reagan's new CIA Director, ordered that this report be withheld. The challenge for the new Reagan administration was to organize a massive campaign to establish terrorism in the imaginations of Americans as the greatest and most overarching threat to their personal security. In short, the first item on the agenda was to terrorize the imaginations of Americans, and then to call forth an aggressive response to the crisis which would be called a "counterterrorism policy." That this counterterrorism policy would

**Jayce Salloum and
Elia Suleiman**
stills from the
video *Muqaddimah
Li-Nihayat Jidal
Intifada: Speaking
for Oneself . . .
Speaking for
Others . . .*,
1990
courtesy of
the artists.

bring the Reagan government close to outright fascism would go unnoticed because, as Hannah Arendt points out in *The Origins of Totalitarianism*, the ultimate goal of terrorism is to eliminate the capacity of a population to think and act, to paralyze their wills. George Bush's Task Force, cited above, was the concrete product which followed the simulation. Counterterrorism was what the Reagan administration wanted all along, but it needed a pretext for developing such a massive national and international police force and a way of preventing Americans from challenging the policies.

William Casey ordered the routine CIA terrorism report rewritten in order to show an entirely different picture of world terrorism. The *Washington Post*'s Bob Woodward reports that Casey told CIA analysts to "forget this mush" (i.e., the original report) and "read Claire Sterling's book."[11] Sterling had just published *The Terror Network: The Secret War of International Terror*. Casey, according to Woodward, screamed at his analysts, "I paid $13.95 for this and it told me more than you bastards whom I pay $50,000 a year." Bruce Clark, the chief author of the original report, resigned in protest, becoming the first of a series of CIA analysts who would resign rather than put their names to politicized intelligence. Casey found the fabricator he needed in General Eugene Tighe of the Defense Intelligence Agency. A long-time cold warrior, who took it as a matter of faith that the Soviet Union was behind all the evil in the world, Tighe produced the conclusions Casey wanted. A third report, called *Soviet Support for International Terrorism*, was also written by Lincoln Gordon, who used information from the National Security Association (NSA). Gordon concluded that the Soviet Union did support national liberation movements in the Third World, but that there was no evidence to suggest a connection between "pure" terrorism of radical gangs like Baader-Meinhof or Red Army Faction and the Soviet Union. A compromise between the three reports was submitted to the White House on May 27, 1981. It concluded that the Soviet Union was not the master manipulator of international terrorism. That report was classified and remained secret throughout the Reagan years.[12]

While the consensus report was known by top administration officials only, another CIA report entitled *Patterns of International Terror, 1980* was made public on June 1, 1981, after being "leaked"

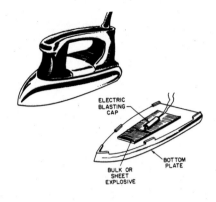

ELECTRIC
BLASTING
CAP

BOTTOM
PLATE

BULK OR
SHEET
EXPLOSIVE

to the press and widely cited. Its thesis that terrorism was an "international network" controlled by the Soviet Union became the accepted theory of "intelligence experts," as they were referred to in the press. Nothing less than a firestorm of terrorism reporting began. *Patterns of International Terror* contained charts showing a dramatic increase in terrorism during the 1970s; Reagan presented these charts in televised news conferences. During the 1980s, literally hundreds of specious reports were released or leaked by the CIA, Pentagon, National Security Council, or State Department. My favorite was a pamphlet prepared by the Defense Department showing satellite photographs of Nicaraguan "war canoes" which were used by Soviet-sponsored Sandinistas to transport weapons across the Gulf of Fonseca to Salvadoran terrorists. It's true, the photographs do show canoes on a beach. But it is not likely that anyone could row a heavily loaded canoe 70 miles across a choppy bay. In all probability, they were just fishing boats. After ten years, there has never been any real evidence to show that the Nicaraguan government supplied weapons to the rebels in El Salvador, but there have been dozens of false revelations.

In the absence of actual proof for Soviet sponsorship, the report relied on the assertion that revolutionary violence is an essential element of Leninist ideology. In this way, virtually every act of violence against capitalist interests in the world could be seen as emanating from the Soviet Union. In a high profile speech in 1985, Reagan proclaimed that Iran, Libya, North Korea, Syria, Cuba, Nicaragua, the IRA, Basque separatists, and virtually every left-wing group were members of a network headed by the Soviet Union: "There is a temptation to see the terrorist act as simply the erratic work of a small group of fanatics. We make this mistake at great peril; for the attacks on America, her citizens, her allies, and other democratic nations in recent years do form a pattern of terrorism that has strategic implications and political goals." He concludes by identifying those goals:

And the strategic purpose behind the terrorism sponsored
by these outlaw states is clear: to disorient the United
States, to disrupt or alter our foreign policy, to sow
discord between ourselves and our allies, to frighten
friendly Third World nations working with us for peaceful
solutions of regional conflicts, and, finally, to remove
American influence from those areas of the world where
we're working to bring stable and democratic government.
In short, to cause us to retreat, retrench, to become
"Fortress America." Yes, their real goal is to expel
America from the world.[13]

The key point about the revised CIA document and its assumption
into Reagan-era doctrine is that it announced in bold print that
"Americans remained the primary targets of international terrorism,
with nearly 2 out of 5 incidents involving US citizens or property."
This simply is not true, unless terrorism can be conflated with all
sorts of criminal activity, especially drug smuggling (which is
primarily aimed at Americans who are willing to pay high prices for
drugs) or all acts of disaffected individuals or groups which employ
violence or destruction of property to gain a hearing from established
authorities, *and* if one lowers the total numbers by discounting all of
the violence committed against people by repressive governments.
This sort of international terrorism would include postal workers who
go berserk and shoot-up their workplaces. It also meant that all wars
of national liberation would be treated as terrorism against the
United States. By definition, the Soviet Union had to be the ultimate
sponsor of terrorism conceived this way since "the Soviets are deeply
engaged in supporting of revolutionary violence, which is a fundamental element of Leninist ideology. Such support frequently entails
acts of international violence. The ostensible position of the Soviet
Union is that they oppose terrorism while supporting national
liberation movements" (*Patterns of International Terror*). Such logic lay
behind the certification by the State Department that Nicaragua was
a terrorist state. To seek national liberation is to be a terrorist, and
U.S. foreign policy from the Casey/Haig period onward has been to
deal with such terrorists by the harshest and most violent means
possible. As Secretary of State George Shultz was fond of saying, it
is not a matter of whether or not we will retaliate, but only when.

The CIA's report began a flurry of activity in Congress and think tanks. On June 26, 1981, three weeks after the CIA report, the Senate held hearings on the subject of "Terrorism: The Role of Moscow and Its Subcontractors" (Senate Committee on the Judiciary, Subcommittee on Security). Articles on terrorism as a network began making the front covers of the national news magazines. *U.S. News and World Report* on May 4, 1981 (the CIA document was officially released on June 1 but was leaked earlier to make it seem classified and shocking), ran an article entitled "Terrorism: Russia's Secret Weapon." The article states that Washington charges that—either directly or through go-betweens—the Kremlin supports some of the world's most vicious guerrillas. Claire Sterling published selections from her book in *Reader's Digest* and also in the *New York Times Magazine*. Daily papers and network news programs were likewise swamped with terrorism stories. A cadre of what soon were called "terrorism experts" began appearing on TV shows like *MacNeil/Lehrer* or *Nightline*. For anyone concerned with the actual plight of victims of terrorism no matter who they are, it is disconcerting to see all of these "terrorism experts" and news programs mindlessly repeating information released or leaked by the government.

I think most of us would regard as instances of genuine terrorism the policies of state repression practiced in such places as Iran under the Shah, El Salvador, Chile, Brazil, and Argentina, Indonesia, Cambodia under the Khmer Rouge, or counterrevolutionary militias such as the Nicaraguan contras, Jonas Savimbi's UNITA in Angola, Renamo in Mozambique, or the Mujahadeen in Afghanistan, but the CIA report rules them out. All of these terrorist campaigns are heavily supported by the U.S. government, so the CIA report simply excludes them, saying, "Most right-wing terrorism falls into the category of domestic violence and is not dealt with in this paper. Right wing terrorism is difficult to categorize and analyze because it is perpetuated anonymously by groups with few or no articulated goals" (p. 10). Those anonymous groups are, of course, the death squads which all the experts pretend to know very little about but which are invariably made up of off-duty police, military personnel, and foreign mercenaries. All of the above-named groups are financed and directed out of Washington. One would think that finding their leaders would not be so hard; Jonas Savimbi was given the royal treatment each time he visited Washington seeking more money and weapons. As Randall Robinson points out in his contribution to this volume, Angola has the highest percentage of amputees of any population in the world. Savimbi, however, is not considered a terrorist. He is just not mentioned at all in official discussions of terrorism. Without any difficulty, any of these terrorist groups could be called "Washington's Sub-contractors," but in the hyperreal world of terrorism they have come to occupy the place of "Freedom Fighters." That is how we are asked to imagine the world.

The CIA report goes on to say that left-wing terrorism can be known by its interest in publicity-seeking. Terrorists, such as Yassir Arafat, are always trying to explain themselves to TV reporters. Death squads in El Salvador, though they may adopt colorful names like "The White Warriors Union," "The White Hand," "The Falange," "The Secret Anti-Communist Army," do not seek TV publicity in the United States. But, citizens of El Salvador are painfully aware of the murders and disappearances of friends and relatives. Americans generally are not sensitized to political murders. What Americans do see incessantly on TV are events like the Hizbullah hijacking of TWA Flight 847, which sat on the runway in Beirut, Lebanon, for seventeen days while the news media showed hooded hijackers holding a pistol to the head of Captain Testrake. And that's the kind of terrorism the CIA is interested in. Think-tank terrorist experts used this photo on the covers of *The Terrorism Reader* and *The Almanac of Modern Terrorism*.[14]

A clear example of this principle is the case of Pol Pot and the Khmer Rouge of Cambodia. The genocide carried out by Pol Pot's government between 1976 and 1979 was brought to the attention of the general public in the film, *The Killing Fields*. But the movie did not reveal who supported them. In 1979 when the Vietnamese overthrew the Khmer Rouge and occupied Cambodia, Pol Pot retreated to the mountains in the west of Cambodia along the border with Thailand to carry out guerilla attacks on Cambodian villages. Pol Pot and the Khmer Rouge have never been classified as terrorists; in fact, they are still recognized by the United States as the legitimate government of Cambodia (this may change as elections take place in Cambodia in May 1993). And since 1985 they have received economic and military support from the United States, some directly,

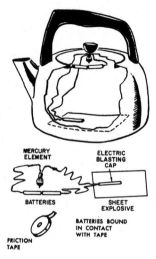

MERCURY
ELEMENT

ELECTRIC
BLASTING
CAP

BATTERIES

SHEET
EXPLOSIVE

BATTERIES BOUND
IN CONTACT
WITH TAPE

FRICTION
TAPE

some through the government of Thailand, and some indirectly through Prince Norodom Sihanouk. Their usefulness lies chiefly in keeping a war against Vietnam going since the Khmer Rouge claim that much of South Vietnam, including Ho Chi Minh City, belongs to Cambodia.

While most of the world believes that Pol Pot should be arrested and tried for crimes against humanity—that is, genocide—the United States has quietly insisted that the Khmer Rouge be included in a three-way power sharing agreement to end the civil war in Cambodia. At the time of this writing, Pol Pot has consistently refused to abide by the UN-negotiated cease-fire. He has refused to give up his weapons, and he continues to attack villages and kill civilians, while the UN busily disarms all other groups. An honest observer might well predict the second coming of Pol Pot and a return to the killing fields. More important for U.S. strategic interests, a return of Pol Pot would almost certainly mean a reopening of the war between Cambodia and Vietnam, just as Vietnam is beginning to develop significant economic relations with Japan, France, and other nations. It does not matter in the imaginary world of U.S. foreign policy that Pol Pot has murdered and terrorized the population of Cambodia for more than fifteen years on a scale that makes most other terrorist incidents seem minuscule. What matters is strategic control of Southeast Asia. In fact, this is the advice now coming from the Rand Corporation's journal, *Studies in Conflict and Terrorism,* in which Harvard Center for International Affairs scholar Kishore Mahbubani chastises the United States for its "morally correct" insistence upon not dealing directly with Pol Pot. Mah-bubani claims that efforts to distance Pol Pot from U.S. policies are only prolonging the agony of the Cambodian people. In order to save the Cambodians from Vietnamese communists, he suggests that the United States stand behind Pol Pot and help him make war on communism. Mahbubani uses the phrase "morally correct" with all the sarcasm we have come to expect in the phrase "politically correct." For Mahbubani, true morality is uninhibited anticommunism.[15]

III. From Politico-Terrorism to Narco-Terrorism: Global Policing

At the outset of this paper, I noted that the hyperreality of terrorism
is a process of stimulating the imaginations of Americans with
certain kinds of images in order to ground a certain kind of social
structure and governmental policy. We are now ready to look more
closely at that social structure. Terrorism evolved through the 1980s
to include "narco-terrorism" and now the "urban terrorism" of gang
and street violence in U.S. cities. "Crips," "Bloods," and all manner of
other "crews" have taken their place alongside of the Red Brigades
and the Abu Nidal Organization. The high profile of violence in the
American consciousness industry—television—runs parallel with the
government's interest in fighting violence. None of it has much to
do with producing a peaceful world; rather, the intent is to create
military and police forces upon which the social order can be based.
Further, it is to create patterns of self-consciousness which amount to
self-policing.

Three things come together at this point: the articulation of a
terrorist network, the creation of a drug/violence crisis on the streets
of America, and the policy of reconquest of the Third World,
particularly Africa, Latin America, and the Middle East. It is no
coincidence that drug smuggling and terrorism are not pointed to in
nations that do not have large and restless revolutionary movements
threatening a pro-U.S. government or in nations like Thailand,
Taiwan, or Turkey where U.S. allegiance is assured. It is similarly no
coincidence that the domestic drug-pusher is always depicted for
popular consumption as Latino or African-American, segments of the
U.S. population most likely to rebel against the oppressive conditions
in their communities, as exemplified by the uprising in Los Angeles
following the acquittal of four L.A. policemen whose savage beating
of a black man was captured on videotape. Government policy under
Reagan, Bush, and now apparently Clinton is about discipline and
policing. In order to ensure consent for the war against self-determination in developing nations, American citizens must adopt the
policing model in their own lives. To do this they must feel the terror
themselves, and drugs provide that experience in a personal way so
that people will beg the government to act decisively and do something against narco-terrorism. The police need a reason to enter the

schools, homes, neighborhoods, bank accounts, cars, workplaces, and even the body itself. Narco-terrorism provides that reason. More than this, the police want you to do this policing to yourself.

If terrorism and narco-terrorism did not already exist, they would have to be invented as a way to teach people to police themselves. From the factual record, there can be no doubt that governmental agencies, particularly the CIA, involve themselves with terrorism and drug traffic as a means of creating political conditions favorable to U.S. interests. Illegal drugs are also one means of raising vast sums of untraceable cash and establishing around the world within developing nations a system of drug-lords who wield great political power and who can be called upon to suppress any stirring of socialist or communist insurrection. Alfred McCoy's *The Politics of Heroin* makes all this very clear, but I think that there is a domestic and psychological effect of increasing the paranoia level of terrorism—and more generally, crime—in the United States that is ultimately more important than foreign repression.

This internal effect is a form of policing the domestic population—what the French social historian Michel Foucault calls "penal mapping of the social body"[16]—which represents an effort on the part of the central government to increase its administrative control. Any crime epidemic provides the pretext for this penal mapping. Foucault's reference is to postrevolutionary and Bonapartist France, but his observations on criminal reforms illuminate, I think very precisely, what we have been seeing under Reagan, Bush, and now Clinton, who so far has shown no inclination to break with the policies of his predecessors in these matters. The point of convergence between nineteenth century France and contemporary America is the preoccupation with the national security state and the desire to wipe out all traces of revolution in the minds of citizens. Foucault writes, "The true objective of the reform movement . . . [was] to set up a new economy of the power to punish, to assure its better distribution . . . so that it should be distributed in homogeneous circuits capable of operating everywhere, in a continuous way, down to the finest grain of the social body" (*Discipline and Punish*, p. 80). Robert Bork was to have been the Supreme Court's chief theorizer of the extension of federal powers, a man whose fundamental opposition to rights of privacy and whose privileging the interests of the state (as in the state has an interest in the lives of children, even unborn children, that supersedes any individual rights) would make legitimate a dramatic increase in state policing of such things as sexual behavior and speech. Bork, of course, was not confirmed, but the process continues nonetheless.

This new interest in punishment is pervasive, from the resurgence of capital punishment to retaliatory strikes against alleged terrorists to federal courts indicting foreign citizens (Manuel Noriega), and it must be read as a strategy for redefining in the public mind the power of the central government as essentially punitive, not liberatory. This is the government's power to make war on its enemies. But who are the enemies of the U.S. government? Clearly, not people like Saddam Hussein, who are tremendously useful in playing out the drama of terror and counterterror. How could the hyperreal world of American politics exist without the likes of Hussein? The enemies are, if we are not afraid to admit it, working people who live in this country and all over the world, people who will have to endure a global lowering of living standards as wealth increasingly accumulates in a few centers around the world. I mentioned a moment ago that the 1993 *National Security Strategy of the United States* calls for preventing potential threats from arising. Lowered living standards in the United States as well as elsewhere are causing exactly such threats, and the way to prevent threats to the national security is to teach people not to rebel, that is, to discipline themselves.

Both crime and the punishment of crime are public spectacles with quasi-religious implications. This point is demonstrated clearly in the popularity of TV crime drama, which is best termed a penal liturgy in which the power of the police is first eclipsed as darkness and crime cover the land, and then restored in the cathartic killing or capturing of the criminal. In America we are in a religious revival right now, and it serves the interests of the police to have this ritual enacted as frequently as possible, whether on television, or in the streets, high schools, and workplaces of America. Everyone must participate and be sacralized. Though I hesitate to take as true anything former-Assistant Secretary of State Elliot Abrams says, his analysis of the convergence of antiterrorism and antidrug policies demonstrates precisely why drugs are an instrument for both foreign

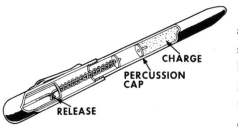

CHARGE
PERCUSSION
CAP
RELEASE

and domestic repression in the same way that terrorism has been. Before discussing Abrams's remarkable paper delivered before the Council on Foreign Relations on February 10, 1986, it is necessary to return to Foucault's analysis of penal mapping. Power penetrates individual consciousnesses when people learn to police themselves in the way the state would if it were standing over them at every moment. The modern problem, according to Foucault, is "to procure for a small number, or even for a single individual, the instantaneous view of a great multitude" (*Discipline and Punish*, p. 216). Now in the late twentieth century that includes maintaining the control of the oil resources in the Middle East, the mineral riches of Africa, and the agricultural wealth of Latin America. Policing in this sense is finally a means of training which is complete when, as Foucault writes, the "disciplinary society . . . stretches from the enclosed disciplines, a sort of social 'quarantine,' to an indefinitely generalizable mechanism of 'panopticism'"—everyone watches everyone else, everyone becomes the police, and "the disciplinary modality of power . . . infiltrates all others . . . serving as an intermediary between them, linking them together, extending them and above all making it possible to bring the effects of power to the most minute and distant elements."

Now to Abrams. His paper is entitled "Drug Wars: The New Alliances Against Traffickers and Terrorists," and it outlines the ways the Reagan government is using the drug crisis both to educate American citizens and to redefine all other governmental agencies on the model of policing. He begins by saying, "The drug problem has long been thought to be a matter for the police or for the local TV news or Friday night melodramas. I want to change that attitude . . . for I believe that few issues we face in the areas of foreign policy and national security have a greater and more immediate relevance . . . than international narcotics." The change Abrams refers to is precisely the change Foucault sees in pre-modern to modern policing, necessitated by the emergence of private individuals, and that is surveillance. People must be trained to watch themselves and each other. Abrams writes, "There has been a dramatic change. There is a bit of the 'narc' in all of us now—from presidents of Latin American democracies, to commanders of U.S. Navy destroyers in the Caribbean, to Assistant Secretaries of State for Inter-American Affairs." Everyone is a narc and everyone is implicated in the government's redistribution of power and its fight against its enemies. Federal agencies are redefined in the movement toward a prison without walls: Abrams again, "I don't know which is more surprising—State Department 'narcs' working closely with Drug Enforcement Administration 'diplomats' or"—and this is crucial—"joint Colombian/ Peruvian military and police anti-drug actions on their common border." This change eliminates the problem of individualism and any concern for privacy rights (such as your bank account or your bodily fluids) in the same way that it eliminates national sovereignty and borders. The reconquest of Third World nations requires, of course, this destruction of national sovereignty, examples of which have occurred in Panama, Iraq, Somalia, and many other places where U.S. or UN forces return nations to the effective status of "trusteeship." In Iraq, the United States has announced its policy of violating Iraqi sovereignty until Saddam Hussein is overthrown, at which time a neocolonialist government can be installed. Abrams concludes his presentation with a call for legalization of military intervention in Latin American nations, ostensibly to combat drugs. One more line from this repugnant man should be enough: "The time has come— now that Latin America is 90% democratic—for our system to recognize that certain legal restrictions which emerged from another era no longer apply across the hemisphere. . . . We must be able to allow our own agencies, civilian and military, to assist the police. And if, in a specific country . . . the military has the mandate, then that is where our aid should be directed."[17]

You learn to police others when you are constantly policed. You become a "narc" when you are subjected to the policies of drug enforcement. We might add to Abrams's list of agencies that have been transformed the Department of Education, whose secretary has several times called for increased drug surveillance in schools, even to the extent of mandatory drug testing for students and faculty. In 1988, Secretary of Transportation James H. Burnley similarly called for random, pre-employment, post-accident, and periodic drug testing for airline pilots and railroad engineers. That pretty much accounts for all of their time. Even when they are not being tested, you can be sure students and transportation workers will be thinking about the test and surveilling themselves whenever they take any sort of chemical into their bodies. What we have now are different minds, different states of consciousness, now grounded in discipline and policing. And most importantly, we have a different relationship between people, one grounded on the model of policing. The same holds true for nations. What we are aiming toward is a period of re-colonization. First the re-colonization of minds and then the re-colonization of the Third World. We are already beginning to see in journals such as *Foreign Affairs* the notion of "failed states"; that is, Third World nations which have had their experiment with self-determination, sovereignty, and democracy and failed in it. Now, it is up to the United States to re-colonize them and re-impose some level of what will be called in the press "civil society." Somalia is only the first example. Paul Johnson makes the secret agenda of counter-terrorism all too painfully clear in the April 18, 1993, issue of the *New York Times Magazine*. His article is called "Colonialism's Back—and Not a Moment Too Soon." His thesis is simply: "Let's face it: Some countries are just not fit to govern themselves."

Terrorism: Misrepresentations of Power

Edward S. Herman

Terrorism is a frightening symbol that brings to mind the image of a bewhiskered and sinister figure carrying a bomb. In earlier years, it used to look like someone from Eastern Europe who was Jewish in appearance; more recently, since the late 1970s, it has a darker complexion, suggesting an Arab. It is a frightening symbol, but it is also a wonderful symbol to mobilize people. In the lingo of media analysis, terrorism is a "snarl" word or a "condensation symbol" that embodies strong negative emotions.

Because of this emotion-laden quality, terrorism is an excellent vehicle for propaganda messages designed to arouse the public and help engineer consent for desired lines of policy. To effectively label one's enemy a terrorist is a vital step in the struggle with that enemy—it is like winning a court victory that identifies your opponent as a criminal.

I. The Uneven Struggle Over Representation

There is, therefore, an ongoing struggle between governments and their enemies and victims over the use of the label "terrorist." The indigenous Indian peasants of Guatemala and the African National Congress (ANC) would have liked to have the governments of Guatemala and South Africa designated as terrorist states in the 1980s. And Martin Luther King, Jr., and the members of the U.S. civil rights movement regarded the FBI as a terrorist organization in the 1960s, with ample justification.[1] But you will look in vain for such labelling in the mainstream U.S. media and scholarship. The struggle over the use of invidious language is an unequal one. The Rand Corporation, Heritage Foundation, and the *New York Times* do not serve the interests of Guatemalan peasants or a Martin Luther King, Jr. They are always talking about terrorism and conducting studies of terrorists, but their use of the word terrorism never includes

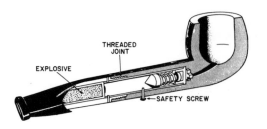

THREADED JOINT

EXPLOSIVE

SAFETY SCREW

the FBI or other agencies and policies of the government. Governments have huge resources and connections that give them a great defamation edge. They are, therefore, usually able to name their enemies and targets of attack as terrorists without much trouble, no matter how absurd the designation. What is more, there is a commonality of interest and powerful linkages among the great powers of the North, so that when upheavals occur in the poorer countries of the South, threatening northern interests, these are easily and quickly portrayed as cases of "terrorism," and the actions of the North and its ruling allies in the Third World are seen as "counterterrorism."[2]

II. The Reagan-Era Representation: Politicization without Limit

In 1981, when Ronald Reagan became President, he quickly latched onto terrorism as a vehicle for gaining public acceptance of his foreign and domestic policies. He declared Libya's President Muammar el-Qaddafi the prime villain; the Soviet Union became the fountainhead of international terrorism. Both were demonized and subjected to an intense propaganda campaign of vilification. At the same time that Reagan went after Qaddafi and the Soviet Union, he enlisted the support of the Argentine military government to help train the Salvadoran and Guatemalan armies and death squads. In a war against the FMLN (Farabundo Marti National Liberation Front), about 75,000 people, almost all civilians, were killed by the Salvadoran military and death squads. Another million people were driven into exile, most settling in other nations of Latin America but several hundred thousand moving to the United States. Similarly, the Reagan administration lobbied hard for congressional aid to the Guatemalan government. Until its war with England over the Falkland Islands, Argentina and its military leaders were very friendly with the Reagan administration and helped in its struggle against what Reagan called terrorism in El Salvador, Guatemala, and Nicaragua. Argentine mercenaries were among the first "contras" to attack the newly established Sandinista government of Nicaragua by terrorizing the civilian population. As is also well known, the Reagan government entered into an alliance with the South African government in the 1980s under a program called "constructive engagement," in which the administration, in effect, bargained on behalf of South Africa in dealing with Angola and Namibia and protected the government as it repressed blacks at home and devastated the frontline states either directly or through proxy armies.[3]

The Reagan administration's Argentine ally slaughtered thousands of civilians in what has come to be called the "Dirty War," which continued long after an Argentine guerrilla movement was wiped out. An Amnesty International report of 1980, entitled *Secret Detention Centers in Argentina*, claimed that torture was carried out in sixty separate government and military facilities in that country.[4] A commission of inquiry appointed by President Raul Alfonsin after the ouster of the military regime in 1983 concluded that the "terrorism" of the military regime was "infinitely worse" than the terror they were allegedly combatting. The Salvadoran government that the Reagan administration advised, funded, and protected was murdering civilians at a rate of 700 to 800 a month, and exposing tortured and mutilated bodies in the suburbs of San Salvador and other towns as a form of public education, during the period of Reagan's mobilization against "terrorism." The Guatemalan government was engaged in even more fierce civilian murder at that time. Another Amnesty International report of 1980 was entitled *Guatemala: Government by Political Murder*, and an AI report of October 1982, which described in detail the murder of 2,600 civilians in Guatemala, preceded by only two months a Reagan visit there in which he declared that the Guatemalan head of state was a devoted democrat and getting a "bum rap."

South Africa engaged in successive invasions of Angola from illegally occupied Namibia. The United Nations condemned the invasions, but the Reagan administration vetoed the condemnations. In addition to the killing of thousands of blacks in South Africa and Namibia, the South African invasion of Angola, its support of Jonas Savimbi, and its sponsorship of Renamo in Mozambique were estimated by the UN to have resulted in over a million deaths in southern Africa during the years of "constructive engagement." A

U.S. State Department report of April 1988 estimated that Renamo alone in the years between 1985 and 1988 had murdered at least 100,000 unarmed civilians.[5]

More directly, the Reagan administration organized the contras in Honduras and financed and planned their attacks on "soft targets" in Nicaragua, with many thousands of civilian casualties. This operation, declared by the International Court of Justice in the Hague, 1986, to have involved the "unlawful use of force," fit with precision the U.S. government's own definition of state-sponsored international terrorism.[6] The Court even ruled that the United States must pay reparations to Nicaragua, but so far it has not paid and, in fact, the Bush administration was successful in getting the new Nicaraguan government of Violeta Chamorro to drop the charges against the United States in return for economic aid.

Qaddafi, by comparison with the United States (in Nicaragua) or Argentina, El Salvador, and South Africa in the 1980s, was a very minor terrorist. A 1987 Amnesty International report on *Political Killings by Governments* listed by name ten people that Qaddafi's regime had murdered, whereas for countries like Guatemala, El Salvador, Argentina, and South Africa, or for the victims of the Nicaraguan contras there are no lists of names because the numbers are too vast. Libya has also supported terrorist organizations abroad, but the numbers killed by Qaddafi's "proxies" do not come anywhere near the totals killed by U.S. proxies in Nicaragua, let alone those in El Salvador or Guatemala, and they are not nearly in the same league with the number of victims of South Africa and its proxies. In any case, it is extremely clear that Qaddafi was a very small-scale operator on the terrorism scene in the 1980s, whereas the Reagan administration in its support of various dictatorships and counterrevolutionary groups around the world murdered hundreds of thousands of people in the same eight years. But that is not the impression you have if you only read *Time* magazine and the *New York Times* or listen to news on the radio or TV.[7]

In the 1980s, Guatemalan and Salvadoran rebels were frequently called terrorists by government spokespersons and journalists, and it is an unpublicized but significant fact that U.S. police aid to El Salvador and Guatemala was provided under an "antiterrorism law," which, of course, implied that the massive state terrorism of

Rita Duffy
Freestate General,
1991
acrylic and
charcoal on paper
55" x 41" x 2"
courtesy of the
artist.

ON-OFF SWITCH

those countries was *combatting* terrorism and was not terrorism itself. ANC and SWAPO (South West African People's Organization) operations were also often labelled terrorism by U.S. officials, as well as by white South Africans, and this was very often hinted at indirectly by terrorism experts in their stress on alleged Soviet aid and support for the ANC.

In short, the Reagan-era usage was not only completely politicized, it was also straight out of George Orwell's *1984*, in which enemy states and the victims of "our" terrorists were identified as the terrorists while we and our clients were consistently exempted from blame. There was even a further element of opportunism that rendered this semantic word play still more farcical. In 1985, when Reagan put forth a list of terrorist states, he omitted Syria; the explanation given with a straight face by the press was that Syria had just been helpful in gaining the release of some hostages held in Lebanon. So it ceased to be a terrorist state, for the moment.[8] This opportunism was evident in the aftermath of the December 1988 bombing of Pan Am Flight 103, where after several years in which the administration claimed to have solid evidence of Iranian, Palestinian, and Syrian involvement, all was suddenly altered when Libya was named as the villain. By coincidence, Syria, Iran, and the Palestinians were involved in the new post-Gulf war "peace process" organized by the United States, whereas Libya was not.

Despite this remarkable use of a double standard and opportunism, the Reagan-era strategy for using terrorism as an instrument of propaganda was an outstanding success, and it continued to be a success under Bush, and very likely it will continue under Clinton. Qaddafi, the perfect condensation symbol, was and remains a target of opportunity and the model of terrorism.[9] Successive lies about the "hit squad" of 1981 and the alleged Libyan involvement in the bombing of a German discotheque in 1986[10] simply did not register here. The Soviet terror network also sold well. Meanwhile, demonstrable U.S.-sponsored terrorism in Nicaragua and the massive terrorism of U.S. clients were treated in a low key and were never designated as terrorism. The hypocrisy and Orwellian properties of the whole system went unmentioned—the United States, then and now, is engaged only in "counterterrorism."

III. How to Represent Yourself as a Victim, Not a Terrorist

How can the country that organized and funded the Nicaraguan contras and supplied them with a terrorism handbook, called *Psychological Operations in Guerilla Warfare,* and that for many years financed and trained the Salvadoran and Guatemalan armies that engaged in large-scale civilian murder get itself represented as a victim of terrorists and deeply concerned with the struggle against terrorism? This obviously demands a potent system of images and semantics, but it also depends upon the existence of a cooperative and powerful base of institutions that will put the images and semantics across to the general public.

Principles of Biased Representation

Basically, what is required for suitably biased representation is that the cultural apparatus centering in the mass media accept and transmit a system of patriotic premises, semantics, and filtered information that always puts us in a good light and villainizes our enemies. A main premise in regular use has been that we are always well intended, trying to foster democracy and responding only to "threats." If we are always benevolent, then we can only be victims, never terrorists or sponsors of terrorists. This was swallowed by the press even as regards Nicaragua, where we supported Somoza family rule for forty-five years and became allegedly interested in democracy only when a non-elite and independent government took power in 1979.

In the semantics of terrorism, four major devices have been employed. One is to define terrorism so as to exclude states, allowing a focus on the terrorism of dissidents and rebels. This deflects attention from the kind of terrorism perpetrated on a large scale by our clients, like Argentina, Chile, El Salvador, and Guatemala. State

Table 1. Killings by state and non-state terrorists: numbers and orders of magnitude[11]

Type of Killing	Numbers Killed	Fraction or multiple of PLO killings (entry 3)
Non-state		
German: Red Army Faction, Revolutionary Cells, and all other non-state, January 1970-April 1979[a]	31	0.1
Italian: Red Brigades and all other non-state, 1968-82[b]	334	1.2
PLO: Israelis killed in all acts of terror, 1968-81[c]	282	1.0
World: all "international terrorists" CIA global aggregate, 1969-80[d]	3,368	11.9
Single incidents of state terror		
El Salvador: Rio Sumpul, May 14, 1980[e]	600+	2.1 +
South Africa: Kassinga refugee camp, May 14, 1978[f]	600+	2.1 +
Guatemala: Panzos, May 29, 1978[g]	114	0.4
Israel: Sabra Shatila, September 16-18, 1982[h]	1,900-3,500	6.7-12.4
Larger dimensions of state terror		
Argentina: 1976-82 "disappeared"[i]	11,000	39.0
Chile: 1973-85[j]	20,000+	70.9 +
Dominican Republic: 1965-72[k]	2,000	7.1
El Salvador: Matanza I, 1932[l]	30,000	106.4
El Salvador: Matanza II, 1980-85[m]	50,000+	177.3 +
Guatemala: Rios Montt pacification campaign, March-June 1982[n]	2,186	7.8
Guatemala: 1966-85[o]	100,000+	354.6 +
Indonesia: 1965-66[p]	500,000+	1,773.0 +
Indonesia: invasion and pacification of East Timor, 1980-85[q]	200,000+	709.2 +
Libya: external assassinations of Libyans, 1980-83[r]	10+	0.04 +
Cambodia: Pol Pot era, 1975-78[s]	300,000+	1,063.8 +
U.S.-sponsored Contras: civilians in Nicaragua, 1981-87[t]	3,000+	10.6 +
South Africa and proxies: in Angola and Mozambique, 1980-89[u]	1,000,000+	3,546 +

Mainstream media, think tanks, and government always frame discussions of terrorism in terms of the unprovoked violence of others to which the West legitimately responds in self-defense. Secretary of State George Shultz said that the question was not if we would respond to terrorism but only when. In this way, the focus of the debate is always on "What Reagan Might Do," never on what was done in the pre-ceding years to create conditions that led to the violent acts of powerless and des-perate people. Magazines like *Newsweek* revel in the options—from all out bombing raids to more subtle and secret infiltration and assassin-ation. No one questions what the victims of U.S. terror must feel as they see American press openly debating what sort of violent attack will be employed next time.

terrorism is a far more important form of terrorism than is the terrorism of dissidents and rebels, as indicated in Table 1, "Killings by State and Non-State Terrorists." The table is a dramatic illustra-tion of why states must be excluded. The table gives numbers for non-state victims, then single incidents of state terror, and then the larger dimensions of state terror. I use as a benchmark the third entry, which lists the number of Israelis killed in all acts of terror attributed to the Palestinian Liberation Organization (PLO) from 1968 to 1981. The number, 282, is an Israeli police estimate. For the purposes of statistical comparison, that number of deaths is equal to "1" and all other totals are expressed as a fraction or multiple thereof. You can see quickly that in El Salvador in a single incident at Rio Sumpul six hundred people were killed. That is just over twice the number of Israelis killed by the PLO during this thirteen-year period. In South Africa, at the Kassinga refugee camp in 1978 more than six hundred people were killed at one time. Again, that is twice the benchmark figure or about twice the PLO total. These are single incidents. When you reach the larger dimensions of state terror in Argentina from 1976 to 1982, the total is 39 times the PLO figure. For Guatemala, it is 354 times the PLO total. The multiple is 1773 for Indonesia. Furthermore, only states terrorize by the use of systematic torture, as Argentina did in the junta years, 1976-83; this reinforces the

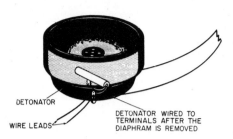

DETONATOR
WIRE LEADS
DETONATOR WIRED TO
TERMINALS AFTER THE
DIAPHRAM IS REMOVED

conclusion about the relatively greater importance of state terrorism. State terrorism is excluded from the terrorism category in contemporary Western usage and propaganda because it is politically inconvenient.

Once you start talking about state terrorism, you are talking about really large numbers and therefore our government has decided not to call this terrorism. They insist that terrorism refers only to the actions of someone such as Abu Nidal or a group such as the Red Brigades. If any name at all is given to the policies of murder, disappearance, torture, illegal arrest or imprisonment, police brutality, bombing, and more that are practiced by the governments of friendly nations like El Salvador, Israel, South Africa, Brazil, and many more, it is "counterterrorism." These policies are allegedly carried out in response to the terrorism of some other individual or group.

Thus, the second semantic trick is differentiating terrorism from retaliation. Suppose you say that everything you do is "retaliation" against something someone else has done, whereas anything done to you is autonomous terrorism based on no genuine grievance or true provocation. You are always retaliating for someone else's violence, and they are always attacking you for no good reason. This also makes your actions a matter of "self-defense," and self-defense is accepted generally as an unassailable excuse. In its dealings with the PLO and Arab nations, Israel is always allowed to be engaged in retaliation and counterterrorism, in spite of the fact that Israel has been making preemptive strikes across borders for more than forty years. It's always the other party's acts that are terrorism.

A third semantic device has been to use the concept of "international terrorism," i.e., cross-border attacks by non-state terrorists. This allows the selective inclusion of states as terrorists, as they can be labelled "sponsors" of "international terrorists." Thus Qaddafi can be brought in as a "sponsor" of Abu Nidal. Of course, South Africa sponsors Renamo in Mozambique and Israel sponsors the South Lebanese Army, and the United States sponsored the contras in Nicaragua and the Mujahadeen in Afghanistan, but I have never seen a mainstream publication describe these last cases as sponsorship of international terrorism. Sometimes, as in the cases of UNITA or the contras, the conflicts are called civil wars, even though one side is clearly an agent and proxy of foreign government.

This brings us to the fourth and pivotal trick: selective attention and indignation. Great attention and much indignation is given to Qaddafi's sponsorship of terrorism across borders, but U.S., Israeli, and South African sponsorship is treated in a low key or ignored altogether by the cultural institutions, as if such actions don't fit the category. I have never seen the Israeli-sponsored South Lebanese Army described in the U.S. mass media as an "international terrorist" organization or Israel called a "sponsor" of international terrorism. The same applies to U.S. sponsorship of the contras and South Africa's support for Renamo.

The Institutional Base of Misrepresentation

The success of all these intellectual and semantic tricks is contingent upon the cooperation of academic and journalistic institutions in the United States. Misrepresentations of terrorism require a strong institutional base. The primary institutions involved here are the government and the mass media. The government, of course, promotes its own line on terrorism in which its enemies are terrorists and it is strictly a victim. The mass media in the United States are highly concentrated and heavily dependent on the government for information. This contributes to their being easily "managed" by the government,[12] a process made still easier when the government has succeeded in identifying and demonizing a foreign enemy, as it does regularly in coping with "terrorism." Representation and misrepresentation in accord with the government agenda on terrorism are easily achieved.[13]

Getting the official line across has been further aided by the development of the "terrorism industry" of institutes, think tanks, and experts who meet the government and corporate demand for terrorism scholarship produced by seemingly "independent" experts. There are many such institutes in the United States, which are linked to similar institutes in other Free World countries like Israel and Great Britain.[14] Notable ones in the United States are the Hoover

Institute for the Study of War, Peace, and Revolution, the American Enterprise Institute, the Center for Strategic and International Studies, the Heritage Foundation, and the Rand Corporation. These are generally funded by large corporations and corporate foundations. Rand is an exception since it is funded mainly by the Pentagon. Experts and officials attached to these institutions have a revolving-door relationship with the State Department, CIA, and Pentagon. Table 2, "Linkages and Perspectives of the Terrorism Industry Experts," shows that some two-thirds of the leading mainstream experts on terrorism are currently affiliated with governments or have been so affiliated in the recent past.

These institutions are very important not only because they house experts and give them an opportunity to research and write, but also because they accredit them. That is, the prestige of institutional affiliation marks them as experts. The people who work at the Center for Strategic and International Studies, for example, have an affiliation with an institution that the mass media accept as legitimate and important. The Center was for a period also connected to Georgetown University, just as the Hoover Institute is connected to Stanford University. The institutions give them authenticity. They receive titles like Senior Scholar or Fellow or other academic-sounding names that tend to impute academic rigor and validity to their research and publications.

The government and corporate supporters of the institutes and experts have a definite special-interest view of terrorism. Their perspectives are reproduced in analyses by the experts, who never find the United States or its clients to be terrorists, but select precisely the terrorists that fit government and corporate demands. Sensible people would conclude that these so-called experts on terrorism are not objective analysts but are in fact no more than adjuncts of the government. But in the mass media, through which their research finds its way to ordinary Americans, that is not how it is represented. On the *MacNeil/Lehrer NewsHour*, for example, Robert Kupperman is introduced simply as a Senior Advisor to the Center for Strategic and International Studies and a "terrorism expert." His connection to the Pentagon goes unmentioned.

The beauty of this system of experts linked to institutes is that it fills the space that might otherwise be filled by real investigative

Table 2. Linkages and perspectives of the terrorism industry experts[15]

Characteristic	Media 16		Big 32	
	No.	%	No.	%
1. U.S. government link	11	68.8	20	62.5
CIA	(4)	(25.0)	(7)	(21.9)
2. British Government link	1	6.3	6	18.8
Army/police	(1)	(6.3)	(6)	(18.8)
3. Net government affiliated	12	75.0	22	68.8
4. Institute/think tank	11	68.8	23	71.9
Big Four[a]	(5)	(31.3)	(13)	(40.6)
Moon related	(3)	(18.8)	(5)	(15.6)
Israel lobby related	(2)	(12.5)	(4)	(12.5)
5. Risk analysis/security	8	50.0	15	46.9
6. Journalist	1	6.3	5	15.6
7. Academic	5	31.1	13	40.6
8. Focus on left and insurgent terror	16	100.0	31	96.9
9. Fit in classification by model:				
Moderate establishment	4	25.0	6	18.8
Right-wing establishment	10	62.5	20	62.5
Dissident	-	-	1	3.1
None[b]	2	12.5	5	15.6

[a]Heritage, Hoover, the AEI, and the CSIS
[b]No model evident in published writings.

reporting and really independent analysis. The media are remarkably gullible in accepting the claims and propaganda thrusts of these think-tank "scholars." The heading "Focus on left and insurgent terror" of Table 2 (line 8) shows that thirty-one of the thirty-two terrorism experts focus attention almost exclusively on insurgent or left-wing terror, not state terror or right-wing terror. That is, thirty-one of thirty-two of the most-respected experts accept the premise that enemies of the United States are terrorists and the friends of the United States are counterterrorists.

This is dramatically illustrated in Table 3: "References by Terrorism Industry Experts to Western Right-Wing and Non-Western Left-Wing Terrorism." This table is based on citations in the indexes to four major books on terrorism: Walter Laqueur's *The Age of Terrorism*, Claire Sterling's *The Terror Network*, Paul

OFF-ON SWITCH

Wilkinson's *Terrorism and the Liberal State*, and Dobson and Payne's *The Terrorists*.[16] These books are a representative sampling of the research published by think-tank scholars. The table lists a dozen major Western-based and right-wing state and non-state terrorists, and then a dozen non-Western and/or left-wing terrorists. It can quickly be seen that the references to the first set in the indexes of the four books are negligible, although the number of their victims is surely larger than that of the victims of the other set, who are cited repeatedly. The ratio of citations, 2 to 733, is dramatic evidence of bias. It is clear that the establishment experts focus only on approved terror and simply don't talk about the terror that is inconvenient or embarrassing to U.S. policy-makers.

The final step in providing a closed view of terrorism that fits the requirements of the powerful is the media's near total reliance on just two sources for reporting on terrorism: government officials and the "experts" located in think tanks. The mainstream media take government officials as truth-tellers even when their latest lies have been exposed the day before. The mass media motto is that "truth comes out of the mouths of the powerful." The media also take the experts as independent and nonpartisan, no matter what their past affiliations. This can reach comic levels. One of the two leading experts on the alleged (but untrue) KGB-Bulgarian plot to kill Pope John Paul II was Paul Henze, a long time propaganda specialist for the CIA and former CIA station chief in Turkey. The *MacNeil/Lehrer NewsHour*, CBS, the *Christian Science Monitor*, and the rest not only took him as a truly independent expert, they also failed even to disclose his credentials.[17]

With this sourcing arrangement, the mass media offer the perspectives of the government and experts as supposedly unbiased news. This provides a model system of propaganda, where the state line is reinforced regularly by nominally independent experts who are in fact virtual agents of the state, while genuinely independent analysts are ignored as lacking proper credentials. Moreover, real

Table 3. References by terrorism industry experts to Western right-wing and non-Western left-wing terrorism

Type of terrorism	Dobson-Payne	Laqueur	Wilkinson	Sterling
Western/right-wing				
Roberto D'Aubuisson	-	-	-	-
Stefano Delle Chiaie	-	-	-	-
Orlando Bosch-CORU	-	-	1	-
Luis Posada Carriles	-	-	-	-
Botha-South Africa	-	(2)[a]	(1)[a]	-
Operation condor	-	-	-	-
Pinochet	-	-	-	-
Videla	(2)[a]	-	-	-
Sharon-Begin-Yaron	(1)[a]	-	(2)[a]	-
Saad Haddad	-	-	-	-
Contras-Reagan-North	-	1	(4)[a]	-
Tecos (Mexico)	-	-	-	-
Total	**0**	**1**	**1**	**0**
Non-Western/left-wing				
Arafat-Fatah-PLO	22	26	10	51
Carlos	11	7	2	40
Abu Nidal	11	16	1	2
Marighela	8	8	6	11
Baader-Meinhof	34	19	4	36
Red Brigades	15	22	2	57
Tupamaros	5	19	6	22
Castro-Cuba	4	19	15	40
Qadaffi-Libya	18	21	13	34
Soviet Union	-	9	11	54
Weathermen	5	7	2	2
Black Panthers	1	2	-	3
Totals	**134**	**175**	**72**	**352**

[a]Means that while individual or group are listed in index, they are not treated as a terrorist in the text, but rather as a victim of terror or as somebody having to cope with terrorists.

reporting is rejected on the grounds that the reporter has gotten too close to the subjects of the story and lost his or her objectivity. This is what the *Wall Street Journal* as well as State Department officials said about Ray Bonner when he reported the massacre of as many as six hundred women and children by the Salvadoran military at El

Mozote in 1980. During the 1980s, it took a remarkable propaganda system to be able to make the Reagan-Botha-Begin-Argentine-Salvadoran-Guatemalan alliance into fighters against terrorism, and the ANC, SWAPO, and the Salvadoran and Guatemalan rebels and peasants into terrorists. We have in the U.S. media system a presentation of the views of the powerful and a gross misrepresentation of the truth. The first step necessary in combatting terrorism is to confront the misrepresentation of terrorism in the establishment media and think tanks and to start calling things by their right names.

Audience: Are there no independent columnists who appear in any of the major newspapers or television networks?

Herman: There are almost none. Alexander Cockburn used to have a column in the *Wall Street Journal*, but they dropped him. He was an important exception. I don't know of even one who is a regular columnist. The left wing in American journalism, which in this case carries the burden of presenting the truth, is represented by someone like Mary McGrory of the *Washington Post*, and we don't even get anything that far left in Philadelphia, where I live. In fact, the editor of the *Philadelphia Inquirer* when asked where the left is said, "We've got David Broder." He considers David Broder a man of the left. There are really none who get published regularly in major newspapers. The same holds for TV news and shows like *MacNeil/Lehrer*.

Audience: How about Gary Wills?

Herman: He is actually an independent thinker and he occasionally has some articles of quality and interest and substance, but he definitely assumes the premises of the establishment. That is the key—do you assume that we are a benevolent nation? Even Anthony Lewis and Tom Wicker in the *New York Times*, who are about as left-wing as columnists get, always assume that we mean well and they only question the methods that we use.

Audience: Would you talk about the relation of economic interests and terrorism. How do the multinational corporations fit in?

62

Leon Golub
Mercenaries 1, 1976
acrylic on canvas
116"x186"
courtesy of the Eli
Broad Family
Foundation,
Santa Monica.

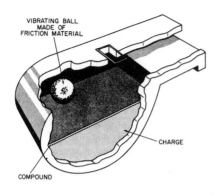

VIBRATING BALL MADE OF FRICTION MATERIAL

CHARGE

COMPOUND

Herman: The relationship is close; the multinational corporation fit is snug. The analysis of who are the terrorists and who are the counterterrorists is shaped by the fact that the U.S. is part of a global economy and that multinational corporations' interests in the Third World are dominant factors in shaping U.S. policy toward those nations and therefore our attitude toward the various contesting factions in these states. A country like Guatemala had a democratic government for ten years from 1945 to 1954, but it was threatening United Fruit Company by allowing trade unions to flourish; and one of the best books on Eisenhower says that U.S. hostility toward the Guatemalan government began in 1947 when it allowed trade unions to form freely. When the government began to talk about land reform which would affect United Fruit Company's holdings, our government became hysterical and found a communist conspiracy. I don't know what we are going to do now without international communism to rationalize things that we do that have nothing to do with international communism. The history of Guatemala presents a textbook case where the hegemonic interest of the U.S. government is tied to the economic interest of various corporations. The result has been thirty years of state terror and over a hundred thousand people murdered, but bananas have become a tremendous commodity in people's diets around the "First World."

There are very important documents that Noam Chomsky and I have cited that I have never seen anyone mention in the major media. One of these is a National Security Council (NSC) document of 1954 on "U.S. Objectives and Courses of Action with Respect to Latin America," which says that nationalist regimes concerned with "immediate improvement in the low living standards of the masses" are a challenge and threat to U.S. interests. The language is dramatic: a regime that is interested in the well-being of the majority of the people is a challenge and threat that we have to cope with. Other NSC documents say clearly that building up the military, educating them to ensure their "understanding of, and orientation toward, U.S.

objectives," is the way we can cope with this threat. There is nothing like state terror to make people forget about improving their standard of living. They are just happy to be alive. Now you can be sure the 1954 document was never quoted in the *New York Times* or *Newsweek* because it tells a painful truth about policy not suitable for general consumption. It is a basic document of U.S. foreign policy, but it shows the extent to which popular governments who are trying to do something for their masses are seen as a threat. Popular governments are a threat to multinational corporations, and the corporate desire for a favorable climate for investment is the dominant consideration in U.S. foreign policy. What that means is that when the Guatemalan government we installed in 1954 started to kill civilians, no one here was about to start calling it terrorist because it was now serving "our" needs. You can be sure that it is not going to be raising the living standards of Guatemalan people. So there is a crucial parallelism between corporate economic interests, the definition of who the terrorists are, and our government's kind treatment of terrorist states.

Beyond Terrorism

Ramsey Clark

Lenora Foerstel: One of the most ironic statements of our time was Richard Nixon's remark that if we are to ensure order and respect for law in this country there is one place we must begin: we are going to have a new Attorney General. The object of this attack was Attorney General Ramsey Clark. In 1961, Mr. Clark joined the Justice Department at the beginning of the administration of John F. Kennedy. In 1964, he helped to formulate the Civil Rights Act and the following year he helped to formulate the Voting Rights Act of 1965. He was appointed Attorney General by President Lyndon Johnson in 1967. From the 1960s on, Mr. Clark has sought to remedy the conditions of violence existing in the United States. He worked to purge violence and racism from this country. In a book which he co-authored with Roy Wilkins, *Search and Destroy: A Report by the Commission of Inquiry into the Black Panthers and the Police,* he states that there is a common thread that runs through the violence of a B-52 raid in Indonesia, the police shooting at Jackson State University in Mississippi, and the slaughter of prisoners and guards at Attica state penitentiary in New York. Mr. Clark points out that until we recognize that all human beings are equal in every way to our children and to ourselves, we will see no wrong in using violence to control and destroy those we believe to be inferior. He organized and introduced the first federal strike force that began to make serious inroads on organized crime and reorganized the archaic Bureau of Prisons to provide new kinds of rehabilitation programs.

A prolific writer, Mr. Clark has published numerous articles and books. In his publication *Crime in America*, he discusses the dehumanizing effects on individuals of slums, racism, ignorance, violence, and corruption; the sense of frustration of those who have no power to achieve their rights; and the effects of poverty, unemployment, malnutrition, and drugs. These are the fountainheads of crime. Tom Wicker, in his introduction to *Crime in America*, writes that Ramsey Clark's voice is singularly competent and remarkably clear.

I am sure that, like myself, most people have felt a sense of great depression and frustration at the violence perpetrated by Bush, Quayle, Cheney, Powell, Schwarzkopf, and others during Desert Storm. From February 2 to February 8, 1991, Mr. Clark traveled in Iraq to assess the damages to human life. He traveled 2,000 miles, accompanied by a cameraman, recording the images of destroyed neighborhoods, burnt victims, children in hospitals without food, drugs, and proper clean water. And when he returned from Iraq, he initiated the Commission of Inquiry for an International War Crimes Tribunal. Many of you may want to read the book *War Crimes: A Report on U.S. War Crimes Against Iraq*, which presents the materials he and others collected. In this book, there is a chapter by Ramsey Clark and a powerful letter written by Mr. Clark to former UN Secretary General Javier Perez de Quellar. In this letter, we are painfully informed of the U.S. violations of the United Nations Charter, international laws, and our own Constitution. Mr. Clark reminds us that every act of justice makes for an order which will ensure human rights, social justice, political and cultural integrity.

Clark: We have an unpleasant subject tonight—terrorism—but it is befitting of the times. It is remarkable to see an art exhibit and participate in a discussion of terrorism at this time. It is not the happiest thing to think about, and many would like to believe that all of that is behind us, but if you look around you know otherwise. Just this month, January 1992, our government warned the people of North Korea that unless they accede to our demands for inspection of their nuclear power plants, they risk our displeasure. Also this month, we caused the Security Council of the United Nations, fifteen members, to vote unanimously that an extradition which has always been handled by treaty and occurs thousands of times a year had better occur or dire consequences will ensue. Our government wants two Libyan citizens it says were involved in the bombing of a Pan Am airliner over Lockerbie, Scotland, and it is using the United Nations to get them.

This event is worth examining for a moment. The United Nations was created to end the scourge of war in the wake of the worst war in human history, World War II, which killed some fifty

Craig Kalpakjian
Station (bullet proof casket),
1990
bullet resistant
plexiglass
23"x75"x17"
courtesy of
the artist.

million people. And now, an institution of the United Nations that ought never to have existed—it was "victor's justice" that gave the Security Council, composed of the nations that won the war, veto power over the vast majority of the population of the planet—this institution created to end the scourge of war became an instrumentality of war in the slaughter in Iraq. Its resolutions which led to war were secured by corruption, outright bribery, public and notorious. Seven billion dollars in aid went to the Soviet Union for its vote; $108 million in emergency military aid went to Ethiopia when we knew that the government was failing and when the only consequence could be more death in the Horn of Africa—but we wanted a vote. And we bribed them. And now we threaten Libya with sanctions and, as our geopolitical leaders not-so-subtly say, and by any means that may be necessary to obtain custody of two Libyan citizens.

There is a man named Robert Manning. He's an American citizen under investigation for sending eleven letter bombs in the United States and under indictment for murder as a result of one of them. He is the prime suspect in the death of Alex Odeh in California. He lives now in the occupied territories and participates regularly in the brutalization of Palestinian people. The United States asked for his extradition, but he has not been extradited. And he has been under indictment here for years.

St. Augustine—how he knew and whether it's true, I'll leave to you— reports that there was a colloquy between Alexander the Great who died in Babylon and some pirates that had been caught harassing Greek ships in the eastern Mediterranean. Alexander asked the pirates, "How dare you molest my ships?" One of the pirates who lost his head, figuratively at first and then actually, said to Alexander the Great, "How dare you molest the whole world."

I don't like beginning with illustrations of a point I hope to make, and I realize that there is nothing crueler than the murder of a beautiful idea by a brutal gang of facts, but about ten years ago I was in Lebanon and I remember having lunch with Gabriel Habib who was, and still is, the head of the Middle East Council of Churches and one of those wonderful scholars who knows everything in his field of study. It is just thrilling to talk to him. We were sitting in a small cafe waiting for my plane and every once in a while we heard a "boom" and the building would shake a little bit. Then all of a sudden we heard "ah-ah-ah-ah-ah-ah-ah"; there was machine-gun fire right outside. As he broke a piece of bread, he said, "Who do you think are the most violent people that ever came to this violent region of the world?" I didn't want to match knowledge with him; I just wanted to know what he thought. So after dodging a couple of times, I said, You tell me. He said, "There is no question; it was the Christian Crusaders. They came and said, these people are heathens and ought to be killed, man, woman, and child. And they did it."

The things that create the greatest terror in life by far are rarely called "terrorism." Because the word is the master and as the Scripture says, in the beginning was the word, so the things that create the greatest terror in the world are rarely called by the word terrorism or perceived as terrorism. And things that we call terrorism, horrible in human terms as they are, are overwhelmingly the acts of powerless people. In his great book *Dark Ghetto*, Kenneth Bancroft Clark wrote of the urban race riots of the 1960s, which seemed so threatening, wild, and irrational, that they are the "exercise of power by powerless people." I was in London a few Sundays back and seven bombs went off in furniture stores. Now, I can't tell you whether M-5 or the IRA set them off. We have been conditioned to disbelief. Nobody happened to be hurt. In 1986 there was a survey by the State Department that showed that twenty-five Americans died as a result of acts of terror that year. The report said that if there is to be peace in the world, something had to be done about it. That same year, there were 7,000 bombings in the United States of which only three were identified as being terrorist political acts and in which no one was killed. In the other bombings, about 140 people were killed altogether. There were more than 50,000 people killed on highways that year and in nearly half of the fatal accidents alcohol was involved. There were 25,500 people murdered in the United States that year. Most of the murders were, as they always are, within families or among friends or by people who know each other pretty well. It was not the frightening figure in the dark, the image portrayed so often in our media, that killed Americans. It is most often a person who has been disintegrating in your midst for a long time and just spills over. No one tried to help or seemed to care. About 45 percent of those murders were with handguns. And we don't have the will to come to grips with handguns.

After the Watts riots in South Central Los Angeles in 1965, sales of guns in Los Angeles County were four time greater between August, when the riots occurred, and the end of the year than for the entire previous year. And most of the purchases were out in Beverly Hills or places like that where you couldn't cause a riot if you spat in people's faces and said the meanest things you could. They would just turn up the air conditioning in their Cadillacs, and if they didn't run over you, they would just drive away. You couldn't even get an angry crowd together out in the suburbs. There were about 12,000 people who died from slipping and falling in 1986. You can say that these things are not comparable to so-called terrorist acts, but then what you really see is that the amount of fear created by the use of the word "terrorism" and the invocation of the image of the shadowy figure of the terrorist is all out of proportion to its human impact.

That same year in early April, someone set off a bomb in a disco in West Berlin. It killed a Turkish woman, an American GI, and a few weeks later another American GI died of injuries sustained in the bomb blast. On April 15, Ronald Reagan, our President, ordered an aerial assault on the sleeping cities of Tripoli and Benghazi. The cities hadn't known war since the end of the desert campaigns of World War II in 1942. The bombing was a surprise attack, in violation of every international law that applies to the conduct of war. These laws were written after the surprise attack on Pearl Harbor on December 7, 1941. At least one hundred civilians were killed and several times that number were injured. There were nine different nationalities with deaths, four embassies were damaged, the French embassy totally destroyed. Reagan administration officials claimed that they had intercepted telephone communications from Libya to East Germany that had discussed the bombing. They hadn't named the disco or anything that specific, but had discussed doing some acts of terrorism. The Berlin police denied any knowledge or any involvement of Libyan persons either in Germany or in Libya and denied having ever been told by the United States that this information existed, as did the intelligence agencies of the Federal Republic of Germany. I guess Turkey could have attacked Greece, claiming that some Greek had set off the bomb.

Terrorism as I understand it in all its forms is the use of fear to cause or compel the conduct of other people. And if you measure it quantitatively in terms of deaths, in terms of injuries, in terms of torture, in terms of fear, state terrorism would be better than 99 percent of the total. A state can't really dominate a people physically by police; it has to dominate people by fear. There can never be enough police to really control the whole population. The power is *in* the people. Stokely Carmichael didn't have it quite right when he said "power to the people." Power is in the people. That is a sociological truism. The question is whether the people can exercise their power, and states—police states, totalitarian or authoritarian states as Jeane Kirkpatrick likes to distinguish them—must use fear to control the people. Fear caused by the sudden disappearance of a friend or family member is a pretty terrifying thing. A neighbor is gone, and no one answers where or why or what has happened. Bodies are left on the road for all to see. I was down in Haiti about four weeks ago with a group of observers to see what was going on there. People who had not been in the human rights business for a long time thought they were discovering things when they moved around the countryside and found bodies lying on the streets. The bodies were left out there specifically to terrorize the people. It wasn't that the military was lazy and didn't want to cart them away. Nor was it that they were particularly proud of the murders. It is a method of terror.

The American people were told for years that the African National Congress (ANC) was a terrorist organization. And because of that it had to be repressed. All the while, the government of South Africa engaged in the most pervasive use of violence, segregation, and fear against the great majority of the population. If you attended a passport trial there in the 1970s and 1980s—the pass being required as a means for separating the races by identifying a person and his or her right to be in a region (you had to have authority to be where you were found)—you would see men and some women shaking with uncontrollable fear as they stood before a judge. They were hunkered down before a judge who was speaking in a language they could not understand, but they realized nonetheless that by his word they may never see their families again. And yet what we heard about in the United States was the terrorism of the ANC.

In Lebanon a few years ago, I was on a trip to Beaufort Castle, which is down south of the Litani River. It was an old Christian monastery built like a fort. From there you could see forever: you could see the Dead Sea, you could see the Sinai, and the whole coast of Israel. It was being shelled at this time by extended range artillery. This was the 181st consecutive day of Israeli assaults by land, sea, and air on Lebanon. It was a policy designed, we were told, to end Palestinian terrorism in Israel. At the time of my visit, it was Ramadan, and as we drove back up the coastal highway, we came upon some lights and cars ahead and pulled up beside a shot-up Volkswagen mini-van. There were five religious women, at least they had on religious clothes, who were all dead except for one. We were told, and from all appearances it seemed true, that commandos had come up from the sea and lain along the road waiting for a car. They fired with machine guns on the first car to come by. It just happened to be this mini-bus and these women were killed. A few days later an English-language newspaper in Beirut ran a story with an interview with General Raphael Eitan, who was the chief of staff of the Israeli army. He was asked how his program to end terrorism was working. He replied, "Wonderfully. For six months there hasn't been a single act of terrorism in Israel." The assaults in Lebanon, like the one on these religious women, were called by another name. And that creates an enormous problem.

When the United States invaded Grenada in 1983, a small island of less than 100,000 people, its army was listed as having 1,200 active and reserve members. It wasn't really an army at all. After the invasion, our government gave 9,000 medals to U.S. soldiers. As a proportion of the population of Grenada, the invasion killed more people than America lost in all of World War II as a proportion of our population. Now that is a statistical argument. You will remember that Mark Twain said, "There are three kinds of lies: lies, damn lies, and statistics." This is a statistic and therefore it has to be examined. It is mathematically correct. More Grenadians were killed in proportion to their population than we lost in World War II in proportion to our population. Fewer than 250 Grenadians were killed, but if you happened to know them and love them, it hurts. Nearly thirty of the casualties were in a mental hospital. It was up on Richmond Hill—everything in Grenada is named after the British because that's where the people who named things came from— and some Navy pilot, who didn't mean to do it, launched

Alison Saar
Briar Patch, 1988
wood, wire, nails,
caulk, iron, wax
9 1/2" x 33" x 10"
courtesy of a private
collector through the
Jan Baum Gallery,
Los Angeles.

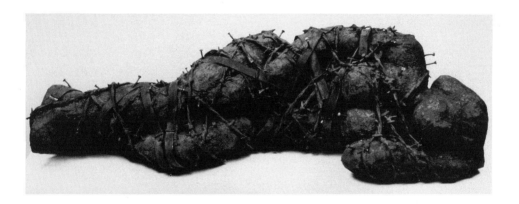

his rockets and they hit the hospital. The point is not whether he meant to or not; he shouldn't have been there in the first place. If you scrambled up Richmond Hill as I did just four days later for a family who had a brother there and wanted to know if he was alive, you found the surviving patients digging out the dead. The stench was almost unbearable. A few of the staff were helping dig out. It was a Third World mental hospital, so you can imagine that it was not much of a place even before the bombing. But after the bombing, it was a scene from hell.

As a result of the invasion of Grenada, terror spread throughout the Caribbean. There had been U.S. Navy war games in the Caribbean every six months for two years. The President of these mighty United States—which has a nuclear warhead for every three people in Grenada and twenty-five full-time uniformed military service personnel for every man, woman, and child in Grenada—went on national television to show pictures of an airport at Salinas Point, which he says could be used for intercontinental bombers and was therefore a threat to the United States. Barbados, 150 miles away, has a 12,000-foot runway, a much bigger airport. Through a British contractor, Grenada was building an 8,000-foot runway. We chose to call it something the Soviets might use.

You've probably not often thought of capital punishment as a form of terrorism. But here is what Josef de Maistre has to say about it, and we should remember who he was and what he believed and consider how many really agree with him. He is talking about the executioner: "All grandeur, all power, and subordination rests on the executioner. He is the horror and bond of all human association. Remove this incomprehensible agent from the world and at that very moment order gives way to chaos, thrones topple, and society disappears." It is a eulogy to terror, to the use of fear to control society. It is the antithesis to the idea of freedom, and that is what Josef de Maistre stood for in the early nineteenth century. Freedom has no enemy like fear because fear completely confines and paralyzes. And the United States of America is the lord high executioner of the planet. Even South Africa, albeit for the moment for political reasons, has suspended capital punishment. We have 2,700 people on death row tonight. We have executed two human beings this week. We are telling our people that freedom compels us to kill you, if you displease us. So be careful what you do.

The forms of state terror are endless. Twain wrote a remarkable and bitter piece toward the end of his life. This was a man who earlier took such delight in the jumping frogs in Calavaras County. Toward the end of his life he was pretty embittered, primarily by American materialism and perhaps because he lost out on its rewards. The "Gilded Age" didn't treat him right; he was cheated out of his royalties and investments. He wrote of the two terrors in France: the Reign of Terror during the Revolution which horrifies us all, as it should, and the terror that endured for one thousand before. He points out that during the few months of the Reign of Terror, which was in its own way a government, such as it was, perhaps ten thousand died. André Chénier, probably the greatest poet of the late eighteenth century, died, not that his poetry made him more valuable than anybody else. The Carmelite nuns one after another went to the guillotine rather than divest themselves of the traditional religious custom and habit in favor of the *sans-culottes*. But Twain suggests that the Reign of Terror was nothing compared to the millions who lived lives of constant fear, misery, and violence for centuries and centuries under the reign of kings.

One of the greatest fears in a society that knows real poverty and hunger is starvation. We don't see that here and we have glib phrases like "you can't use food as a weapon." But we know that eight million infants starve to death every year. I am not talking about catastrophes like doubling the infant mortality rate in Iraq, as we did by our destruction of their essential facilities like water, electrical power, sewer, communications, hospitals, schools, farming, and much more. There are twice as many infants dying in Iraq today as there were fifteen months ago because the water is still bad, food is scarce, there is no fertilizer, there is no power for irrigation, and no importation of medicines. It is not an insignificant number, although if it is your baby, even one death is enough. Before the war, there were 69 deaths before the first year per 1,000 live births; today it is about 140. In Iraq there are about 750,000 births a year. To find out how many babies are dying because of the long-range effects of the war, if you want to call it a war, you just have to multiply 750 (how many thousands there are) times 71 which is the additional infant deaths since the bombing. More than 50,000 babies have died who would otherwise have lived. And that calculation doesn't account for the injuries to other babies who do survive, it doesn't figure the death rate for children under five, which has tripled, it doesn't tell you about whole categories of illnesses which become death sentences because you can't get medications. Some are pretty numerous, like those people with diabetes who die because they can't get insulin. If you needed dialysis in Iraq and remained there during the embargo, you are dead because dialysis is not available. Whole categories of illnesses condemn people to death because of the conditions we have imposed on this nation.

In a sense, you could call the American policy toward Iraq with all its destructiveness a reign of terror. There were 110,000 aerial sorties over a forty-two-day period; that is one every thirty seconds. They dropped 88,000 tons of bombs; that's equivalent to seven Hiroshimas. Ninety-three percent were free-falling bombs, none of this fancy stuff you saw on television. The war on television was little more than forty-two consecutive days of commercials for militarism and military hardware. The United States lost thirty-eight planes. That is a regrettable and needless loss, but it is a smaller number than we suffer in equivalent war games where you don't use live ammunition. The Iraqis had no defense against our attacks, and we knew it. We bombed them until we had done all the destruction that we wanted, and then we quit. We assaulted defenseless troops, and we knew it. I could give you endless quotations like "It was like shooting sheep in a pen, fish in a barrel, a turkey shoot," on and on. We didn't lose a B-52 over Iraq. During Rolling Thunder, that great tragedy of aerial assault on Vietnam in 1966, our air losses were ten times greater than in Iraq. The reason for this is that since 1966 we have spent billions, even trillions, of dollars perfecting weapons with which to terrorize the world.

If you don't think these arms are to terrorize the rest of the world, then try to think of any other possible meaning for the Trident II nuclear submarine. We have commissioned twenty of these submarines. This is a submarine that can launch twenty-four missiles while submerged, so it is almost impossible for anyone even to know where it is. Each missile can contain up to seventeen independently targeted nuclear warheads. Each warhead can have a range of 7,000 nautical miles, a span of 14,000 miles, which is more than halfway around the world, and can strike within 300 feet—they say— of a predetermined target. It is a first-strike weapon designed

Mary Lum
*An American F-16
Fighter-Bomber
Passing by a
Mosque in Incirlik,
Turkey, as It
Returned to Its
Base after a
Mission against
Iraq*, 1991,
from the *Historical
Present* series
charcoal drawing
with text
8" x 10"
courtesy of
the artist

to hit an enemy's nuclear missiles in their silos before they are launched. Each warhead can have an explosive capacity of ten times that of the bomb that incinerated the people of Hiroshima. One finger can press one button and hit 408 centers of human population, destroying a million people each, if you target them that way. It is utter madness. What quality of moral value could ever permit the construction of such a monstrous machine? And what utility could it have but to strike fear in anyone who dares challenge us or dares act contrary to our will. Is it conceivable that we could use them? Well, maybe it is, but God help us. And yet we build them. And until this week, the Trident II was never mentioned in any nuclear arms reduction proposal by any American administration. Yet it is the supreme strategic weapon.

And what do you think Saddam Hussein thought in November 1990 when I met with him? I told him that it is not a pleasant thing to say, but Hiroshima happened. I didn't say that as a threat, but as an historical observation. You have to act to save your children, I told him. He knew that out in the Persian Gulf there were nuclear warheads that could destroy all of Mesopotamia. He was under no illusion that the Republican Guards could cope with that capacity for violence. Even in conventional war, as it turned out, his planes did not rise to meet enemy aircraft bombing Iraqi villages. Thirty percent of the planes were flown to Iran, the old enemy, and parked there, not because the pilots were frightened but because they were ordered to get them out before they were destroyed.

And what is the meaning of all this military now? Why are we so insistent that if we can't have Subic Bay in the Philippines, we've got to have a naval base in Singapore or someplace else? Why do we want a permanent military facility in the Persian Gulf, such as we now have in Kuwait and Saudi Arabia? What kind of terror will Germany and Japan have to suffer if the United States decides to talk about them like it is talking about Cuba, Iraq, Libya, or North Korea?

Japan has a constitution that in Article 9 prohibits the use of military force even in self-defense. General Douglas MacArthur imposed it. But interestingly there is a peace movement in Japan which wants to live by that Constitution now. There is also great militarism there as well; never doubt it. Of the many highly militaristic religions that the planet has known, Shinto is in the forefront. Many Japanese didn't want to participate in any way in the Persian Gulf war, but they were finally coerced into giving some billions of dollars. It may not be important except psychologically and as a matter of principle that this war has broken the Japanese constitutional ban on participating in war. And if we start trying to use fear to cause them to do something about how they make and sell automobiles, rather than doing what we ought to do—which is build better ones ourselves—we may see an arms race which would make the one we have just been through seem like child's play because of the technological skills that will be involved. The last arms race between the United States and the Soviet Union was the greatest crime against humanity in history, and if we don't understand that, then we are bound to repeat it.

My father worked for President Truman and I loved him as a man of unique integrity and candor. In his memoirs, President Truman describes being on the U.S.S. *Augusta* a few days after the Potsdam Conference in early August 1945. President Truman reports that he was sitting in the galley drinking coffee with the sailors when the word came from the bridge: "Big Boy dropped on Hiroshima. Results exceed our greatest expectations." President Truman says he turned to the sailors and said, "Boys, this is the greatest thing in history. Let's hurry home." You can puzzle for a long time about what he meant by that. On the surface you can say that he meant that finally the war was going to end quickly and American lives were going to be saved. But I think most people already thought the war would end quickly. How much longer could it go on? And why would that be the greatest thing in history? What I think he meant was that we now have absolute power. We are good. And they are evil. They being whoever opposes us. Now they will do as we say. And there will be peace. You could call it "Pox Americana," not "Pax," because we now have power over everything on earth.

The use of fear as a means of coercing conduct is the most dangerous practice of the species. Whether it is battering a woman or threatening to, threatening a child, beating it once in a while so it knows for sure that you will really do it. That's what the acts of a police state are. That's what the bodies in Haiti are. You don't kill everybody; you just lay them out there so people know you will really do it. And the people will be terrorized. And through that coercion we create the climate from which other acts of violence emerge. I remember some heartbreaking debates in South Africa about the meaning of Martin Luther King and his insistence on nonviolence as the means to change the police state conditions created by the white government. They would look out and sadly, almost unanimously say, "Not here. It would never work here."

We have to address all uses of fear. For years off the coast of Nicaragua, we practiced war games. I remember believing that the Sandinistas would fall from adrenal exhaustion because they could never be sure when the expected invasion was coming. We used this fear as a means of domination. I remember waiting for a car to come get me in Baghdad in November before the bombing. I was talking to a young woman who told me she had cancelled her wedding and she was saying how terribly frightened she was that she would not survive, that she would never marry, that she would never have children. She is a woman who had lived seven years in Montreal, an Iraqi, a human being like you and me. I can guarantee you that the fear in Libya at this time is enormous, as the United States contemplates what means it will use to punish Libyans for whatever part they may, or may not, have had in the bombing of Pan Am Flight 103. In 1986 the bombing of Tripoli and Benghazi came at 2:30 in the morning. Libyan cities were quiet and people were asleep, but in the United States it was just in time for the evening news on the East Coast. That's when the reports came in. We did exactly the same thing in Iraq. We had it live from both places: from Libya and from Baghdad. Then we could flash to Washington for an immediate response.

We are the victims of "double-speak." We are shown what we are supposed to see and we do not see what we are not supposed to see. Our government didn't keep the bombing of Cambodia secret so the Cambodians wouldn't discover it. They had a pretty good idea it was happening every time the ground shook. The secrecy was to deceive the American people, you and me, and that is why our anger was so uncontrollable and why we took to the streets and the campuses, like Kent State and Jackson State. Some got killed and some of the survivors got prosecuted.

The fear that we strike in all these countries is a form of terrorism. The fear of economic sanctions is a form of terrorism of

Green Team Video Collective
still from the video *The Generation
after Martial Law: Taiwan*, 1990
curated by Ching Jan Lee
60 minutes
Shu Lea Cheang produced and
coordinated the series *Will Be
Televised*—five one-hour programs
of video compiled from five
regions in Asia that documented
movements for social and political
change within those countries.
Courtesy of the artist.

the worst sort. If you have been hungry for a long time and things are getting worse and you are told your food is going to be cut off, you can get pretty desperate.

If you want to end terrorism, you have to renounce all uses of fear to coerce others. They are irrational, they are cowardly, they are destructive, and we know it. And our use of fear is no better than anyone else's use of fear and 99.44 percent of all terror comes from governments. Ask the people who lived in Chile under General Augusto Pinochet or in Argentina or in Greece under the Colonels, or in all the tyrannies of the planet, including so many that we have supported. I believe—and it is an article of faith with me—that infants born healthy (and that is a big task to get infants to be born healthy) to people who love each other in a society that understands the importance of values and that doesn't glorify violence will grow up to be loving, gentle people who will not hurt others. This is the great goal of life. A university in a whole year with all its instructors couldn't begin to cover the different ways the people of the United States glorify violence constantly and ignore its horrible and destructive consequences. And the love of things—Mammon—these are what pass as values in our country today. Children born healthy in a society that understands the importance of values and the desire to live by them will rarely hurt each other. And they won't use fear to coerce the conduct of others. And that is hard work.

You don't do it with prisons, which are an instrumentality of both segregation and fear. There is a good reason why very few men—it's little different for women but there are not that many women prisoners—come out from a long time in prison without physical disabilities like stomach ulcers. The reason is constant tension. You walk through the blocks at San Quentin or Attica or any major prison and you feel the violence in the air, the constant fear, and the acid is eating your insides out. All we seem to know to try to stop antisocial conduct is the use of more fear, and it is destroying all of our institutions. After all, it does reflect upon our character since these are our children in prison, they really are, they grew up here among us. Because of our own fears, we can only think of ways to make others fear us rather than addressing the causes of crime and resolving the crime problem by doing something about the causes. Where was the love? Where was the health? Where was the opportunity? Where was the family that could have given them a chance? And when they act out, we in fear want to smash them down, confine them, and execute them. We are the largest imprisoner on the planet.

I was talking with someone recently about the twentieth anniversary of the uprising at Attica prison. There is a jury out in Buffalo, New York, right now deciding whether or not there will be civil damages for the survivors of the slaughter at Attica prison. It was the bloodiest day in the twentieth century in America in a confrontation at a single place. Thirty-nine people were killed, including nine people called hostages, all by gunfire and no inmate had a gun. We were told immediately that some had their throats cut and some were emasculated, but autopsies showed that no one was hurt except by gunfire. The police just came in with a fusillade and killed all these people. The Attica rebellion occurred because of overcrowding in the New York prison system in 1971. There were 12,500 in there in 1971. In the last twenty years, the population of New York state has not grown, but now there are in excess of 60,000 prisoners in New York. They are overwhelmingly minorities. They are young men from poverty, from urban ghettos, and we are growing them and we are manufacturing a new quality of meanness in their segregation and brutalization and constant fear in prisons.

And then we let ourselves go to extreme tactics in response to great tragedies like Pan Am Flight 103. Our government now says that Libya blew that plane up. Why did it earlier say that Syria did it? Why even earlier did they say that Iranians may have been involved? Still earlier they said Palestinians. Why has our government never shown us what it really knows about the West Berlin disco, as if that act could possibly give anyone a justification for killing all those people in Tripoli and Benghazi a week later. With laser-directed bombs, the first wave went straight for Qadaffi's home, his office, and his field tent. Two bombs were aimed at his house and his tent because he is a Bedouin and so he spends some time in his tent. Everyone at the house was injured and a baby was killed. Then we argue about whose baby it was, as if it mattered. A baby is dead. Our Secretary of Defense, Caspar Weinberger, said that it was impossible that we killed civilians. I brought a lawsuit against the U.S. government on behalf of more than 340 people killed or seriously injured. During the bombing and immediately afterwards, people leaped into their cars to rush out into the desert. In the panic there were a series of accidents and in one case a car crashed into a truck, fire broke out, and four people were burned to death. Stark fear. The terror of an alien aerial attack, a surprise in the middle of the night.

If we want to end all terrorism, we have to stop practicing terrorism in our lives, in our families, in everything we do. And then we can live in a world without fear of others.

Foerstel: I want to thank you on behalf of everyone. That was a very, very powerful statement. I now have a little grandchild who is just eight months old. I think when you are young and don't have children you may not be as sensitive as when you are older and so very aware of the vulnerability of a child. I watch how she watches everything we do and I know the enormous power of the nurturing we are trying to give that child. I wish that everyone could feel as I do about the importance of the point that you made about the love and nurturing we must give in order to make a healthier society. I want to thank you for that.

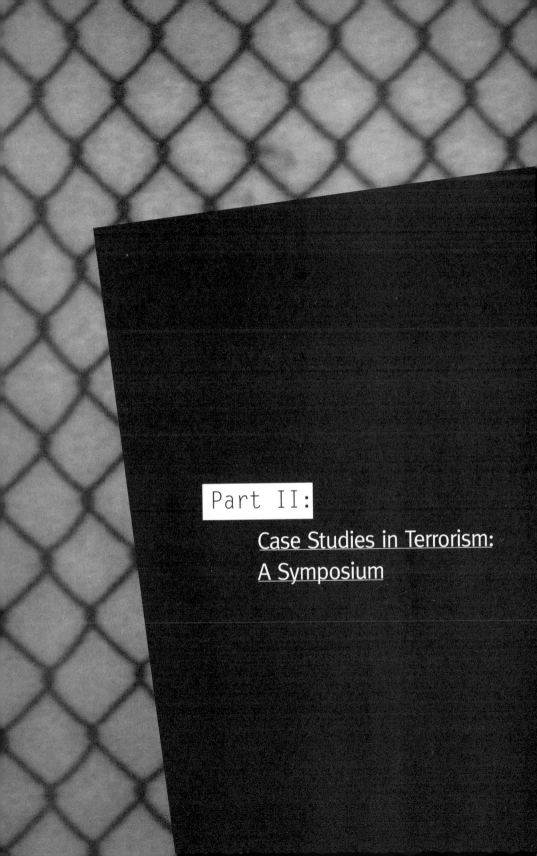

Part II:

Case Studies in Terrorism:
A Symposium

Case Studies in Terrorism:
A Symposium

William Schaap
Angela Sanbrano
Randall Robinson
Robert Merrill
Ward Churchill
Alexander Cockburn, moderator

Cockburn: Our panel will flow very naturally out of Ed Herman's excellent overview. We have an extremely well-qualified panel on the platform here, all of whom have intimate experience with the domestic and international struggles which have provoked the whole infrastructure of the terrorism industry, from the inflicting of appalling violence to the ideological labelling in the press. All of this has arisen in reaction to national struggles for liberation. Our speakers will each make a presentation and then go to the floor from which there will also be very interesting things to say and we will try to set up an interesting dialogue between the people on the platform and the people on the floor.

First I would like to introduce Bill Schaap, director of the Institute for Media Analysis. Many of you will have read *Lies of Our Times*, which has addressed itself in recent years to the way the media misrepresent current events in favor of the agenda of the state. He has had decades of experience in studying the Central Intelligence Agency and the kindred organizations of the national security state. Out of this experience has grown *Covert Action Quarterly*, something many of you might also have read. So without further ado, I would like to give you Bill Schaap.

Schaap: Thank you, Alex. I am very happy to be here at this incredible event. It has renewed my faith in the National Endowment for the Arts and I want to thank Jesse Helms for making this weekend possible.

There has been a lot of discussion of the real terrorism practiced by the United States and its allies, and some analysis of the ways in which terrorism practiced and supported by the United States almost invariably goes by other names, most of which contain key buzzwords like "freedom" and "democracy," sometimes prefaced by "fledgling" or "emerging." Always look twice at any organization that has "freedom" and "democracy" in its name. That's why the contras in Nicaragua were the Freedom Fighters and people like Alfredo Cristiani are said to represent the democratic forces. This is why people like Lindsey Gruson of the *New York Times*, for example, would say—and I might add verbatim three times in three days—that "the regime of the dictator Ephrain Rios Montt was remembered more for stability than brutality." The question, of course, we ask is: remembered by *whom* more for its stability than its brutality? You would have to ask the friends and relatives of the tens of thousands of people in Guatemala who were murdered, disappeared, or tortured how they remember General Montt.

I want to look a little bit at the other side of the coin: the ways in which the forces opposed to the U.S. government are characterized as everything bad and particularly as terrorists. Other speakers will be discussing liberation movements, virtually all of which up until recently—I make this qualification because of the Croatian Liberation Front and its ilk— have been characterized by the U.S. government as terrorists. I want to consider the strategy that the U.S. government employs in demonizing its enemies and comment on the ways the mass media in this country are used to perpetuate those myths and transformations. I will do this by concentrating on some specific examples. I want to stress that we are really going into the area of the "big lie." Reality has very little to do with this kind of strategizing: you paint your enemies as terrorists by accusing them of horrible things, and you don't worry in the least about the evidence or events that actually occurred.

How many of you remember Secretary of State Alexander Haig holding up a photograph of hundreds of bodies burning in a pyre and saying that it showed the Sandinistas burning the bodies after they had massacred 10,000 Miskito Indians. If you remember the incident, a great photo-op, you probably don't remember that the photo turned out to be of earthquake victims from ten years earlier being burned by the Red Cross. This was after the devastating earthquake that struck Managua in 1972. Haig's outright lie is a good example of the "where there is smoke there is fire" syndrome because after his fallacious announcement, the debate in the American press was over whether the Sandinistas had massacred 10,000 Miskitos, or maybe only 2,000 Miskitos, or maybe only 200. In fact, the answer was zero since this was not a real incident at all.

Little switches can make the victims into the terrorists. There is another example from Nicaragua when the conservative leadership of the Catholic school in Masaya denounced the Sandinista government. Hundreds of townspeople who supported the government marched past the school in protest. Inside the school were armed men who shot at the demonstrators in the street, several of whom were wounded or killed. The Associated Press Central American affiliate, that paragon of objectivity, sent out a radio photograph of a number of demonstrators in the street diving for cover and hiding behind walls. The caption read, "Church supporters dodge Sandinista bullets." The Sandinista supporters didn't have any guns. It was, in fact, the church supporters who were shooting at them. Maybe the Associated Press caption writer just made a mistake! Such mistakes are not that uncommon, after all, you might say. It happened in Jamaica during Michael Manley's unsuccessful 1980 campaign when an opposition supporter fired on a pro-Manley march and the wire service dispatch said that a Manley supporter fired on an opposition march. The Associated Press (AP) affiliate said that it was a typographical error at the telegraph office.

But if you think it was a mistake, you have to remember that we are dealing with the people who also said that Grenada was a threat to U.S. national security, and we are also dealing with the people who believed that. Reagan said that Grenada was a threat to the international sea lanes. But Grenada didn't even have a navy, and no one in the American press pointed that out. Not one ship. Not only can the manipulators present such nonsensical propositions with a straight face and get away with it, they can also change friends into enemies and vice-versa in the blink of an eye. When you look at the incredible speed with which Manuel Noriega and Saddam Hussein were transformed, you begin to think that it is impossible to overestimate the

Greg Barsamian
Putti, 1990,
electric motor,
programmed
strobe light, wire,
foam, electric eye
8" x 18"
courtesy of
the artist.

shortness of the average American's political memory. Nobody remembers that they read something completely the opposite just days before the release of the current line. If you look at the papers two or three months before the Iraqi invasion of Kuwait, you see a completely different U.S. attitude toward Saddam Hussein. There is a great story in the *Washington Post* that uses the word "moderate" about eight times and uses the word "pragmatic" about six times. "Moderate" and "pragmatic" are the words we use for our friends. We don't call the other side "moderates" or "pragmatists." The Syrians fit this category as well. They are our allies at the moment, but they used to be our enemies. That switch happened almost overnight, and it was driven by the momentary needs of the Bush administration to solidify Arab opposition to Iraq. The rest of the reality of Syrian President Hafez el-Assad's record just vanished into thin air.

Another example of complete fabrication involves the charges that the plot to kill Pope John Paul II originated in the KGB and was carried out through Bulgarian operatives. Ed Herman's *The Rise and Fall of the Bulgarian Connection* is a case study in the exposure of this kind of manipulation. The plot to kill the Pope was really a case in which a right-wing Turkish fanatic, Mehmet Ali Agca, who had already been imprisoned for the 1979 murder of left-wing newspaper editor Abdi Ipecki of *Milliyet*, and who belonged to a fanatical right-wing group, the Grey Wolves, said he shot at the Pope in order to defend the honor of Muslim fundamentalism. In the American media he was converted into a left-wing terrorist. No one raised any questions about his background. The connection between the Bulgarians and the Soviets was accepted because it satisfied the kind of logic which demands that all evil acts originate from our enemies. The *New York Times* even said that all this right-wing stuff was the creation of a cover story to make him appear to be a right-winger when he was actually a left-winger working for the Soviets to stop the Pope's support for Solidarity in Poland. Nobody in the mainstream media pointed out that this guy was involved in the murder of a left-wing newspaper editor in Turkey before Solidarity ever even existed. This was an instance of creating a cover story even before the reason for the cover story had come into being. Nobody pointed that out.

One of the things that is clear from all of this outright fabrication and that helps the disinformationist get away with murder—

both literally and figuratively—is the elimination of any sense of history, any understanding of history, particularly when it might be embarrassing. Ramsey Clark mentioned yesterday that in all the discussions of the Gulf war there was very little about the history of Mesopotamia in general or about Iraq and Kuwait in particular or about the governments in the area. That shortness of memory and *absence of historical perspective* make the manipulation and the demonization of our enemies of the moment so much easier. In the campaign against Saddam Hussein there was almost no political analysis of the other autocratic regimes in the area, and what did appear was pretty weak since the discussions did not approach a real analysis of the total absence of democracy in Kuwait or Saudi Arabia. In fact, Iraq had made more progress toward democracy than either Kuwait or Saudi Arabia, but any discussion of that sort would have undermined the image of a "Hitler" that was being imposed on Saddam Hussein. It was almost as if some overnight conversion came to every mainstream journalist. Following some prophetic dream, they all woke up one morning and began calling Saddam Hussein a "Hitler." Now, they never woke up and decided to call Augusto Pinochet, the former dictator of Chile, a "Hitler," or decided to call General Suharto, who murdered as many as 800,000 people in Indonesia because they were members of PKI, the Indonesian Communist Party, a "Hitler." They never called a string of leaders in Guatemala and El Salvador "Hitlers," but all of those people were responsible for vast numbers of deaths, the kinds of killings that can only be called genocide.

Many of you may have seen the issue of the *New Republic* at the time of the build-up to the Gulf war which had a cover photo of Saddam Hussein with his moustache retouched in order to make it look like a Hitler moustache. The headline was "Furor in the Gulf." They didn't say anything about the photograph. The editors just let the impression of the photography stand. This is pretty tricky stuff. If you have any friends who are professional photographers, then you know that retouching of photographs has become a major problem in the industry. Retouching has become so good that you can't tell when a picture has been altered or even re-composed. If the magazine editors don't point out what alterations they have made, then incredible manipulation of public opinion becomes possible. Photographs carry with them a presumption of objectivity and history. Their nature is always presumed to be documentary and not editorial. But in fact, photographs now regularly contribute to the editorializing intentions of the media. This is only a further example of the erasure of history.

Staying with the Middle East for a moment, another point I want to make is that the media in this country would never in a million years use the word "terrorism" with respect to the government of Israel. Ed Herman pointed out that they would very rarely use it in connection with *any* ally, but in the case of Israel it becomes an even more compelling contradiction because you have events like the Sabra and Shatila massacres in 1982 during the Israeli occupation of Beirut. Within Israel itself, there is the use of collective punishment of Palestinians, the bulldozing of homes of innocent Palestinians and legally sanctioned detentions without charges or trials for vast lengths of time. The Israeli occupation of Arab lands in the West Bank and Gaza Strip is accomplished with precisely those policies that Ramsey Clark outlined yesterday as the very definition of terrorism: the maintenance of political rule by the instillation of terrible fear in the population.

The idea of a complete terror state where all the people or at least a large proportion of the people are ruled by complete terror is exemplified all over the globe, but it is never pointed out in the media unless the nation happens to have a communist government or be an enemy of the United States. Compare the terrorism of the supposed Iraqi threat of the use of chemical weapons with the terrorism of the omnipresent U.S. threat of using nuclear weapons. This is almost never touched on. The United States is the only nation that has actually dropped nuclear weapons on an adversary. And it has used nuclear weapons, as Daniel Ellsberg points out, dozens and dozens of times since. Most people think that the only time the U.S. has used a nuclear weapon was against Japan, but if you are held up at gun-point, the robber used a gun. And in that fashion, the U.S. has used nuclear weapons many times.

Occasionally an enemy state clearly acts unlike the image it has been given in the press, and the media has to go through some fancy steps to maintain the image. For example, after the Iraqi invasion of Kuwait, Cuba, which was a member of the UN Security Council at the time, joined with all the other members in condemning the invasion. The vote condemning the invasion of Kuwait was unanimous, but it was described in the *New York Times* as "The Cubans say they condemn the occupation and annexation of Kuwait by Iraq." It is a very interesting way of putting it. The *Times* did not write that any other country "said" it condemned the invasion; the *Times* just wrote they "condemned it." Effectively, the *Times* implied that Cuba might have been lying. In this way, Cuba's image as a terrorist state is preserved.

Finally, there are occasions in this country—a glimmer of optimism— when people suggest that our own government might be engaged in terrorism, and we have to fight against the obfuscation of those disclosures. A very good example is the appeal by the Conference of Catholic Bishops in Washington in late 1990 for restraint in the growing determination of the Bush administration to advance toward war. This is the same Conference of Bishops that supported very strongly the Vietnam war. The Conference voted 249 to 14 to support an appeal for restraint by the United States, saying that Catholic teaching considers it essential for warfare to be moral, that there be a just cause, that all alternatives be exhausted and so on. They said that there is a great danger of the U.S. violating these principles if war breaks out. And what do you think was the *New York Times* headline about this: "Debate on Persian Gulf Enlivens Bishops' Meeting." You had to get down to about paragraph twenty to see that the Bishops had voted against the war build-up.

Detecting fabrication in the mass media is a case-by-case affair. The examples could be multiplied endlessly, but unless we insist on a genuine understanding of history and a sincere analysis of real events, we will be helpless victims of political policies that have absolutely no concern for human life.

Cockburn: Thank you very much, Bill. If people want to look at a very interesting example of retouching and the presentation of composed photographs as though they are reality, a recent issue of *Sports Illustrated* set up one of those dream games that sports correspondents endlessly write about between two teams who have never played. The whole game is actually made up of computer-simulated images that are so photographically realistic that no ordinary reader could be expected to tell that they were fakes. So if you are ever in a trial and you want to challenge the idea of photographic evidence, I think *Sports Illustrated* might be a useful little weapon for you there.

Our next speaker has just returned from Mexico, where she attended the signing of the peace accords brokered by the United Nations between the government of El Salvador and the Farabundo Marti National Liberation Front (FMLN). She is Angela Sanbrano who is the executive director of one of the organizations that most vigorously challenged U.S. policy in Central America, the Committee in Solidarity with the People of El Salvador (CISPES).

Sanbrano: Thank you very much. It is great to be here this morning and it is great to see many friends who have been struggling for many years to change U.S. policy toward Central America. I want to thank the Maryland Institute, College of Art for organizing the exhibition and the symposium on the politics and imagery of terrorism because those of us who have been victims of the ill-defined and manipulated term understand the importance of educating ourselves and the public, not only about how the term is defined by the government but also about the tactics used to attack those of us who challenge U.S. policy at home and abroad. Most importantly, we should work to redefine the term, to recapture the term "terrorism," and bring to justice the real terrorists. For example, the United States has been waging a war against the people of El Salvador for twelve years. The basic issue in the war is the refusal of the dozen or so aristocratic families who own almost all the wealth in El Salvador to share economic and political power. During the 1980s, the U.S. government spent more than $6 billion dollars supporting the Salvadoran government and training and supervising a military which systematically murdered more than 75,000 people and disappeared another 8,000 people. Over one million people, a fifth of the population, have been forced to flee the country. This is a tiny country of five million people, about the size of the state of Massachusetts.

The army and particularly the elite battalions trained here in the United States have carried out some of the most horrendous crimes in modern history. The Bishop of that country, Archbishop Oscar Romero, was machine-gunned in his church because he called upon the army to stop killing peasants and he called upon the United States to stop military aid to the army. Hundreds of religious people were killed, including four North American religious women in 1981. Six Jesuits and their co-workers were killed in 1989 and the army carried out massive bombings in the countryside. They massacred thousands of people, many killed by uniformed soldiers and many others killed by the infamous death squads, either off-duty soldiers, Treasury Police, or hired killers who terrorized the population with random killings of up to about 800 people a month during the most violent years of the early Reagan era. The point of this terror was to stop absolutely any demands by Salvadoran peasants for land reform and to prevent anyone from supporting the FMLN.

There are many cases that illustrate this point, but I will mention just two. The first is a story told by Rufina Anaya who survived the massacre of her village, El Mozote, in 1980. Her husband and her four children were killed. According to what she saw, the army troops first fired mortars over the community; then they invaded the village and forced all the people to go to the village square, where they were forced to lie down. Then the soldiers took all the men to the chapel and forced everyone else into their homes. The soldiers took the people out in groups beginning with the men, most of whom were elderly. The men were told that they were being taken to the lieutenant so that they could later be released; instead they were all killed. The people, who were still inside the houses, heard the machine guns firing. Next, the women and children were taken out of their houses. The women were raped and then shot. While the soldiers were killing a group of women, Rufina escaped and hid behind the bushes and this is how she was able to see the whole massacre. She later heard the screams of the children being shot and bayoneted and then burned. All of the people of the town were being killed. One thousand people. No one knew about it for a long time. The people were too terrorized to talk.

The second example concerns the massacre at Rio Sumpul. In this case, there was a public outcry. On June 24, 1980, the archdiocese of Santa Rosa of Compagne across the border in Honduras denounced the massacre and said that the Salvadoran and Honduran governments were responsible. They said that women were tortured before

being killed and that babies were tossed in the air and shot. People who crossed the river into Honduras were forced back across by Honduran soldiers. In the late afternoon, when the killing ended, a minimum of 600 people were dead.

Now if this is not terrorism, I don't know what is. And yet the American administration, President Reagan, Alexander Haig, Thomas Enders, and Elliot Abrams were calling the Salvadoran peasants and the FMLN rebels terrorists. On the government's part there were well-understood political goals that have been accomplished by means of this terrorism. These massacres occurred in 1980 and the United States continued to fund the killer army for many years and this funding continues to this day. A congressional report released in 1988 said that El Salvador was approaching the record for dependence on U.S. aid held by South Vietnam during the height of that war. In 1991, a peace accord was signed between the FMLN and the Salvadoran government. The real question is not the peace accord, however, but whether the United States will continue funding the military.

CISPES, the organization I belong to, has tried to bring the testimonies of the victims of the repression to the American people so that they might bring pressure on their government to stop the terror in El Salvador and change U.S. policy so as to support the people of El Salvador, whose only crime was in trying to bring about change in a country that was ruled by a military which maintained its power through terror. Because we were being successful in organizing public opinion against U.S. intervention in El Salvador on the side of the military, the United States government declared us to be supporters of terrorism and began a long campaign to destroy us. In early 1981, the FBI began an investigation of CISPES under the heading of "foreign counterintelligence terrorism." The investigation led to information being collected in over 300 files on 13,198 individuals and 11,000 organizations. Every single organization that was doing anything connected with the churches, unions, civil rights organizations, or human rights organizations that came in contact with CISPES or activities related to CISPES was investigated. They were called spin-off investigations. All of the fifty-nine FBI field offices and personnel at all levels were involved in the investigation. The FBI placed informants or spies in our committees. We became aware of this illegal investigation because one of the informants turned on the FBI and exposed the case.

The FBI visited members of the committees, members of their families, their neighbors, their employers, they carried out several break-ins, wire taps, they photographed our activities, they followed people around in their cars, and they worked very closely with the National Guard and the National Police in El Salvador. They sent lists of people who were involved in CISPES activities, both North Americans and Salvadorans, to the Salvadoran National Guard. Those lists generated a wave of terror that occurred in Los Angeles in 1987. One of my friends, a Salvadoran woman, was kidnapped in Los Angeles. She was tortured; they cut and burned her skin. Then they raped her and showed her a picture of her child and told her that if she didn't stop talking about El Salvador her child was going to be killed. And later she received a letter containing nineteen names— my name was included—which said that if we did not shut up and stop talking about El Salvador, then we were going to be killed. They went as far as to develop a plan to attack CISPES and specifically some individuals. We have in information that we got from the New Orleans FBI documents a clear statement of the intent. This is a quote from an FBI field officer's memorandum: "It is imperative at this time to formulate some plan of attack against CISPES and specifically against individuals. . . ." The names which followed on the memorandum were deleted. The FBI told us the names were deleted for reasons of privacy. The FBI report goes on, "who defiantly display their contempt for the U.S. government by making speeches and placing propaganda for their cause while asking for political asylum." In other words, our activities under their definition were subversive. That is what they believed we were doing, but, in fact, we were talking about what was going on in El Salvador.

The FBI carried out a massive investigation for several years and yet never filed criminal charges against anyone in the organization. Why? Because all of the activities that we were carrying out are protected by the Constitution. We were able to make a public disclosure of the illegal investigation because all of the groups involved got together and we took the offensive as soon as we were able to prove that the FBI was illegally investigating us. We claimed that the spying, the harassment, the attacks, and the surveillance were part of an overall counterinsurgency strategy of the U.S. government to carry out the war against the people of El Salvador. The tactic used in El Salvador was to brand people as terrorists or subversives and this justified the government's programs of arresting people or disappearing them. Counterinsurgency strategies led to the death squad killings and assassinations. The FBI was trying to get the same thing started here in the United States. By labelling us as terrorists and subversives, they were justifying all the harassment against us.

We were not silenced, however. We took the offensive and claimed that our constitutional rights were being violated and our right to dissent was being violated. We had a press conference in front of the FBI building to expose them and called for a congressional hearing. This hearing started to generate a lot of interest because some congressmen were identified in the FBI files. They wanted to find out why the FBI had been investigating them. We filed a lawsuit under the Freedom of Information Act and got all of the FBI files—well, not all of them, but many of them. We filed an injunction forcing the FBI to put all of the information in the Archives so that the FBI and the federal government cannot use the information without special permission.

We accomplished something, but we have a long way still to go. We must continue to challenge the use of the term "terrorism." We must redefine the term, and most of all we must challenge the media when they use the term and force them to bring out our point of view. I remember during the Reagan administration when we were carrying out our protest activities, we used to have a favorite chant that went "Who is the terrorist?" The response was, "Reagan is the terrorist. Who is the terrorist? Reagan is the terrorist." So I think we were clear about who were the real terrorists and we exposed them. We exposed their terrorism and we are going to continue to do so until we stop the political manipulation of the term as a cover-up for what is really happening in countries like El Salvador.

On March 15, 1993, our efforts and charges were finally confirmed by the report of the United Nation's Commission on the Truth. The report was established as part of the peace agreement signed by the government of El Salvador and the FMLN. Among other things, the Commission investigated the worst human rights abuses and made recommendations to prevent a repeat of those abuses. The report found that about 87 percent of the terrorist violence was committed by the military and its secret death squads. It said:

The Commission finds that death squads, often operated by the military and supported by powerful businessmen, land-owners and some leading politicians, have long acted in El Salvador and remain a potential menace. . . . This problem is so serious that the Commission calls for a special investigation of death squads in order to reveal and then put an end to such activity. The Commission is especially concerned by the close relations between the military, hired assassins and extremists within the Salvadoran business community and some affluent families, who resorted to killing to settle disputes. This practice must end.

The Commission also is concerned that Salvadoran exiles living in Miami helped administer death squad activities between 1980 and 1983, with apparently little attention from the U.S. government. Such use of American territory for acts of terrorism abroad should be investigated and never allowed to be repeated.

Of the findings, the *Seattle Post Intelligencer* stated, "The Truth Commission . . . stands as an indictment of the Reagan and Bush administrations and their Latin American functionaries in the U.S. State Department, who turned blind eyes to the bloody horrors taking place in El Salvador while pushing about $6 billion in mostly military aid to the small nation's oppressors. It is a disgrace that the Atlacatl Battalion responsible for the killings of six Jesuit priests and the El Mozote massacre had been trained by U.S. military officers."

Also, the *Washington Post* reported that "elements of the U.S. government have unavoidably had contact with Salvadoran organizations and individuals strongly suspected of being involved in or associated with political violence." The *Post* article also cited Neil Livingstone, a consultant who worked with Oliver North and reviewed U.S. policy in the early 1980s. Livingstone concluded

Thomas Enders

Massacre at El Mozote

One of the chief architects of U.S. policy in El Salvador responds to the UN Truth Commission report without apologies, "Death was a way of life in El Salvador," he says. That was his job; he did it and it worked. (Published by the *Washington Post*).

Discovery of the bodies of villagers killed in a massacre at the Salvadoran town of El Mozote in 1981 has brought charges that the U.S. Embassy and I (as the assistant secretary of state for the area) covered up or condoned the crime. These accusations require a response.

The incident occurred in a part of El Salvador controlled by guerrillas throughout the war, through which government forces occasionally swept. Correspondents brought there by insurgents reported seeing bodies of villagers killed by a U.S.-supported military unit. The embassy sent representatives, approached but could not reach El Mozote, made inquiries of neighbors and reported it could not confirm systematic violence by government units. I repeated the conclusion to Congress.

I was wrong. For 11 years no outsider appears to have gone to these rebel strongholds. Last year, the U.N. Truth Commission did. It found the bodies.

A coverup? The guerrillas—not the embassy—controlled the evidence.

Why didn't we go back to the village? A military expedition would have been required. And El Salvador was gripped in some of the heaviest fighting of the war as insurgents attempted to prevent their countrymen from voting. Salvadorans did anyway, in millions, in the first step toward resolution.

In testimony I did not deny the killing. I have responsibility for not having been able to confirm it.

For the rest I make no apologies. One of the century's most savage civil wars is now over.

In 1981 death was a way of life in El Salvador. Leftist guerrillas with outside support shook the country. A weak civilian government could not control its security forces, which attacked civilians and political opponents as well as combatants.

Now the violence has ended. Elected governments have gained the legitimacy to negotiate with the enemy and reform security forces. Insurgents agree to compete as a political party. The country that emerges is not a mini-Cuba, derelict and despotic. It is an open society, anguished but at peace. It will grow and prosper.

What happened in between? America engaged. We sustained the effort under three administrations: late Carter, Reagan, Bush. We accepted the opprobrium of helping a flawed army as the only way to end human rights abuses while preventing communist takeover. Under our influence, violence against civilians peaked, fell and ended.

The war is over. You can say it took too long, or cost too many lives. But there is one major conflict less to deal with in this war-ridden decade. That could not have happened had we not engaged. For all the scars—some of them self-inflicted—that was worth being part of.

The writer was assistant secretary of state for inter-American affairs, 1981-1983.

that "death squads are an extremely effective tool, however odious, in combatting terrorism and revolutionary challenges."

Cockburn: Thank you very much, indeed, Angela, for those excellent remarks. Among the many techniques the state-influenced media have is either writing a lot about something and misrepresenting it, or suddenly falling silent and not writing at all. It is the moments of silence that we need to watch very carefully, especially after the peace accords in El Salvador. What is going to happen next? Remember in the Carter era, it was announced that no more aid would go to the Guatemalan military because of its abominable human rights record. Actually, the levels of military aid never dropped—not once. When the mainstream press announces that something wonderful has happened, that is when vigilance ought to be redoubled.

Our next speaker is Randall Robinson, director of TransAfrica. He has enormous experience and knowledge of one of the longest-running and most steadfast parties fighting state terror, the African National Congress (ANC).

Robinson: I always say if you want to know what the American people really think and you are not afraid to discover what it is, go to Fort Wayne, Indiana. I was afraid but I went anyway. I was addressing an audience in Fort Wayne on the subject of South Africa and a lady—a nice lady, wonderfully sincere, middle class and middle aged, and genuinely earnest—approached me after the talk saying that she was shocked by the fabric of my comments because they sounded like so much fiction in the face of the real and dramatic changes in South Africa. "What's all this you are talking about," she said. Earlier I had spoken with someone a wee bit more sophisticated, Mary McGrory of the *Washington Post*, and Mary told me that she thought that F. W. de Klerk, the president of South Africa, was a very nice man and a wonderful fellow. I said, "How can you be certain, Mary?" "Well," she said, "he has that twinkle in his eye."

I think if you polled Americans on South Africa, the general view would be that South Africa has dramatically changed. Democracy is in the offing. Fundamental reforms have been undertaken. Mr. de Klerk is worthy of the Nobel Prize. While all of this has happened, the whites have relaxed control of the country and liberalized and democratized the society. The mainstream of South Africa, however, comprised of the black majority, is descending into some endless and senseless violence claiming tens of thousands of lives, a more consuming violence than we've ever seen in response to apartheid itself. This is, I believe, what ordinary Americans tend to think.

The fact is that we seem to forget because it is not carried in the news here that when Nelson Mandela went to jail twenty-eight years ago he couldn't vote. He went to jail in an effort to accomplish that. And now at age seventy-four, twenty-eight years later, he still cannot vote. Much was made of de Klerk's repeal of certain pillars of the apartheid system, one of which was the population registration act, which is the real centerpiece of apartheid in South Africa. Everybody had to register according to race under that act, and from those lists the South Africans learned how they would discriminate in this area and that. Well, in fact, the law *was* repealed, but its repeal applies only to those born after the effective date of the repeal. So it has no meaning to twenty-eight million living black South Africans who remain on the population registration rolls. We were told that the Group Areas Act, pursuant to which all South Africans are segregated, was repealed, but communities, white communities, still retain the right to maintain the "standards and norms" of the communities. It means that they have the authority to accept and reject as they see fit. In fact, of the one hundred or so apartheid laws that TransAfrica has looked at, the vast majority, over 70 percent, are still very much on the books in South Africa.

Nonetheless, Mr. de Klerk has the image in the United States of a very special and wonderful guy. I was in South Africa in October 1991 at Mr. Mandela's invitation. He asked me to bring a delegation of prominent African-Americans there to meet with the ANC leadership to talk about a range of things. In the two days while we were there, some fifteen people were killed. Another fifty were killed while we were en route back to the United States. Some of them were killed on a subway platform in a township.[1] They were just innocent bystanders waiting to go to work and someone drove by in a car and sprayed the platform with a machine gun and mowed them down. These sorts of things just continue. In September 1991, all of the contending groups in South Africa got together at the Carleton Hotel in Johannesburg: the government represented by Mr. de Klerk, Mangosuthu Buthelesi, chief minister of KwaZulu, the African National Congress, and the South African Council of Churches. There were over fifty groups in all. At the conclusion of the meeting, they signed a peace accord. Mr. Buthelesi said at the meeting that the peace accord would not work. He knew this because there were about six thousand of his supporters outside bearing weapons, the only blacks in South Africa who are allowed to do so because the government has determined these to be "cultural" weapons. Many people were killed en route home from the signing of the peace accord, as if to fulfill Mr. Buthelesi's forecast of what was to happen.

The government has armed Mr. Buthelesi; it trains his people and transports them to attack points.[2] I think that it is important to make clear that this business of a third force in South Africa is real.[3] We don't often hear about it in the press here, and you can't trace it all the way up to Mr. de Klerk and the government, but we know it is real. The South African Defense Forces are divided into four parts. One branch is the so-called Special Forces and it operates independently of everyone (thus guaranteeing deniability for government officials). These people have historically cooperated with the Mozambique National Resistance Organization (Renamo) by training and supplying them in their terror campaign against the government of Mozambique. Renamo was founded by former Portuguese colonists who were not willing to give up their economic interests in Mozambique. Renamo maintains offices in Pretoria, South Africa, and in Lisbon, Portugal. Surprisingly, Renamo was even defined as a terrorist organization by Ronald Reagan, and the State Department's report on Mozambique charges Renamo with the killing of at least 100,000 people in its effort to destabilize the government of Mozambique. For the South African Special Forces to be involved with Renamo tells a lot, I think.

The Special Forces have also worked with the Cela Scouts in Rhodesia. They have done much the same with the Kovet people in Namibia.[4] They have operated in Angola in support of Jonas Savimbi's UNITA (National Union for the Total Independence of Angola), and, of course, they operate very vigorously in South Africa now. They have organized death squads that

operate broadly in South Africa. This is called the Civil Cooperation Bureau. They do the clever work of the pseudo-terrorist. This tactic was first refined by the British and the Portuguese during the colonial period and further by the Rhodesians and now by the South Africans in the resistance to decolonization. You may recall having seen something in the press a few months ago about a train massacre in South Africa. This violence was not attributed to the ANC. But it didn't matter so long as the story involved blacks killing blacks because that fact would diminish the luster of the ANC and all of the black South Africans at the negotiating table. It turns out the people who committed the massacre were pseudo-terrorists; that is, they dressed in the uniforms of the government's enemy so that responsibility for the atrocities could be attributed to the ANC. What gave them away was that they didn't speak any South African language. The killers were probably from Mozambique and were brought in by the South African government or Special Forces. They were spread around the country to do these kinds of killings.

The high levels of violence and terrorism in South Africa serve only one purpose: to spoil the environment in which any negotiation for democratic reform and majority rule can take place. I think I should describe some of the possible outcomes that might take place in this climate of violence. Nelson Mandela said to us during our meetings in October and again a few weeks ago when he was in this country that his principal concern was this violence. As you know, he spoke at first of Mr. de Klerk as an honorable man; he has since regretted deeply that he described him so. He now believes that if Mr. de Klerk doesn't have direct responsibility for this escalating violence, then he has at least done nothing to stop it because it serves his interests, the interests of white South Africans, and the interests of Mr. Buthelesi.[5] It serves the interests of all the minorities in the country by forestalling majority democracy. The fact is that the ANC enjoys about 60 percent of the public support, Mr. de Klerk holds about 8 percent, and Mr. Buthelesi even less, about 6 percent. Mr. de Klerk must understand that the violence stands in the way of a genuine democratic election. If so, the violence serves his interests since an election would almost certainly bring to power the African National Congress and Mr. Mandela. Mandela would like to see this election take place before the constitution is written. He would like to see a constituent assembly elected to write the constitution. Mr. de Klerk does not want a constitution so democratically written. He wants it written by a select committee in a smoke-filled room, and then he wants to have elections pursuant to that constitution.

I think there are other, very dangerous and likely outcomes of this process. First, there is the likely outcome of a right-wing coup in South Africa. We have got to understand that while we can't be certain how decent and sincere or how indecent and insincere Mr. de Klerk is, we know that the majority of the Security Forces in South Africa both in the army and the police are not National Party sympathizers. They are sympathizers of the Conservative Party, which arose in 1982 precisely in opposition to a perceived "softness" of the National Party toward the anti-apartheid movement. We know as well that most of the guns in South Africa are not in the black community; they are in the white community. White South Africans are armed to the teeth and trained to shoot to kill. We know that the Afrikaner Resistance Movement led by Eugene Terre'Blanche is openly Nazi and might well have the capacity to pull off a coup or to subvert anything that is going on in negotiations. Mr. de Klerk is pressured from both sides: the democratic forces for majority government and the right-wing, white supremacist forces. He believes that if enough of this violence continues to spiral upward and the impression can be created that the ANC and others on the radical right are responsible for it, then he could win an election. He could win an election with Mr. Buthelesi's supporters and other conservative blacks who want stability and peace in their country more than democracy. Here again, this kind of race warfare serves his purposes.

The government also feels—and I think that this is the most likely scenario for the government—that as this violence goes on and on, Western nations will lose any appetite they might have had for democratic reform in South Africa and all outside pressure on the white government will cease. After all, with the blink of a headline in this country that Mr. de Klerk was going to release Mr. Mandela from prison, our news media forgot that thousands more were left in jail after he was released. But that was of no consequence to people in this country. Mandela's release was a big windfall for Mr. de Klerk, and the government probably benefited more from Mr. Mandela's release than even Mr. Mandela did. But nonetheless, the impression here was that things were changing. Steven Solarz (D-New York) in the Congress, my good, decent, wonderful, very adamantly liberal friend from New York, has put together a proposal to send millions and millions of dollars to South Africa to rehabilitate the country. Some of the money would go through the government's office for housing development, even before democracy occurs. Mr. Solarz is a man of great faith. But I think the white government believes that if it continues on the path of moderate reforms that sound different from apartheid, but are nowhere near genuine democracy, while covertly escalating terrorism and violence, then everyone in the rest of the world will tire of the ANC's demands for elections and there will be no more sanctions, no new measures in order to force the government to come up with something real. South Africa is now allowed to participate in the Olympics, and economic sanctions have been lifted in Japan, the United States, the Commonwealth countries. And yet the domestic violence is continuing to escalate. Around the world, the impression grows that the violence is attributable to the black community and not the government. Black-on-black violence is all we hear in the press.

I think that is precisely how state terrorism and violence serve the purpose of the white minority, not only in South Africa but throughout southern Africa.

Cockburn: Thank you, Randall. Next we have Robert Merrill, who teaches here at the Maryland Institute and was one of the planners of this symposium.

Merrill: I want to take as my starting point a chapter in Richard Falk's book *Revolutionaries and Functionaries: The Dual Face of Terrorism* (New York: E. P. Dutton, 1988) called "The Myth of the Good Terrorist." It may be true that everyone says they abhor violence, but violence and terror are nonetheless used quite widely as a means to political ends. Randall Robinson just made that perfectly clear. Leaders on all sides "heroize" those who commit even the most outrageous acts against those who can be labelled as the enemy. "Good terrorist" is, of course, an oxymoron; they aren't called "good terrorists." They are called something like "heroes of the revolution," "freedom fighters," "liberation armies," "democratic fronts," "counterterrorists," "special operations teams," or something very similar. But they are all considered "good." The idea or the myth of the good terrorist helps us get at the roots of political violence in a way that condemnations cannot since it reveals to us what the various sides value. Terrorism has something about it that is inextricably linked to the modern political experience, the great founding events of which were the American and French Revolutions. These were not just struggles for power among ruling elites; they were also revolutions in ideas about fundamental relations and rights in society. In both cases, terror as we know it today was practiced by those we now regard as our founding fathers (the patriarchal lineage is intended here since it is not at all certain that "founding mothers" would have chosen violence as a means to political ends).

The link I am getting at is between terrorism and the struggle for liberation or freedom. We in the "First World" live in societies that have a revolution as their founding experience, and at the heart of that revolution was an insurgency force taking on the vastly superior army of an oppressive government with "unconventional" fighting tactics. The French Declaration of the Rights of Man and Citizen makes the stance of human rights against an abusive government clear. So does the American Declaration of Independence, a document cited over and over by "Third World" revolutionaries and so-called terrorists:

When in the course of human events, it becomes necessary for one people to dissolve the political bands which have connected them to another, and to assume among the powers of the earth, the separate and equal station to which the laws of nature and nature's God entitle them . . . That to secure these rights, governments are instituted among men, deriving their just powers from the consent of the governed, that whenever any form of government becomes destructive of these ends, it is the right of the people to alter or abolish it, and to institute a new government.

This founding or "originary" experience—to use a term from myth-theory—is often invoked to justify or dignify present political actions. Whatever is done in the spirit of the revolutionary fathers automatically gains an almost sacred social stature. If you read White House and State Department policies, you will be astounded, as I always am, at the number of times the revolutionary spirit of America is invoked to legitimize present policies. When I see it invoked by all sides, even the most reactionary, I can't help thinking of Peter Weiss's wonderful play *Marat/Sade* and the line spoken by the director of the insane asylum at Charenton to the inmates who are demanding their rights within an abusive and medieval asylum: "Do we have to listen to this sort of thing? . . . We're all revolutionaries, nowadays."

Ronald Reagan called the guerrilla band he assembled to overthrow the government of Nicaragua "freedom fighters" and he said they fought with the moral equivalence of the American Founding Fathers. He went on to place the contras in the same category as resistance fighters against other totalitarian regimes:

You see, when the Sandinistas betrayed the revolution, many who had fought the old Somoza dictatorship literally took to the hills and like the French Resistance that fought the Nazis, began fighting the Soviet-bloc Communists and the Nicaraguan collaborators. These few have now been joined in struggle by thousands of Nicaraguans. (Address to the Nation, March 16, 1986)

Beyond the point that the statement is factually false—the contras were originally made up of National Guardsmen and expatriate businessmen loyal to Somoza or at least to the aristocratic class Somoza represented—it is clear that to be a "good terrorist"—since there is ample evidence to show that the contras were terrorists plain and simple—one has to fight against dictatorship, fascism, and political oppression. Like it or not, this is a well-accepted principle in moral and legal theory about conditions necessary for a just war or just self-defense. One has a right to defend his or her freedom against an oppressor. The means to that defense need only be proportional to the threat coming from the oppressor. In self-defense cases, it is the attacker who is regarded as violent; the defender's act is said to be justified by the violence of the attacker. In Reagan's view the contras were defending their inherent rights to liberty and self-determination. But this is the same claim that is made by the Palestinian Liberation Army, the Irish Republican Army, the Basque ETA, the African National Congress, the Sandinistas, the FMLN in El Salvador, and many other irregular armies across the face of the globe.

So behind the claim of who is the terrorist and who is the freedom fighter is the more fundamental claim of who is the revolutionary. Do the contras and their supporters in the United States represent the true revolution in Nicaragua or do the Sandinistas? This I think is where the confusion about terrorism comes from, for it is simply true that abhorrent acts of violence, even against innocent civilians, are committed by all sides. But when those acts are committed in the cause of revolution, they can be justified. Former Secretary of State George Shultz justifies counterterrorism—which, I must add, is a much greater form of terrorism than plain terrorism—in this manner: "As times change, so does the challenge of human rights. Two centuries ago, it meant revolution, spelling out fundamental principles in our Constitution. Today, [as] we continue to observe those fundamental principles . . . an important part of the struggle for human rights has also meant the struggle against terrorism" (Current Policy, No. 1045, February 12, 1988). Thus, counterterrorism today continues and even extends the American Revolution, both in principle and in act—if you take Shultz at his word. So counterterrorists are the true revolutionaries—again, if you believe Shultz. We must, however, be clear about the meaning of "revolutionary."

In the late twentieth century, the revolutionary belief in inherent human rights has become the core doctrine of the United Nations. It underlies the Charter and more specifically the Universal Declaration of Human Rights (1948), the International Covenant on Economic, Social, and Cultural Rights (1966), the International Covenant on Civil and Political Rights (1966), and the Declaration on Principles of International Law Concerning Friendly Relations and Co-operation among States. In spite of the recent Gulf war corruption of the UN, in which the United States bribed members of the Security

Council to vote for the war, the development of international law and relations between nations under the leadership of the UN has been co-extensive with the process of extending the entire spectrum of human rights accepted in the developed world to peoples of the so-called Third World. The name for this process is decolonization:

All peoples have a right to self-determination. By virtue of this right they freely determine their political status and freely pursue their economic, social and cultural development. (from Part I, a statement common to both Covenants cited above)

In principle, therefore, UN doctrines stand on the side of oppressed people in their wars against colonial domination or economic exploitation and against powerful nations which seek to maintain political control or economic benefit in a foreign land. This bias in international law is what provoked the unceasing harangue from Jeane Kirkpatrick, Reagan's ambassador to the UN, about the "unfair" advantage Third World nations enjoyed at the UN. Her harangue was, of course, disingenuous since the real power at the UN is vested in the Security Council, in which the United States holds a commanding position, and the sad fact is that the UN is hopelessly split between its own theory and practice. Nevertheless, Kirkpatrick showed herself to be a powerful propagandist against the universal application of human rights doctrines.

Most of the terrorism we see in the world since World War II has involved decolonization struggles: wars by disorganized and powerless people against highly developed colonial powers and the reactionary repression of those liberation movements. A useful resource here is Patrick Brogan's *The Fighting Never Stopped: A Comprehensive Guide to World Conflict Since 1945* (New York: Vintage, 1990). If you check Brogan's lists, you will see that there have been more than three hundred wars, civil wars, or rebellions in which some 17 million people have been killed since 1945. Brogan makes the mistake of separating terrorist "incidents" from what he calls "wars," but it is pretty obvious that the "incidents" taken together constitute the "wars." Nearly all of the fighting has occurred in former colonies, as indigenous people make demands for rights that UN doctrines say are inherent in human beings. The Universal Declaration of Human

Rights (1948) recognizes that rebellion will be the inevitable result when an oppressive government denies essential human rights to people: "It is essential, if man is not to be compelled to have recourse, as a last resort, to rebellion against tyranny and oppression, that human rights should be protected by the rule of law." In 1947, the UN specifically outlawed colonialism as a crime against humanity (see the Declaration on Principles of International Law Concerning Friendly Relations and Co-operation among States). But this has not stopped the "First World" from seeking to control the wealth of its former colonies. An important distinction must be made at this point between colonialism and neocolonialism. Colonialism exists when the foreign power actually controls the administration of the government, army, and economy in the colonized nation. Indigenous people have no essential rights and do not even own the nation they inhabit. Neocolonialism exists when the powers of government and the military have been turned over to indigenous people, sometimes even by carefully staged "democratic elections." But the new local govern-ment functions as a tool of the former colonial power. Moreover, the old colonial power through its corporations or banks retains control of the economy, often by sinking the neocolonial government in massive foreign debt. All this is made plain in the charters of the World Bank and International Monetary Fund. Often, indigenous people are left poorer and more abused under neocolonialist regimes than under colonial ones.

Neocolonialism describes the political conditions of much of Africa, Latin America, the Middle East, and Southeast Asia. In Zaire, for example, the present ruler, Mobutu Sese Seko, was installed in a CIA-sponsored coup and U.S., Belgian, and British corporations control most of the economy. Mobutu's government is brutal and corrupt. Mobutu runs the military, from whose ranks he originally rose. Living standards and human rights are perhaps even worse now than they were before decolonization.

In another telling case, that of Angola, indigenous people fought a fifteen-year-long revolu-tion against Portugal, 1960-75, only to be embroiled in a civil war that continues to this day. One side in the civil war is Jonas Savimbi's National Union for the Total Independence of Angola (UNITA), which receives support from white South Africa, Portuguese corporations, and the U.S. government. Until 1988, Cuba provided support for the Angolan government forces. Neocolonialism, therefore, includes the refusal of "First World" nations to permit genuine political self-determination in former colonies. This refusal takes the form of introducing massive amounts of sophisticated weaponry into small, developing nations and fomenting bloody civil wars between ethnic or ideological factions. Such a civil war in Angola has all but destroyed any chance for civil rights and economic development.

Phrased as I have just done, it is pretty easy to see who is the terrorist and who is the freedom fighter. The question is simply which side stands for the principles of human rights and self-determination as articulated in UN conventions and international law. It is clear that people do have a right to use violent means to protect themselves, their freedom, or their nationhood. As unfortunate as it may be, it is sometimes necessary, but we must as honest observers see the vastly greater and prior violence against whole populations that provoked the use of violence as a self-defense. Not to see the violence of neocolonialism is to decontextualize a terrorist incident. We cannot fall into the trap of decontextualizing or de-historicizing any act of violence. In the purview of international law, national liberation struggles are recognized as legal, moral, and, in fact, at the very foundation of the human rights tradition in the modern world. In our debate about terrorism, then, we have to determine where each side stands. To do that, we need good information, which is obviously not always available through our press and government spokespersons. But nonetheless, while it may be difficult right away to understand a terrorist act, eventually we must determine the relation of the act to the struggle for self-determination or the attempt to repress self-determination. We need to be asking these questions right now about the civil war in Peru between the government of Alberto Fujimori (backed by the U.S. military) and the Sendero Luminoso (Shining Path). We can't just take our State Department's word because it is a party to the conflict.

This slant in international law has made counterterrorism very difficult for the United States: its economy remains dependent upon a steady flow of wealth from the Third World into U.S. banks and yet international law makes that a criminal act. How do you remain an exploiter nation and at the same time claim to be a revolutionary one? For this reason, Abraham Sofaer, legal advisor to Reagan's State Department, wrote in a 1986 issue of *Foreign Affairs* that "the law applicable to terrorism is not merely flawed, it is perverse." To Sofaer and other government functionaries, it is perverse for international law to recognize intrinsic or inalienable rights in individuals because that makes it impossible for governments to use these laws to repress those who resist when their rights are infringed. The problem is, as the citation above from the Covenant on Civil and Political Rights makes clear, that no rights inhere in states or governments. The sovereignty of governments can be overthrown, but the sovereignty of persons cannot. Governments exist solely to protect the rights of persons. When governments engage in stealing wealth from a group of people, as ours has done with Middle Eastern oil for fifty years, there is nothing in international law to use against indigenous resistance movements. To Sofaer this is not fair: "At its worst the law has in important ways actually served to legitimize international terror, and to protect terrorists from punishment as criminals. These deficiencies are not the product of negligence or mistake. They are intentional." Indeed, they are intentional.

The only exception to the principled bias in human rights law occurs when an individual can be brought under criminal law. In criminal law, states enjoy a tremendous advantage over accused or convicted people. Because of the nature of international law, the appeal of American leaders in combatting terrorism and insurgency, therefore, cannot be to international law, the laws of war between states, or the laws of war within states (civil war). Instead, the U.S. has consistently tried to portray its own foreign policies as revolutionary and thus in the spirit of international law, and the actions of all those who oppose neocolonial exploitation as violations of criminal law. In Nicaragua, Angola, Afghanistan, Vietnam, etc., the United States portrayed itself as on the side of genuine revolution. Leaders and nations where resistance to colonial domination occurs are branded as criminals or outlaws with labels such as "dictator," "strongman," or "terrorist." The best example is Panama's Manuel Noriega, who was captured in a military invasion (i.e, laws of war should have applied) but tried in the U.S. criminal courts and sentenced as a criminal, in spite of successful pleas to retain his prisoner-of-war status.

L. Paul Bremer III, Ambassador at Large for Counterterrorism, was the man in the Reagan government responsible for shifting the debate on terrorism from the domain of revolution and international law to the area of criminal justice. He concludes in a 1988 report that "more and more, we are seeing the world debate focusing on the criminal effects of terrorism, not on the 'causes'" (Current Policy, No. 1047, February 4, 1988). Precisely! That was what Reagan hired him to do. In a paper written a year earlier, Bremer tells why it is important to treat insurgents as criminals: "Democratic nations must treat terrorists as criminals, for to do otherwise legitimizes terrorists not only in their own eyes but in the eyes of others" (Current Policy, No. 947, April 23, 1987). Here he admits that at least some insurgents do have legitimate causes—that is, legal claims—that might gain a favorable hearing if brought to a court which based its decisions on international law. This, of course, happened when Nicaragua successfully sued the United States in the World Court for its terrorist acts against the Nicaraguan people. But in a criminal court, terrorists' actions could not gain any sort of legitimacy because the violent act—the criminal *effect*—would be lifted out of its geo-political or historical context and viewed as an isolated and horrifying incident.

The effect of Bremer's work as special ambassador for counterterrorism—"terror tsar"—has been to criminalize the heroic struggle for decolonization. He has criminalized the very principles upon which the United Nations was founded and, indeed, the principles of the American Declaration of Independence. There are some very important implications of this shift. Bremer seeks to persuade us that terrorism is not war because the Geneva Conventions which regulate the conduct of warring parties give certain rights and protections to legitimate combatants, and thus the laws of war offer a means by which terrorists can meet their enemies on a level field or, if captured, escape the much harsher criminal justice system: "Terrorists and their sympathizers invoke the banal phrase that 'terrorism is the poor man's war.' By this argument, terrorists are presented as merely soldiers, forced by circumstances into an unconventional mode of conventional war, but, nonetheless, entitled to the same privileges extended to 'lawful combatants'" (Current Policy, No. 947, April 23, 1987). International laws regarding prisoners of war restrict the kinds of judicial procedures, rules of evidence, access to counsel, and the kinds of punishments that prisoners of war can receive. Generally, prisoners of war must be repatriated when hostilities cease. Should Noriega have been repatriated to Panama?

Counterterrorists like Bremer rightly see international law as a severe limitation on their ability to combat insurgency, so they will just not call it war. But the Geneva Conventions of 1949 and subsequent Protocols in 1977 have specifically included terrorism, insurrection, and rebellion in the larger category of war for the specific purpose of providing the fullest legal framework in which to resolve such disputes. The status of "lawful belligerents"—that is, those who are entitled to the protections of laws of war—was first articulated in the 1907 Hague Convention IV. It was enlarged in the 1949 Geneva Conventions I, II, and III to include resistance and guerrilla movements, provided those movements adhered to other requirements imposed on regular armies such as having a recognized chain of command, wearing identifiable insignias, carrying arms openly, and conforming to other laws and customs of war (such as not attacking innocent civilians or using prohibited weapons). In the 1977 Protocol Additional to the Geneva Conventions, the language pertaining to insurgency movements was again expanded: "The situations referred to in the preceding paragraph include armed conflicts in which peoples are fighting against colonial domination and alien occupation and against racist regimes in the exercise of their right of self-determination, as enshrined in the Charter of the United Nations and the Declaration on Principles of International Law concerning Friendly Relations and Co-operation among States in accordance with the Charter of the United Nations" (1977 Geneva Protocol I, Part I, Article 1). Article 44 eases the requirements of wearing insignias and carrying arms openly in order to afford recognition as "lawful belligerents" to terrorists and guerrillas who for obvious reasons could not wear uniforms and openly carry their weapons.

It seems pretty clear from the texts and the modifications over time that the laws governing war intend to fold so-called terrorist incidents into a larger conflict between an irregular army and a vastly superior government. One of the classic examples of so-called terrorism in recent years is by any fair account a legitimate act of war. This was the bombing of a Marine bunker in Beirut, Lebanon, on October 23, 1983. Some 241 Marines died in the attack. This event is always referred to in the United States as a terrorist act. But the target was a strictly military installation containing armed Marines who were in combat supporting the minority and foreign-backed Christian government of Amin Gemayel against majority insurgent Lebanese Muslims. The fact that the bomb was delivered in a truck and was not a laser-guided "smart bomb" launched by a stealth bomber seems to be the essential factor in choosing to label the act as terrorism and not just another violent episode in a larger but legitimate war. Rand Corporation terrorism "expert" Brian Jenkins, explains it this way: "We make a moral distinction between bombs dropped on cities from 20,000 feet and a car bomb driven by suicidal terrorists" (*U.S. News and World Report*, July 1, 1985). Morality, Jenkins suggests, depends upon technology and distance from the killing. In effect, whatever his side does is moral and whatever the other side does is immoral. That kind of reasoning is bankrupt to the core, but nonetheless common in the terrorism debate.

Sheik Ibrahim el-Amin, a spokesman for Hizbullah, described the attack in a way that directly refutes Bremer's position: "[The truck bombers] fought these people in the only way they could. These people don't have the same strong quality of weapons as the enemy. They have only the willingness to die [to] become an example for all freedom seekers in the world. They are not terrorists. We have not gone to America; the Americans came to us. We haven't sent an army to America—not even a *New Jersey*. We haven't bombed the American people—not even a car bomb" (*Newsweek*, July 8, 1985). The reference to *New Jersey* is to the battleship which had been lobbing 16-inch shells into Druse and Shi'ite neighborhoods every night for months, killing indiscriminately civilians and fighters. These shells carry about one ton of explosives. The reference to a car bomb is to a massive bomb which exploded in front of Islamic Jihad leader Sheikh Mohammed Hussein Fadlallah's house, killing some eighty people and wounding hundreds more on March 8, 1985. It is admitted by almost everyone that this bomb was placed and detonated by CIA operatives under the personal orders of William Casey. Sheik Amin expresses what Bremer and other U.S. government officials are at pains to conceal: in fact, there are good reasons behind the actions of so-called terrorists and those actions are, indeed, part of a larger, ongoing war. The use of the term "random" as an adjective in front of "terrorism" is almost always a distortion of the truth and an attempt to de-historicize the act.

To regard the actions of Hizbullah or the Islamic Jihad as simply "criminal"—as Bremer and U.S. policy do—means to focus on the effects of the acts. The effects are, indeed, horrifying, as are all the effects of war. If you don't like the effects, stop the war. But to focus on effects alone is to sensationalize the horror in order to traumatize American TV watchers and divert their attention away from the causes of those effects, to imply that the effects are random or senseless. Of course, as anyone knows, if you don't address the causes of something you can hardly hope ever to alleviate the unwanted effects. In fact, to deny the causes and to incite outrage against the "criminal" effects is a prime way to ensure that the causes and effects will continue to exist.

In addition to criminalizing the struggle for human rights, Paul Bremer and others were able in the 1980s to shift the focus from the causes to the personalities of individuals involved. In a paper called, "Myths about Terrorism," Bremer cites as the primary myth my whole argument about addressing the causes of terrorism. He says it is a myth to think you can "solve the 'underlying problems' and the terrorism will cease." Bremer would like us to believe that terrorism has nothing to do with underlying political problems such as oppression, colonialism, deterritorialism, racism, and so on. In the Middle East, he argues that terrorism has most often been used to disrupt the peace process; that is, those who sponsor terrorism don't really want peace and stability in the Middle East (as if the present peace process sponsored by the United States were even aimed at a resolution of the real problems in the Middle East). What they really want is personal attention:

Passengers of
TWA Flight 847
were held hostage
in Beirut, Lebanon,
for seventeen days
while members
of Islamic Jihad
demanded the
release of Lebanese
prisoners being
held in Israel.

Individuals frequently join groups because of a need to
"belong." Moreover, it is not at all clear that terrorists themselves are motivated by a desire to solve
underlying problems. In fact, recent psychiatric research makes it clear that many individual terrorists are
not motivated by their so-called cause. For example, Dr.
Jerrold M. Post of George Washington University concludes that the "cause" is not the fundamental reason
most terrorists join up. The "cause" provides the rationale, but the motivation is the terrorist's desire to
belong to a group. Social isolation and personal failure
are frequently seen in preterrorist histories. Studies
in Italy and Germany have shown that members of the Red
Army Faction and the Red Brigades often came from incom-
plete family structures and had shown a high frequency of
educational and job failure. Fully a third had been
convicted in juvenile court before they joined a terrorist group. While the leadership remains focused on the
political goal, many of the rank and file join not out of
a deep ideological commitment to a "cause" but because

the terrorist group, in effect, offers a "home," a "family." (Current Policy, No. 1047, February 4, 1988)

Bremer thinks the underlying cause of terrorism is personal failure. It is interesting that he cites the work of Dr. Jerrold Post, a leading political psychiatrist who was responsible for the psychiatric phase of the demonization of Saddam Hussein. By now we should know exactly what that sort of psychiatry is useful for. It seems remarkable that Post and others can make such elaborate psychiatric analyses without ever having to examine the "patient" personally; rather, they construct a pseudo-psychological profile based on what the State Department or CIA tells them about the person. This profile always suggests someone who is criminally insane and who poses an immediate threat to other people. Hussein was a "malignant narcissist." Apparently, the only cure for a mental disease like that is death. Counterterrorist policy is based on a principle that if someone can be seen as criminally insane, then he can be apprehended or exterminated by whatever means are required. The rule of law just doesn't apply here. Certainly, political and essential rights can be ignored in the case of the criminally insane.

According to Bremer's logic, the PLO (Palestine Liberation Organization) does not want an independent homeland in Palestine; rather, it is simply a crime family whose members gain some psychic comfort in indiscriminate acts of violence. Americans have learned to recognize this profile from innumerable crime dramas on TV. Bremer would like us to imagine that there really isn't much difference between a leader of any anticolonial movement and a serial killer like Ted Bundy who seemed to play a game with police and perhaps really had some deep wish to be caught and executed. At least that is the way people like Post describe him.

Even deeper behind the Bremer campaign is the dreaded "Stockholm Syndrome," a situation in which hostages or victims gain an understanding of the motives of their captors and end up sympathizing with them. This happened in 1985 when TWA Flight 847 was hijacked and held for seventeen days in Beirut, Lebanon. The hijackers were demanding an end to the Israeli occupation of Lebanon and the return of several thousand Lebanese Shi'ites held in Israeli prison camps. Among the Americans on the plane, Allyn Conwell became the spokesman, conducting live interviews on such shows as ABC's *Good Morning America* while under captivity. He expressed sentiments of sympathy with his captors, saying that the blame for the war in Lebanon should really be placed at the feet of Israel and the United States. He said that Lebanese factions did not mean harm to Americans. These were not forced confessions; live television coverage was unprecedented and unrepeated since. These were open and spontaneous conversations with U.S. reporters. On the last night of captivity, hostages and captors held a farewell party, complete with cake and an exchange of gifts.

This event was a nightmare scenario for the Reagan counter-terrorists since millions of Americans got to know some history of the Lebanon crisis. They saw Amal Militia leader Nabih Berri act with real efficiency and concern for lives on both sides. In all but the hardest of the hard-liners, some feelings of sympathy were aroused for the plight of the Lebanese, caught between the insistence of the West that the government and military remain in (minority) Marionite Christian control, the determination of Muslim fundamentalists to create a Muslim government, the Syrian desire to re-annex Lebanon, and the Israeli occupation and policy of treating large parts of Lebanon as a "free-fire zone." It was no longer possible to accept Bremer's proposition that all of these fighting groups in Lebanon were criminal psychopaths engaging in random acts of terrorism, and that there were no underlying political problems.

On the same day that Allyn Conwell spoke to the world via television, President Reagan addressed the national convention of the American Bar Association in Constitution Hall in Washington, D.C. His task was to retake the air waves and reassert the fundamental message of his administration's counterterrorism policy. In order to shift the focus away from local political struggles, he revived Claire Sterling's discredited theory about a terrorist network:

Most of the terrorists . . . are being trained, financed, and directly or indirectly controlled by a core group of radical and totalitarian governments—a new, international version of "Murder Incorporated." And all these states are united by one, simple criminal phenomenon—

their fanatical hatred of the United States, our people, our way of life, our international stature.

Now it is a criminal network, not a revolutionary one. But it is a strange criminality, one motivated by a fanatical hatred. It is the whole criminal insanity rap, again. Reagan goes on:

So the American people are not—I repeat, not—going to tolerate intimidation, terror, and outright acts of war against this nation and its people. And we're especially not going to tolerate these attacks from outlaw states run by the strangest collection of misfits, looney tunes, and squalid criminals since the advent of the Third Reich. (Current Policy, No. 721, July 8, 1985)

The logic of this speech is that "we are the true revolutionaries and our enemies are criminally insane." He invokes the American revolution several times. What we do, therefore, is done for the sake of freedom, human rights, and the increased dignity of humans. Other groups which may have an announced policy of supporting national liberation struggles—principally, Cuba, Libya, the Soviet Union—are really "outlaw states," that is, false revolutionaries or simply criminals.

I think we have to see that the refusal of the U.S. government even to credit the underlying causes of terrorism actually constitutes the greatest escalation of terrorist violence in the world today because it is a policy which determines that the terrible conditions in occupied Palestinian territories, of blacks in South Africa, or of landless peasants in Latin America won't ever be changed. No human rights will be extended to the postcolonial world. In effect, it is to say that complaints about those conditions are not legitimate. Those who seek change are not listened to; they are driven to the last resort of violence, sometimes even against innocent people, anyone who is accessible. The American mis-understanding of terrorism— undoubtedly willful—is best finally illustrated in the report *Terrorist Group Profiles* which presents the information collected by George

Bush as the head of the Vice President's Task Force on Combatting Terrorism. It reads much more like a collection of criminal files than a record of political struggles. The African National Congress, which has been engaged in a struggle for self-determination through majority rule in South Africa for more than eighty years and which would be accepted by almost any fair-minded person as an exemplary revolutionary movement, is described in the Bush report exclusively in negative terms. Its objectives include overthrowing the current South African government and establishing a socialist totalitarian government. The emphasis is upon the increasing scale and randomness of violence, as if to suggest that what might have originated as an organization with high political ideals is now degenerating into criminality and anarchy. The report concludes that the only way to deal with these groups is with an increased world police force. Lock them up and throw away the key! If you think about it for even a moment, you can't help concluding that this policy is just more of the very same oppression people are fighting all over the world.

Cockburn: Thank you very much, Bob. No people and indeed no person knows better about actually existing terrorism inside the United States than people in the American Indian Movement. I think the experience and the eloquence of Ward Churchill is a very good way to end the formal presentations. After this we will get along to discussion.

Churchill: My subject today is domestic terrorism or death squads in the United States. During the first half of the 1970s, the American Indian Movement (AIM) came to the forefront of a drive to realize the rights of treaty-guaranteed national sovereignty on behalf of North America's indigenous peoples. For the government and major corporate interests of the United States, this liberatory challenge represented a considerable threat, given on the one hand that Indians possess clear legal and moral rights to the full exercise of self-determination and, on the other hand, that their reserved land base contains substantial quantities of critical mineral resources. Upwards of half of all known "domestic" U.S. uranium reserves lie within the boundaries of present-day Indian reservations, as do as much as a quarter of the high-grade low sulphur coal, a fifth of all the oil and natural gas, and major deposits of copper and other metals.[1] Loss of internal colonial control over these resources would confront U.S. elites with significant strategic and economic problems.

Predictably, the government set out to liquidate AIM's political effectiveness as a means of maintaining and reinforcing the federal system of administering Indian Country. For a number of reasons, the crux of the conflict came to be situated on the Pine Ridge Sioux Reservation, home of the Oglala Lakota people, in what is now the state of South Dakota. Throughout the mid-1970s, what amounted to low-intensity warfare was conducted against AIM in this remote locale by the FBI and a surrogate organization calling itself the Guardians of the Oglala Nation (GOONs).[2] The Bureau and its various apologists—often "scholarly experts" like Athan Theoharis and Alan Dershowitz—have consistently denied not only that a *de facto* counterinsurgency effort was mounted on Pine Ridge but any direct relationship between the FBI and the GOONs. Those uttering claims to the contrary have been publicly dubbed "left-wing McCarthyites," accused of engaging in "innuendo" and attributing "guilt by association."[3]

Writer Peter Matthiessen, one of the more comprehensive and careful analysts of the "AIM-GOON Wars," has also been the target of two frivolous but massive and prolonged lawsuits, designed to suppress his 1983 book on the topic, *In the Spirit of Crazy Horse.* Matthiessen's sins were allegedly a "defaming of the characters" of David Price, an agent heavily involved in the repression of AIM, and William "Wild Bill" Janklow, former attorney general and then governor of the State of South Dakota, who headed one of the many white vigilante groups operating in the Pine Ridge area during the mid-1970s. Both Price and Janklow, it appears, received substantial support from governmental and corporate quarters—as well as financing from such overtly right-wing entities as the Heritage Foundation—in keeping the Matthiessen study off the shelves for nearly a decade.[4] As a consequence, it was not until the spring of 1991 that the American public was accorded an opportunity to read what this much-celebrated author has to say about the events in question.

A major chink in the stone wall of official and quasi-official "plausible deniability" has now appeared. This assumes the form of Duane Brewer, former second in command of the Bureau of Indian Affairs (BIA) police and eventual head of the Highway Safety Program on Pine Ridge. Along with his superior in the constabulary, Delmar Eastman, Brewer served by his own admission as a primary commander of the reservation GOON squad and participated directly in many of the organization's most virulent anti-AIM actions. In a previously undisclosed interview, undertaken by independent filmmakers Michel Dubois and Kevin Barry McKiernan in 1987 and televised in part through a 1990 PBS television documentary, Brewer does much to nail down exactly how the GOONs were utilized by the FBI within a wider campaign to destroy AIM and "Indian militancy" more generally.[5] His statements should go far in establishing that the federal government has resorted to employment of outright death squads within the borders as an integral aspect of its programs of domestic political and social repression.

The Pine Ridge Bloodbath

During the three year period running from roughly mid-1973 through mid-1976, at least 69 members and supporters of AIM died violently on Pine Ridge. Nearly 350 others suffered serious physical assaults, including gunshot wounds and stabbings, beating administered with baseball bats and tire irons, having their cars rammed and run off the road at high speed, their homes torched as they slept.[6] Researchers Bruce Johansen and Roberto Maestas have determined that the politically motivated toll on Pine Ridge made the murder rate for the reservation 170 per 100,000 during the crucial period.[7]

By comparison, Detroit, the reputed "murder capital of the United States," had a rate of 20.2 per 100,000 in 1974. The U.S. average was 9.7 per 100,000, with the average for large cities as follows . . . Chicago, 15.9; New York City, 16.3; Washington, D.C., 13.4; Los Angeles, 12.9; Seattle, 5.6; and Boston, 5.6. An estimated 20,000 persons were murdered in the United States in 1974. In a nation of 200 million persons, a murder rate comparable with that of Pine Ridge between 1973 and 1976 would have left 340,000 persons dead for political reasons in one year; 1.32 million in three. A similar rate for a city of 500,000 would have produced 850 political murders in a year, 2,550 in three. For a metropolis of 5 million, the figures would have been 8,500 in one year and 25,500 in three.[8]

As Johansen and Maestas go on to point out, their figures do not include the "typical" high rate of fatalities experienced on Pine Ridge and most other American Indian Reservations. Rather, the "murder rate of 170 per 100,000— almost nine times that of Detroit—takes into account only death caused by *physical* repression of Indian resistance."[9] Nowhere in North America has there been a comparable rate of homicide during the twentieth century. To find counterparts, one must turn to contexts of U.S.-sponsored political repression in the Third World.

The political murder rate at Pine Ridge . . . was almost equivalent to that in Chile during the three years after a military coup supported by the United States deposed and killed President Salvador Allende. . . . Based on Chile's population of 10 million, the estimated fifty thousand persons killed in the three years of political repression in Chile at about the same time (1973-1976) roughly paralleled the murder rate at Pine Ridge.[10]

Under a provision of the Major Crimes Act (18 U.S.C.A. sec. 1153), murder on an Indian reservation is an offense falling under jurisdiction of "federal authorities." Since a least as early as 1953, this has specifically meant the FBI.[11] Not one of the murders of AIM people on Pine Ridge during the mid-1970s was ever solved by the Bureau, despite the fact that in a number of instances the assailants were identified by one or more eyewitnesses. In many cases, investigations were never opened. When queried with regard to this apparent inactivity on the part of his personnel, George O'Clock, Assistant Special Agent in Charge (ASAC) of the FBI's Rapid City Resident Agency (under which jurisdic-

tion Pine Ridge falls) until mid-1975, pleaded "lack of manpower" as the reason.[12] At the very moment he spoke, O'Clock was overseeing the highest ration of agents to citizens over a sustained period enjoyed by any resident agency in the history of the bureau.[13] As he himself later put it, the normal complement of personnel for Rapid City was four agents, three investigators plus the ASAC. During the anti-AIM campaign, however, things were different.

Most of the time before the 1970s, there were just four agents assigned to this resident agency and we covered the western half of South Dakota . . . which included the Rosebud and Pine Ridge Indian Reservations. Then, from 1972-73 to the time of my retirement, the resident agency almost tripled in size insofar as agents and FBI personnel were concerned. . . . [Actually, by the summer of 1975, the resident agency had more than quadrupled.] There were probably eighteen agents assigned there. [After that] there were many, many more, at different times, thirty to forty agents working. . . .[14]

All told, O'Clock admits, between January 1973 and the end of 1975, "there were at least 2,500 different Bureau personnel temporarily assigned to [his office]." A peak number of "probably 350" was reached during July of 1975, with an average of "about 200 to 250" maintained for the six months beginning on July 1 and ending on December 31, 1975. Far from there being a "lack," O'Clock now acknowledges there were in fact *too many agents in the area*" (emphasis added) to be effective, or even to be kept track of by administrators. Consequently, by August 1975 Norman Zigrossi, who succeeded O'Clock as Rapid City ASAC, was actively reducing a *100-agent surplus* in his roster.[15] In other words, the Rapid City office was consistently overstaffed throughout the crucial three-year period, and at times the entire western South Dakota region was absolutely saturated with FBI personnel. It is also readily apparent that these personnel engaged in a virtual orgy of investigative and other activities while posted to the Pine Ridge locale.

For instance, while professing to be too shorthanded to assign agents to look into the killing and maiming of AIM members and supporters, O'Clock managed to find ample resources to investigate *the victims*. Some 316,000 separate investigative file classifications were amassed by the Rapid City FBI office with regard to AIM activities during the 1973 siege of Wounded Knee alone.[16] This enormous expenditure of investigative energy made possible the filing of 562 federal charges against various AIM members during the second half of 1973.[17] The result, after more than two years of trials, was a paltry fifteen convictions—far and away the lowest yield of guilty verdicts to investigative hours invested and charges filed in FBI history—all of them on such trivial matters as "interference with a postal inspector in performance of his lawful duty."[18]

Nonetheless, O'Clock's effort cannot be assessed as a failure. The method inherent to his endeavor was perhaps best explained in 1974 by Colonel Volney Warner, a counterinsurgency warfare specialist and military advisor to the FBI on Pine Ridge, when he observed that convictions weren't the point. By virtue of simply causing charges, however spurious, to be filed, Warner said, the Bureau was able to keep "many of AIM's most militant leaders and followers under indictment, in jail or [with] warrants out for their arrest." Concomitantly, the movement's financial resources were necessarily diverted to legal defense efforts. By pursuing such tactics, Warner argues, AIM could be effectively neutralized as a political force: "The government can win, even if no one goes to [prison]."[19] Meanwhile, what the U.S. Commission on Civil Rights described as "a reign of terror" on Pine Ridge continued, unimpeded by interference from the FBI.[20] Indeed, all indications are that the Bureau not only encouraged, but actively aided and abetted it.

The GOONs and the FBI

A number of studies have concluded that the GOONs were responsible for the bulk of the AIM fatalities on Pine Ridge. In those cases in which witnesses identified the murderers, the culprits were invariably known members of the reservation GOON squad. Yet, in most instances, no formal FBI investigation resulted.

On the afternoon of March 21, 1975, Edith Eagle Hawk, her four-month-old daughter, and three-year-old grandson were killed when their car was forced into a deep ditch alongside Highway 44, between Scenic [South Dakota] and Rapid City. Edith Eagle Hawk was a defense (alibi) witness for AIM member Jerry Bear Shield, who was at the time accused of killing a GOON, William Jack Steele, on March 9 (charges against Bear Shield were later dropped when it was revealed that Steele had probably died at the hands of GOON associates). The driver of the car which struck the Eagle Hawk vehicle—Albert Coomes, a white on-reservation rancher who was allowed by the Wilsonites to serve as an active GOON—also lost control of his car, went into the ditch and was killed. Eugene Eagle Hawk, who was badly injured but survived the crash, identified a second occupant of the Coomes car as being Mark Clifford, a prominent GOON. BIA and FBI reports on the matter fail to make mention of Clifford [who survived and escaped the scene].[21]

On other occasions, the victims themselves, or their associates, were investigated and sometimes charged—with attendant publicity to establish the "violence-prone" characteristics of their organization—with having perpetrated the violence directed against them.

On June 19, 1973, brothers (and AIM supporters) Clarence and Vernal Cross were sitting in their car by the side of the road near Pine Ridge [village] when they began receiving rifle fire. Clarence died of gunshot wounds. Vernal, severely injured [by a bullet through the throat] but alive, was charged by Delmar Eastman with the murder of his brother (charges were later dropped). Nine-year-old Mary Ann Little Bear, who was riding past the Cross car in a vehicle driven by her father at the time of the shooting, was struck in the face by a stray round, suffering a wound which cost her an eye. Witnesses named three GOONs—Francis Randall, John Hussman, and Woody Richards—as the gunmen involved [but no investigation resulted].[22]

The tally in these two incidents alone stands at five fatalities, three serious injuries, one blatantly false charge filed by the BIA police, and no subsequent FBI investigations. And, to be sure, there are many comparable incidents. The question, of course, is why such a pattern might exist. That the GOONs had a tangible relationship to the federal government has all along been clear, given that the group was formed in late 1972 through a BIA grant of $62,000 to then Pine Ridge Tribal President Dick Wilson for the purposes of establishing a "Tribal Ranger Group."[23] From 1973 onward, funding of GOON payrolls seems to have accrued from the Wilson administration's misappropriation of block-granted federal highway improvement monies (the "Rangers" were officially expanded to include a "Highway Safety Program" for this purpose).[24] Most federal housing funds allocated to Pine Ridge during the two terms of Wilson's presidency also appear to have been devoted to members of the GOON squad for services rendered.[25] Many of Wilson's relatives[26] as well as perhaps one-third of the BIA police force on the reservation were quickly rostered as GOONs.[27]

The *quid pro quo* seems originally to have been that Wilson would receive quiet federal support in running Pine Ridge as a personal fiefdom in exchange for his cooperation in casting an appearance of legitimacy upon an illegal transfer of the Sheep Mountain Gunnery Range—approximately one-eighth of the total reservation area—from Indian to Federal ownership. Although it was a matter of official secrecy at the time, the motivation for this federal maneuver concerned the discovery of rich molybdenum and uranium deposits within the Gunnery Range; both are considered critical strategic minerals by the Pentagon, access to them a matter of "National Security."[28] The GOONs were necessary to quell resistance among traditional grassroots Oglalas to any such transaction.[29] When AIM moved in at the request of the traditionals, the ante went up appreciably, and the GOONs shifted from intimidation tactics to outright death squad activities, thus pursuing not only their original objective but the broader federal goal of eliminating AIM as a viable political force as well.

On the face of it, the FBI's main complicity in the bloodbath which ensued was to conscientiously look the other way as the GOONs went about their grisly work. This would be bad enough. However, there has always been ample indication that the Bureau's role was much more substantial. For instance, when, during the siege of Wounded Knee, U.S. Marshals on the scene attempted to dismantle a GOON roadblock (at which an FBI man was continuously posted, according to Brewer)—the occupants of which Chief U.S. Marshal Wayne Colburn had decided were uncontrollable and a menace to his own men—head of FBI Internal Security Section Richard G. Held flew to the site by helicopter to "straighten things out." Held, assigned to the reservation as a "consultant," informed the chief marshal that "the highest authority" had instructed that the GOON position would remain in place. Similarly, when several GOONs were arrested by Colburn's deputies after pointing weapons at both the chief marshal and U.S. Justice Department Solicitor General Kent Frizzell, the FBI again intervened, causing the men to be released prior to booking.[30]

More importantly, toward the end of the Wounded Knee siege—a period when Colburn was actively disarming the GOONs after it appeared possible that one of his men had been seriously wounded by a round fired by the Wilsonites—those who were relieved of the hunting rifles and shotguns which until then had comprised their typical weaponry suddenly began to sport fully-automatic, government-issue M-16 assault rifles.[31] A much improved inventory of explosive devices and an abundance of ammunition also made appearances among the GOONs during this period. At about the same time, the Wilsonites experienced a marked upgrade in the quality of their communications gear, acquiring scanners and other electronic paraphernalia which allowed them to monitor federal police frequencies. To top it off, it began to appear as if the GOONs' operational intelligence had undergone considerable improvement during the seventy-one days of the siege.

It has been substantiated that the U.S. military provided no ordnance or other equipment to nonfederal agencies during the siege of Wounded Knee. It is also clear that the U.S. Marshals, for reasons of their own, were genuinely attempting to reduce rather than enhance GOON weaponry while the siege was going on. In any event, Colburn withdrew his personnel as rapidly as possible from Pine Ridge in the aftermath of Wounded Knee, leaving the FBI as the only federal force on the reservation until mid-1975. And, in the months following the siege—both the quantity and quality of GOON fire-power increased steadily. All things considered, it is widely believed among reservation residents—and several researchers have also concluded, by process of elimination, if nothing else—that the FBI not only equipped but provided field intelligence and other support to the death squads operating on Pine Ridge from 1973 through 1976.[32]

Brewer's Revelations

Although much which might have been covered is not addressed in the existing interview with Duane Brewer, what *is* included is often quite explicit. For instance, he readily confirms the oft-leveled accusation that in order to be employed on Pine Ridge during the Wilson era, especially in the Tribal Rangers or Highway Safety Program, one was virtually required to serve simultaneously as a GOON; if "you were a GOON and supported Dick Wilson and hated AIM, you had a pretty good chance of getting a job" under-written by federal funds. "[W]e had people from all over," he says. "Some of them you never had to ask to do anything, you know, like for Dick, you know. They were ready to do anything."

A lot of them liked Dick Wilson and his ideas. And they thought that was pretty nice, a GOON squad. Hell, you don't see that very often in this world, Of course, it is going on all over the nation now, and different presi-dents and leaders have their crew of people. And, you know, I guess that's all, that's politics. You have your certain followers. But, in them days, you had real dedicated people. They would hurt somebody for their leader if they had to. And if anybody tried to hurt him or anything, then [they] were too outnumbered to go messing around. A lot of dedication.

    The GOONs were organized on a community-by-community basis, according to Brewer, into "crews" of about a dozen men apiece, each headed by one or another of "ten to fifteen pretty hard core individuals" such as Chuck and Emile "Woody" Richards and Wilson's eldest son, Manny (Richard, Jr.).[33] Brewer's own crew—of which BIA police and SWAT team commander Marvin Stolt, Manny Wilson, and John Hussman served as operational lieutenants, and which at its high point in 1975 rostered at least twenty-two other individuals—functioned more-or-less exclusively on the western side of Pine Ridge. Chuck Richards's group covered the northeastern quadrant of the reservation, Woody Richards's the southeastern area. Additionally, ad hoc units were formed from time to time. Combined operations between standing units occurred in all areas, as needed.

The result of such organization was a relatively constant reservation-wide fire-force of "about 100 men," sometimes expanded to twice that number, throughout the critical period. The GOONs themselves were augmented, not only by BIA police but also by non-Indian vigilante groups such as the "Bennet County Citizen's Committee," "Charles Mix County Rangers," "Faith Chapter of the John Birch Society," and other Bircher-oriented "ranchers' associations" in South Dakota, Wyoming, and Nebraska. At present, "maybe ten or so" of the hardest-core GOON squad members have buried much of their best weaponry as well as ample stocks of ammunitions and explosives around the reservation. They stand ready, in Brewer's view, to resume their role as a nucleus of GOON leadership "in case that's ever needed again." They are motivated, he says, "by a lot of hatred."

a. The Relationship of GOONs to the FBI

With regard to how he and his underlings got along with the agents on Pine Ridge during the GOONs' formative period, Brewer's estimation is that "we had a pretty good working relationship in those days." Part of this emerged, he believes, because his own BIA police-cum-GOON unit served as a sort of regional roving patrol, dispensing a bare-knuckled "law and order" against AIM on various reservations.

During the time I was an officer, we travelled all over the country following the Movement. We went to the Treaty

Convention up at Fort Yates. We spent a lot of time in Rosebud. We went to Fort Totten when they [AIM] took over the jail. It was always Pine Ridge's little crew that went. So, we kind of had a reputation. . . . [U]sually when they [FBI] send you off like that, they tell you, you know, you don't cut them any slack. So, you know, you bust a few heads. It don't really take, you don't take any shit. . . . You haul 'em in. You show them authority because there is no law and order. . . . I got to travel quite a bit when I was an officer. I enjoyed all of it.[34]

The choice to use Brewer's unit as an inter-reservation fire brigade against AIM was not merely the result of their attitudes towards "radicalism" and the appropriateness of suppressing it through liberal applications of gratuitous violence, but also the result of a conscious federal policy—based in recognition of those attitudes—of equipping them for this purpose.

[After a while] we had all the weaponry. We had fifteen AR-15s. We had long-range projectile smoke, I mean gas guns. We had a [tear gas] fogger. We had everything. So, it was our squad that usually went. And you get there, and you hear people say, "The Pine Ridgers are here." So, of course, a number of times we went to places, some officers busted heads. . . . We were pretty cocky guys, I guess you might say. Tough guys, is what you'd say. They're fighters from around [Pine Ridge].

He affirms that "the FBI was with the GOONs" because "we was fighting in the same thing—we wasn't supporting AIM. And I imagine it's because we got a lot of jobs that, you know, like kicking the hell out of some of these different [AIM] people, giving them trouble." Asked whether this meant the FBI "looked the other way" when GOONs engaged in physical assaults upon AIM members, he replied somewhat disingenuously that "we never, ever done anything with them [agents] around, but they probably would have. . . . So anything we could get away with, we would."[35]

I had a good relationship with them [FBI] because I
helped them a lot. . . . They probably thought I was a
funny guy, you know [laugh]. Have all these weapons and
stand out as much as we did in them days. And all the
situations we was involved in. Yeah, we wasn't afraid [of
being arrested]. . . . I probably have maybe four or five
FBI agents who are real good friends. They tried to get
me into the FBI academy, tried to help me out, to get me
out of this place.

Intelligence with which to conduct his more extracurricular
anti-AIM operations was no particular problem because "the agents
would come to my house" and "give [us] all kinds of information and
things. . . .They were probably giving [the GOONs] a lot more than
they were supposed to. Which is good, hell, every little bit helps."
Basically, "we could get information from them" whenever it was
needed. Queried as to whether this meant the FBI thought it was
"okay to rough up AIM supporters," Brewer responded, "I imagine
they did. . . I think they did. . . .They never did investigate any of
them incidents [of GOON violence], you know." At another point,
in response to a similar question, he replied that when the FBI
brought information to his house, it was because "they wanted to
see us go out and educate" AIM members and supporters: "I got
the feeling they was hoping that I'd kick the shit out of somebody.
Or have a war."

b. General GOON Violence

Asked to explain the term "educate" in the context he was using it,
and thus the sort of activities the FBI had at least tacitly endorsed,
Brewer offered the concept of "butt kickin'. Good word. We would
educate them, like I said, we would kick their butt. Then they ain't
going to come around and bug you any more." He went on to explain
that the intended result of an "educational butt kickin'" was for the
victim to "know that any time they move any part of their body it
hurts 'em, [and] it could have been worse. I've educated a few who
will never forget me, you know, or have never forgotten."

I think [education occurs] when you, you give them a
severe beating, and, like I said, you don't cut no slack.

You beat their face, you beat their arms and legs, and work them over good. So, like I said, when they wake up the next day, every time they move they're going to think about you and decide whether they want to come back and mess with you again, or just let you go. And, you know, you do it good enough and they're not going to be thinking about coming back for more of the pain. They're going to forget about it.

The Wilsonites' repertoire of "educational" techniques was often even more extreme. At one point, Brewer recounts how a GOON named Sonny Dion "beat this [AIM] guy up so bad and then he used a saw and was trying to saw this guy up." Other GOONs apparently shocked at the extent to which Dion was "getting out of hand," intervened to prevent consummation of this macabre act. Brewer goes on to note that Dion was eventually "shipped out"—that is, he was charged by the BIA police and eventually sent to federal prison—not for his murderous assault upon the AIM member, but for turning his brutal attentions upon another GOON, Chauncey Folsom, shooting him six times in the back with a .22 caliber revolver (the victim lived).

For his part, Brewer points out, Folsom was a key player in a notorious event that occurred on February 27, 1975, at the Pine Ridge airport. In this incident, some fifteen car loads of GOONs headed by Dick Wilson himself surrounded an automobile occupied by Bernard Escamilla, an AIM member charged with several offenses during the Wounded Kneed siege, his legal counsel, National Lawyers Guild attorney Roger Finzel, and two paralegal assistants, Eva Gordon and Kathi James.[36] Wilson ordered the GOONs to "stomp" their quarry. Thereupon, Brewer admits, he personally led the charge, smashing the car's windshield. Other GOONs, whom Brewer does not identify, sliced open the top of the car (it was a convertible), dragged Finzel and Escamilla out and, according to a *Rapid City Journal* article published the following day, "stomped, kicked, and pummeled [them] to the ground. [GOONs] took turns kicking and stomping, while one slashed Finzel's face

with a knife, [also] cutting Eva Gordon's hand as she attempted to shield him." Folsom, who as Brewer put it, "was a really huge guy," proceeded to "educate" Escamilla, a much smaller man, "beat him up real bad, and then just sort of dumped him in a ditch full of water. Things kind of got out of hand, I guess."

No federal charges were ever filed against Wilson or any of his GOONs in this matter, although Finzel and Gordon provided detailed and mutually supporting depositions, naming several of the assailants.[37] Instead, the FBI busied itself administering polygraph examinations to the victims (which they passed with flying colors). Wilson, meanwhile, had conducted a press conference in which he claimed to know nothing about the incident other than that the violence was caused by "Russell Means and a large group of followers, last seen heading east out of Pine Ridge" village.[38] When they were nonetheless indicted by a federal grand jury, Wilson and his men quickly pleaded guilty to a misdemeanor charge in tribal court (the judges of which Wilson himself had appointed) and were assessed $10 fines. Assistant U.S. Attorney General Bill Clayton thereupon announced that no federal prosecutions would be initiated because any felony charges brought by his office would constitute "double jeopardy." When asked by interviewers whether the whole thing hadn't been whitewashed, as critics have long contended, Brewer replied, "Yeah, I guess maybe it was."[39]

At one point the former GOON leader denies having person-ally killed anyone: "No, I never did. I never did kill anybody. Like I said, I might have smoked them up pretty bad where they thought they were gonna die. But I never did really kill them." However, he also says, "I've come close, I think, you know. I've beat some people with clubs that I was worried wouldn't live," and "I worried *the few times that I did kill* somebody" (emphasis added). Further he readily admits that the GOONs as a whole did regularly commit homicide: "Some, let's say different incidents."[40] Certain of these "incidents" concern the much-rumored murder of at least thirteen individuals engaged in transporting supplies through GOON and federal lines during the 1973 siege of Wounded Knee.

I don't know if they killed them on the spot. Because, like I said, there would be witnesses. More likely, they

took them off by themselves, if they did this. Like I
say, I don't know! [laugh] . . . They probably, they
might have done it. I know that there was one group of
guys [Woody Richards's crew] that had that roadblock
that, uh, done a guy in pretty bad just beatin' him with
a weapon. . . . They ended up really pistol whippin' him
and usin' weapons on him, you know? More, I've never
heard of them ever taking a guy to the hospital as bad as
he was beat up. . . . He was probably killed somewhere.[41]

A customary GOON squad practice was to conduct drive-by
shootings of the homes of movement people: "You know, if there was
too many AIM members there, or something, maybe [the GOONs]
would take a cruise by and shoot them up." Often, Brewer recalls,
"we would set it up" so that drive-bys "would be blamed on AIM."
During the course of his interview, he drove reporters through the
Cherry Hill Housing Project, where "a lot of AIM people used to
live," pointing out specific dwellings which had been shot up and/or
fire-bombed by GOON patrols.

I know it was done quite a bit. Any time [AIM] gathered
up . . . [the GOONs hit] the AIM people. A lot of times we
had a little war. Somebody would go by and they would
open up. I guess the housing that was really the one that
was shot up the most was probably Cherry Hills. There was
a lot of 'em. That's where AIM, the majority of them
lived there at one time, the supporters of AIM. So it was
shot up a lot. Them houses are a real mess.

Nor was Cherry Hill the only such target: "I know [the
GOONs] fire-bombed a house in Crazy Horse
[housing project] once because one of the guys
that lived there was an AIM supporter." Brewer
also acknowledged that it was GOONs who, on
March 3, 1973, fire-bombed the home of
journalist Aaron DeSersa and his wife, Betty, in
order to "send a message" that they should
suspend publication of an anti-Wilson tabloid
based in the reservation village of Manderson.
Betty DeSersa was badly burned in the ensuing

blaze. Among other targets of GOON fire-bombing were the home of elderly traditional Oglala Lakota Chief Frank Fools Crow on March 5, 1975, and that of his assistant, Matthew King, on March 3. The home of AIM member Severt Young Bear, near the reservation hamlet of Porcupine, was shot up on at least six occasions and fire-bombed twice in a little more than a year.[42]

In another of many more noteworthy incidents, this one occurring on November 17, 1975, BIA police officer/GOON Jesse Trueblood shot up an "AIM house" belonging to Chester and Bernice Stone in Oglala, another reservation village. He seriously wounded all five occupants and permanently maimed two of them, an adult named Louis Tyron and three-year-old Johnny Mousseau. Trueblood himself was found dead in his patrol car shortly thereafter, shot in the back of the head with his own service revolver. The FBI, incredibly, listed the cause of death as "suicide." Brewer concurs that the federal finding was absurd—"Jesse had a disability which prevented him from lifting his arms in such a way that he could've shot himself like that"—but says he has "no idea" who did the killing. It is commonly accepted around Oglala that Trueblood was murdered by a prominent GOON leader (not Brewer), who availed himself of the opportunity presented by the confusion of attending the drive-by to settle a romantic dispute with this erstwhile colleague.

c. GOON Weaponry

Asked about the source of the increasingly sophisticated weaponry the GOONs came to possess, Brewer alludes repeatedly to the idea that the FBI armed his group—both directly and through indirect conduits—with items such as Thompson submachine guns and M-16s: "Some of it was given, like I told you, in a little [indecipherable word] in Rapid City where they would give you some weapons and in another location where they would tell you to come up with this amount of money and we'll turn over all this to you. . . . We had M-16s," he says, ".30 caliber carbines, a lot of . . . military stuff." Supplies of ammunition for such hardware were lavish: "There's sometimes that you, like at one time I probably had five bandoliers full [of .223 caliber rounds for an M-16 rifle]. And boxes and boxes of ammo for this, the 9mm [a type of pistol preferred by Brewer]. . . . It looked like it was probably police stuff, [and] it was always cheap when we got it."

"All this" included more than ammunition and automatic weapons. Brewer itemized provisions of "plastic explosives, det[onation] cord, [and] fragmentation grenades," as well as dynamite and blasting caps, to the GOONs. He contends that certain of the less exotic—but nonetheless expensive— weapons used by the GOONs, such as .300 Weatherby rifles (ideal for sniping purposes) were provided at little or no charge by white vigilante groups. Some of the M-16s, he says, accrued from BIA police inventories provided by the federal government. Most of the rest of the hard-to-get gear came in clandestine fashion from FBI personnel and/or "black drug-gun dealers" in Rapid City motel rooms, usually located at the Holiday Inn.

[Y]ou'd go to their room with this big suitcase and [they'd] show you a bunch of weapons, grenades, det cords, blasting caps, whatever, and give you some. "Here take this." A couple guys I know of walked around with blasting, you know, blasting caps in their shirt pockets.

In those instances where the "black gun dealers" effected transfer of weapons and explosives, agents were in the motel, monitoring the activity.[43] When asked whether the agents were aware that the GOONs were in possession of illegal paraphernalia, Brewer responded, "Sure." As an illustration, he recounted an occasion when, with FBI agents in adjoining rooms, a GOON "playing" with a newly-acquired weapon accidently discharged it in the Holiday Inn, blowing a hole in the floor. No investigation was made, nor was any other action taken by the Bureau. Brewer also mentions repeatedly that agents visiting his home were routinely shown illegal weapons in his personal possession, and often informed of how he planned to use them. Such matters failed to evoke a negative response—never mind an arrest—from the agents. To the contrary, they customarily advised him to "be careful" as he went about his business.

At another point Brewer explains that as a reward for his engaging in a fist fight with AIM leader Russell Means, he was rewarded with "a .357 magnum, 6-inch barrel . . . [worth] three hundred and some bucks, brand new. Real nice. I carried that a long time."[44] He also states categorically that the FBI supplied the GOONs with special types of "armor piercing ammunition," which was "real expensive" and "restricted to law enforcement personnel," so the gunmen could hit their AIM targets even if "they were in a brick building or something." This led to a question concerning "the best way to hit a house," to which the GOON leader responded:

Best way to hit a house is probably just to, like I say, have your lookouts and when there is nobody around and it's nice and quiet, have your, like I said, your assault car with all the weapons in it. And do it from the road. Don't cruise up to the house because then you got return fire. Then you got a war. Most of the points of shooting up a house is just to prove that we didn't approve of [AIM] gathering, you know, and we want them to know that we're on our toes and watching them.

When asked why the Bureau might provide—or arrange provision of—so much costly ordnance to an irregular force like the GOONs, Brewer was unequivocal: "They just didn't want them [AIM] people to survive. I thought that maybe they was, I think they was hoping that we would just kill them all, you know."

d. GOON Murders

The former "Head GOON" offers considerable perspective upon the FBI's "inability to cope" with the wave of violent death of Pine Ridge. Take, for example, one of the more mysterious homicides involved in the entire reign of terror on the reservation, that of Jeannette Bissonette—not especially a prominent activist—at about 1 a.m. on the morning of March 27, 1975. Careful observers have all along suspected the victim was mistakenly killed by a GOON sniper who confused her car with a similar one driven by traditionalist leader and AIM supporter Ellen Moves Camp. The FBI, for reasons it has never adequately explained, insisted the killing must have been done by "militants" and expended an appreciable quantity of investigative energy attempting to link Northwest AIM leader Leonard Peltier to the crime. However, Brewer frames the matter a bit differently.

```
I know there was [innocent] people killed during that
time, like that Bissonette lady down in Oglala. We didn't
do that type of stuff [ordinarily]. That was, must have
been, a freak accident. They must have mistaken her for
somebody else. I, I think that is what happened. But, you
know, the weapon we used to kill that woman was also a
weapon [provided by the FBI].
```

He also extends an interesting interpretation of what the FBI described as the "justifiable homicide" of AIM supporter Pedro Bissonette (brother of Jeanette) at a police roadblock near Pine Ridge village on the night of October 17, 1973. Brewer suggests the killer, BIA police officer/GOON Joe Clifford, may have been not so much politically motivated as he was enraged by the fact that Bissonnette had undergone a stormy marriage to his sister: "They had a real fiery romance, I guess. And it didn't end well. So maybe there was enough hatred [on the part of] this officer to, enough to end the guy's life. . . . Maybe [Clifford] was worried that [Bissonette] was coming back to raise hell with his sister or something." In either event, whether it was motivated politically or on the basis of a personal grudge, the killing plainly added up to murder rather than the "self-defense" explanation officially registered by the FBI and confirmed by government contract coroner W. O. Brown.[45]

Concerning the murder of AIM supporter Byron DeSersa near the reservation hamlet of Wanblee on January 30, 1976, Brewer states that he did not participate directly, since the locale was outside his normal area of operation. On the other hand, he candidly acknowledges providing "some of the weapons" used by GOON leader Chuck Richards, Dick Wilson's younger son, Billy, and others in committing the crime. Still, he holds his silence about the implications of two FBI agents arriving on the scene shortly after the murder, being informed by witnesses as

to the identity of the killers (who were still assembled close at hand), and then making no arrests. Similarly, he stands mute with regard to the significance of Delmar Eastman's subsequent dispatch of a BIA police unit, not to arrest DeSersa's murderers, but to remove them safely from Wanblee when it became apparent that area residents might retaliate.[46]

On the matter of the execution-style slaying of AIM activist Anna Mae Aquash, whose body was found in a ravine near Wanblee on February 24, 1976, Brewer admits there is strong evidence pointing to BIA police investigator (and GOON affiliate) Paul Herman. But, as Brewer puts it, the FBI couldn't "tie him in" to the Aquash murder because the nature of her death failed to conform to Herman's particular mode of killing.

```
[Herman] got sent off [to prison] shortly after that. He,
uh, he killed a young girl, burnt her with cigarette
butts, just done a whole bunch of things. Anna Mae
Aquash, she wasn't done like that. She was shot . . . if
this guy was a maniac and burnt his victims with a ciga-
rette and done things, why didn't he do it to [Aquash]?
. . . She wasn't, you know, sexual[ly] tortured, none of
it, none of that stuff. Just a clean death.
```

The problem with such reasoning is striking. Although government contract coroner W. O. Brown—whose conclusion in this connection Brewer apparently wished his interviewers to accept—failed to find evidence that Aquash had been tortured or sexually abused, he also "determined" that she had died of "exposure."[47] Independent pathologist Garry Peterson, retained by the victim's family to perform a second autopsy, concluded immediately that her death had been caused by a "lead slug consistent with being from a .32 or .38 caliber handgun . . . fired point-blank into the base of the brain." Peterson also observed that the victim appeared to have been "beaten" and that there was "evidence of sexual contact" shortly before she was murdered. This says much to Brewer's contention that the Aquash murder was "out of character" with Paul Herman's lethal style. By implication, it says even more about the FBI's continuing insistence—announced even before its conclusion in the Herman investigation was officially reached—that the victim was "probably"

144

killed by her "AIM associates," ostensibly because she was "suspected of being a government informant."[48]

At present, the FBI's investigation of AIM's possible involvement in the murder of Anna Mae Pictou Aquash is officially ongoing, a circumstance which exempts the Bureau from legal requirements that it disclose relevant documents to researchers. Meanwhile, by its own admission, it never got around to interviewing coroner Brown as to how he arrived at his novel cause-of-death finding.[49] Nor has it bothered to question two of its agents, Tom Green and William Wood, as to why they decided it was necessary to sever the victim's hands and ship them to FBI fingerprint lab for post mortem identification purposes. In the alternative, they might have instructed Dr. Brown to conduct a much more conventional cranial X-ray, for the purposes of identification by dental chart comparison, but, of course, this would have instantly disclosed the bullet lodged in the victim's skull.[50] Finally, the Bureau's sleuths have failed to interrogate agent David Price, who, by several accounts, had threatened Aquash's life during a 1975 interrogation session.[51]

e. The Oglala Firefight

By the spring of 1975, the level of GOON violence on Pine Ridge was so pronounced—and the lack of FBI response so conspicuous—that local traditionals requested that AIM undertake a policy of armed self-defense in order that opposition to Wilson might continue. AIM responded by establishing defensive encampments on properties owned by traditionals at various points around the reservation. Substantial evidence derived from FBI internal documents suggests the Bureau seized upon this situation as affording the opportunity to provoke an incident spectacular enough to bring about public acceptance of another massive paramilitary invasion of Pine Ridge.[52] Deployment of literally hundreds of agents in an extremely aggressive capacity, it was thought, would prove sufficient to finally break the backs of AIM and its supporters, already weakened by the war of attrition waged against them during the two years since Wounded Knee.

In the event, a camp set up by the Northwest AIM Group on Jumping Bull family property, near Oglala, was selected as the target at which the catalyzing confrontation would occur. Two agents, Ron Williams and Jack Coler, were sent there during the late morning of June 26, 1975, and opened fire on several of the Indians they encountered. Almost immediately, the lead elements of a large and already-assembled force of more than a hundred agents, BIA SWAT personnel, and GOONs attempted to force their way onto the property. From there, things seem to have gone somewhat awry from the Bureau point of view. Many more AIM members were present than anticipated, and the government reinforcements beat a hasty retreat to the cover of roadside ditches while Coler and Williams were cut off from their expected support. In the extended firefight which followed, both agents were killed, as was an AIM member named Joe Stuntz Killsright. Despite the presence of perhaps 200 police personnel, GOONs, and white vigilantes by mid-afternoon, the remaining AIM members escaped.[53]

Despite this undoubtedly unanticipated outcome, the Oglala firefight served its intended purpose for the FBI. Public endorsement of the sort of "crushing blow" desired by Bureau strategists was inherent to the situation, especially after it had been "packaged" by Bureau propagandists. Hence, before nightfall on June 26, counterintelligence expert Richard G. Held—detached from his normal duties *before* the firefight and standing by in Minneapolis, ready to assume command of the Pine Ridge operation—was on site.[54] With him, he brought a young counterintelligence protégé, Norman Zigrossi, his son, Richard Wallace Held, head of the FBI's COINTELPRO (Counterintelligence Program) Section in Los Angeles, and a number of other specialists in "political work."[55] They "hit the ground moving," to borrow a phrase from the vernacular of their trade.

By the morning of June 27, SWAT teams imported from Chicago, Minneapolis, Milwaukee, and Quantico (Virginia) were on the reservation, giving the Bureau a military-style presence—complete with armored personnel carriers, Bell "Huey" helicopters and other Vietnam-type equipage—of some 250 agents (as O'Clock mentioned above, this number had swelled to 350 by mid-July). For the next several months, this huge force conducted sweeps back and forth across Pine Ridge, abruptly kicking in doors to perform

146

warrantless searches, making arbitrary arrests, and engaging in air assaults upon assorted "centers of AIM resistance," all in the process of conducting what the FBI called its "RESMURS" (for Reservation Murders) Investigation.[56] Subjected to these sorts of official tactics, the AIM leadership reversed its position, quietly withdrawing from the reservation as an expedient to relieving the pressure imposed upon their traditional allies.

The firefight ultimately served much broader purposes as well. "Under the volatile circumstances caused by the deaths of Agents Coler and Williams, the Senate Select Committee on Government Operations (the so-called Church Committee), which had already issued the first subpoenas for a scheduled probe into the sort of activities encompassed by the FBI's anti-AIM campaign, *especially* those on Pine Ridge, agreed to an "indefinite postponement" of its hearings.[57] In actuality, this exploration of the Bureau's repressive behavior in what has been called its "post-COINTELPRO era" was simply and permanently shelved by the committee (or, in any event, we are still waiting for it to start, 18 years later). And, of course, a few days after the firefight, the U.S. Department of Interior felt the time was appropriate for Dick Wilson to finally sign the instrument transferring title over the Sheep Mountain Gunnery Range to the National Forest Service.[58]

The Bureau and its supporters have always contended that no government plan to provoke a confrontation existed. The presence of large numbers of GOONs and BIA police in close proximity to the remote location in which the firefight occurred was, they say, the sheerest of coincidences, a matter which proves nothing at all. FBI media liaison Tom Coll initially claimed that AIM was the "group with a plan," having "lured" the agents into a "carefully prepared ambush" where they were "fired upon with auto-matic weapons from a "sophisticated bunker complex," "riddled with fifteen to twenty bullets" apiece, "dragged from their cars" and "stripped" and—in one version— "scalped." Coll was even thoughtful enough to quote Williams's last words, having the dead agent plead for his life, begging his "cold hearted executioners" to "please remember my wife and children before you do this."[59]

After FBI Director Clarence M. Kelley finally admitted that none of this was true, the Bureau switched to the story that it maintains to this day: Coler and Williams were merely attempting to serve a "routine warrant" on a nineteen-year-old AIM member named Jimmy Eagle and ended up being brutally murdered for their trouble.[60] Duane Brewer tells a rather different story:

The thing that we was to do was use CB radios, have people placed, positioned in different places, on hills and things. And we was going to have an assault vehicle go to about three houses that we figured they was at, and shoot them up. . . . We would do the shooting, shoot the place up and make our run and go to Rapid City. Stay up over night, party around and then come back the next day, you know. Not be in the area when it happened. But, like I said, *we had three or four different plans* [emphasis added] that we was going to use. . . . [B]ut our intentions never were, was to go right down into that place. That was just one of the places that we was going to hit. We could have hit them from the road, you know. . . .

A second variation of the planning was for Brewer's GOONs to shoot up some of the Jumping Bull houses, precipitating a return fire from the few AIM members expected to be gathered there. A force of FBI agents and a BIA SWAT team would then use this as a pretext to arrest everyone on the property, "and we [GOONs] could cover for them on the way back. *We had three different plans*, I guess. We sat down there at the creek I don't know how many times and went over that" (emphasis added). As it happened, however, Coler and Williams were sent in to get things rolling, but "we never really knew they had this, the Jumping Bull Hall, the Jumping Bull place with all these warriors down there. And that's when they killed them agents." Asked why he and his men hadn't responded to Williams's radioed pleas, once the firefight had begun in earnest, for someone to "get on the high ground" adjacent to the Jumping Bull property and provide covering fire while he and his partner withdrew, Brewer responded:

If we could have got ourselves into that position where we went to the top of that hill, they [AIM] would have had us before we got out of the, got to the highway, the way they were set up. That would have been a losing battle there.

In the end, little more than this need be said about the circumstances in which Northwest AIM leader Leonard Peltier was brought to trial in 1977 and convicted of two counts of first degree murder in the deaths of Williams and Coler. This, after an all-white jury in Cedar Rapids, Iowa, had acquitted his co-defendants, Bob Robideau and Darelle "Dino" Butler, both of whom openly acknowledged at trial having shot at the agents, by reason of their having plainly acted in self-defense.[61] Tellingly, Judge Gerald Heaney, head of the three member panel of the Eighth Circuit Court of Appeals which last reviewed Peltier's case, appeared on national television in 1989 to admit he was "deeply troubled" during his own investigation of the matter. The reason for the judge's discomfort? In his own words, "It became increasingly apparent to me that the FBI was at least as much to blame for what happened as Peltier."[62] More lately, Heaney has joined Hawaii Senator Daniel Inouye and other members of Congress in signing a petition to George Bush requesting that Peltier be pardoned. Needless to say, Bush left office with the petition unanswered.

Death Squads in the United States

At one point toward the end of his interview, Brewer was asked how he justified the sorts of things he'd been involved in as a GOON. Almost pensively, he acknowledged that, "Well, you really can't. There really is no justification for it. . . . It's just what we done at the time, and there is no way you can go back and change what's already done." Exactly. And no number of evasions, withheld documents, denials, or other lies on the part of the FBI and its friends will make the truth of what the Bureau did to AIM and its supporters any less true. The Federal Bureau of Investigation played much the same role on Pine Ridge during the mid-1970s that the CIA has played vis-à-vis Roberto D'Aubisson's hit teams in El Salvador throughout the 1980s. The GOONs, for their part, fulfilled exactly the same requirements on the reservation that other death squads have played throughout Latin America over the past four decades and more. Structurally, the forms and functions assumed by all parties to such comparisons are essentially the same.

The FBI's employment of outright death squads to accomplish the repression of AIM may be the most extreme example of its kind in modern U.S. history. It is nonetheless hardly isolated or unique in principle. To the contrary, ample evidence exists that the Bureau has been experimenting with and perfecting this technique of domestic counterinsurgency for nearly thirty years. There can be little question at this point that the Ku Klux Klan, riddled with FBI *agents provocateurs* such as Gary Thomas Rowe and overlapped as it was with local police forces in the Deep South, was used by the FBI during the early-1960s against the civil rights movement in much the same fashion as the GOONs were later used against AIM. The same circumstances are at issue with regard to the Klan, in alliance with other neo-Nazis, murdering five members of the Communist Workers Party in Greensboro, North Carolina, during November 1979.

Certainly, the special unit of the State's Attorney's Police which assassinated Black Panther leaders Mark Clark and Fred Hampton in Chicago on December 4, 1969, was functioning as a death squad under at least nominal control of the Bureau. Similarly, the Windy City was afflicted with a neo-Nazi/police/FBI/military intelligence amalgamation known as the Legion of Justice during the first half of the 1970s. No less striking is the combination, evident in the late 1960s and described at length by *provocateur* Louis Tackwood in *The Glass House Tapes*, of state and local police red squads with the Bureau's Los Angeles COINTELPRO Section and area vigilante groups, for the purposes of physically destroying the "California Left." As Tackwood and other Bureau-sponsored infiltrators of dissident organizations have stated, often and categorically, assassination of "key activists" is a standard part of the tactical methodology utilized by American political police.

Bearing this in mind, there was the Secret Army Organization (SAO), developed under the aegis of the FBI in southern California during the early 1970s; its express purpose was to liquidate "radical leaders." On another front, there was the death squad formed by

Portland, Maine, police (with apparent cooperation from the local FBI resident agency) during the same period as a means of "coming to grips" with the area's antiwar and prison rights movements. Then again, there is the example of the consortium in Puerto Rico—consisting of a special police unit tightly interlocked with the island's FBI field office, the CIA, U.S. military intelligence units, and right-wing Cuban exile groups—which was responsible for scores of bombings and beatings over the years. Also attributable to this entity are, at the very least, the execution-style murders of labor leader Juan Caballero in the island's El Yunque rain forest in 1977, and of *independentista* activists Arnoldo Dario Rosado and Carlos Soto Arrivi near the mountain village of Cerro Maravilla on July 25, 1978.

Comparable illustrations might be recited at length had we more time, but the pattern will by now be clear to anyone willing to face the facts. And it should be coupled to the fact that not one FBI man has ever served so much as a minute of jail time because of the conduct involved. These realities must serve to inform and temper the understandings of activists and scholars alike, the former in terms of their appreciation of what they are up against as they struggle to achieve positive social change in the United States, the latter in terms of the paradigms by which they attempt to shed light on the nature of power dynamics in America. In either case, it is plain enough that there is no longer any real excuse for continuation of the generalized self-delusion among American progressives that such terrorism is "anomalous" within the context of the contemporary United States. True death squads are not only possible in the United States, they have been a relatively common phenomenon for some time. It is already well past the point where we should have gotten the government's message and begun to conduct ourselves accordingly.

I realize that what I have said does not correspond well with the image of the terrorist you are used to seeing in the media. Since this is an assembly devoted to examin-ing images of terrorism, I want to give you an image of terrorism before I sit down. I am and have been for twenty years a member of the American Indian Movement and therefore, *ipso facto*, in official portray-als I am the terrorist. I will extend the image a little further. Meet my colleagues, the other terrorists

(members of the panel). Now those of you in the crowd who have a mirror, hold it up and look at yourselves. We have a commonality of interest which goes beyond abstract political agendas and goes beyond moral issues; it goes to self-interest in the most primary sort of way. If you are an individual who attempts to exercise social conscience and act upon your beliefs in a constructive way in this society, the chances are that if you are effective you will ultimately be portrayed as a terrorist. I have just given you a sample here of what happens when they construe you in that fashion.

The agendas of my colleagues here on this panel are my agenda for that reason. Your agendas are mine, and I would hope that mine would be yours because we have to join together on the basis of that elemental self-interest to alter the situation that threatens each and every one of us every day.

Cockburn: Thank you very much, Ward, for those very eloquent remarks. I congratulate the members of the panel. What they have provided has been a very wide overview of the uses of terrorism in the agendas of the state and of power. I was particularly glad to hear Ward talk about resources on Indian lands. Underlying everything is the fundamental agenda of the search for economic advantage. If you asked what is the cause of the suffering in the world today, you would have to look at the struggle for economic advantage and all of the suffering that derives from it. When you are talking about terrorism, you have to think all the time about not just the death squads or the man in the uniform, but you have to think about a man like Alan Greenspan, the Chairman of the Federal Reserve, or Paul Volker ten years ago, who by their economic decisions are literally condemning people to death, as if they went out in a field and put someone in a ditch and shot him in the back of the neck.

Audience: I have a comment about some personal experience and I want to direct my remarks to Bill Schaap. I am worried about the portrayal of Jews as terrorists, as seemed to be the tendency of the panel. In Israel, members of the UN Peace Keeping Team are taught Arabic to speak to Arabs but not Hebrew to speak to Jews. A friend of mine who was in Israel saw members of the UN Peace Keeping Team and the Red Cross distributing posters with blatantly anti-

Jewish messages. The anti-Jewish messages were not in the writing. You did not have to be literate to understand the message fomenting what I thought was anti-Jewish terrorism. I am very glad that we are now in peace talks between Israel, Palestinians, and neighboring Arab nations. Nevertheless, I wanted to express that in my opinion the Holocaust survivors paid for every scrap of land they have in Israel. The only land they took was taken when they were first attacked. I am a little upset at some of the things that were said about Israel and terrorism or the implications of state terrorism as you defined it. I am grateful for the cross section of opinion here, but I did escape the Holocaust and not all of my family did. I am very reluctant to paint the Jews with the brush that implies terrorism. I don't think that is an accurate characterization. I would appreciate your comment.

Cockburn: Bill, do you want to comment? But first I would point out that one person who accepts the name terrorist and proudly and eloquently defends it is former Prime Minister Yitzhak Shamir.

Audience: That is not true! Where did you hear that?

Cockburn: It has been in the press constantly since the opening of the peace talks in Madrid where the delegation from Syria held up old posters identifying Shamir as a terrorist. You can see those posters if you look in any of the news magazines.

Merrill: Much the same can be said for Menachem Begin, who is actually listed in the *Almanac of Modern Terrorism* as the leader of Irgun, a terrorist organization which blew up the King David Hotel in 1946 to drive the British out of Palestine.

Audience: I would like to see them.

Schaap: I don't recall using the word Jew when I spoke, and I would never confuse opposition to the policies of the Israeli government of the day with anti-Semitism or religious bigotry. I think one of the most insidious arguments today which is used against

people like myself and I hope millions of others is that if you say one thing against the government of Israel then you are either an anti-Semite or, as in my case if you are Jewish, you are a self-hating Jew. This argument is being made an article of faith by the *New Republic*, *Commentary*, and other publications which will go to any length to support policies of the U.S. and Israeli governments. Not enough people are objecting to it. I have as many trees planted in Israel in my name as anyone in this room, and my mother was vice-president of Hadassah, and I *still* think that the current Israeli government is a bunch of fascist thugs. I do want to debate one particular point. I don't think it is very nice for anyone to throw rocks at anyone, Palestinians included. On the other hand, most of the people on one side have rocks while the people on the other side have guns. If you look at the numbers of how many Israelis have been killed and how many Palestinians have been killed, the disparity is mind-boggling. It is not a one-on-one conflict.

It is true that most of the settlers in Israel in most of the areas paid for the land they occupy. But it is also true that when Hitler took over a Jewish businessman's business and sold it to a German businessman, that German businessman paid for that business. And he paid for that land too. That doesn't make it right.

Audience: That is an insidious comparison. You really don't want to make that comparison. You don't get anywhere with that. . . .

Audience: No. No. That isn't right. . . .

Schaap: I don't think that the settlement on the West Bank is justified on the theory that at some point whether it was fifty years ago, a hundred years ago, or a thousand years ago, that somebody took the land from somebody else. . . .

Audience: They paid for the land. . . .

Schaap: I think you have to deal with the reality of an occupied land.

Cockburn: Can I break in here. Let's not disintegrate into anarchy. Please allow the person to finish the point before breaking in.

Churchill: Perhaps a better analogy is right here. Most of the people in this country occupying individual domiciles paid for the land, too. The problem is that the seller didn't own it.

Audience: I will let that point go, but I want to point out that I have worked very hard teaching multiculturalism in the work that I do. It is important to understand both sides to any conflict. I also work for the Southern Poverty Law Center, and people in this country should understand the racism and terrorism that still exist here and not point to Israel all the time.

Audience: My question goes to many of the difficulties some of us experience in trying to organize opposition to the policies you have discussed. There is an institutional defense of these policies which makes them almost unassailable. In discussing the consternation many of us felt in opposing the Gulf war last year, a Spanish friend of mine remarked that he had always felt a great deal of affection for the American people but the experience of the war had shown him that it is true that the American people are lied to but, unlike other people, they want to be lied to. Lots of people throughout the world are lied to by state apparatuses, and certainly Franco's Spain was a good example, but nowhere else do people seem to want it so bad. Why is this? What makes it so easy to lie to the American people? Why are Americans so hungry for lies about themselves?

Cockburn: I might remind people that at the start of the American public relations industry early in this century, Edward Bernays, Freud's nephew, who wrote many of the primers for the manipulation of opinion, called this the engineering of the consent of the governed.

Robinson: We don't have a viable democracy in any meaningful sense without an enlightened citizenry. I think that our citizenry of all the industrialized citizenries is the least enlightened. I recall a story of a test that was given to people from many different countries and the United States finished at the very bottom. One in eight Americans could not even find the United States on a global map. I recall seeing a debate on CNN

during the war between a British expert on the Middle East and Charlton Heston. Mr. Heston—and you all know he was an appropriate American choice—was asked to name one country that bordered Iraq. He took a stab and ended up in the Pacific somewhere. It was quite embarrassing. I really don't think you can have thoughtful public debate given the appalling state of American education, especially the appalling lack of a multicultural education. Everything is the present and future in this country. No one has any sense of what Sir Percy Cox did in creating these artificial nations in the Middle East in the first place. Why were they created, what was the role of the Ottoman Empire, what was the responsibility of the British? Somehow we demonize Saddam Hussein without understanding that there was a border dispute before him and there will be one after him. Americans really aren't in a position to understand these things. If Ronald Reagan can become President, so can Vanna White. There is no easy answer to your question. We are quite massively a stupid population.

Sanbrano: I think that the people in power in this country, the people who control the economy and the media, are very skilled in defining and justifying the terrorism abroad and here. All they have to do is define the terms and the media does a great job of putting the line out to the people. And the line is repeated hundreds of times in hundreds of different places, from newspapers, TV news, TV comedies, Johnny Carson, radio talk shows, and so on. They are all saying the same thing, so what they see gathers a credibility as if it were true. The few people who tried to protest the invasion of Panama, for example, were intimidated from speaking out because they did not want to be seen as supporting Noriega. Noriega was demonized as a drug dealer, and most Americans could not separate the invasion from the demonization. We had a hard time trying to mobilize people to protest the invasion of Panama. The same thing happened with Hussein and the invasion of Iraq. Right now they are trying to demonize Fidel Castro, in the event that they decide to invade Cuba. Because of the economy and the recession, someone has to be blamed. It is not the executives on Wall Street, but immigrants and undocumented workers. We constantly hear news stories about the people who cross the border to take jobs away from American people. What we get is the African-American community against the Latino community, the middle class is against the poor. We have to educate each other about who the real enemies of the people are.

Audience: I have a question relating to the invasion of Panama. I don't support Noriega or the drug trade, but I heard a remark by William S. Burroughs about the United States using drugs as an excuse to police the world. I was very skeptical when I first heard him say that, but the more I read about this issue the more likely it seems. Right here in this city, Mayor Kurt Schmoke's wife's cousin's house was stormed by the police and the old lady was thrown on the floor. She suffered a broken hip and other injuries. The only reason it was reported in the *Baltimore Sun* was because she was a cousin of the mayor's wife. Then I read in the *Nation* about a DEA raid on a city in Colombia. There were no drugs in the city at all, but the DEA terrorized all the people of the city. And then I read in William S. Burroughs about an Asian country that is being funded by the United States while it is known as a drug-money laundering place. I wonder if you would comment on the connection between the drug war and the policing of the world.

Merrill: The drug war is another monumental fraud. First there was international terrorism and now we have narco-terrorism. The number of people who die each year from illegal drugs is only a tiny fraction of the number who die from the use of alcohol or cigarettes. The government isn't waging war on alcohol and it subsidizes tobacco farmers. The Bush administration has spent a total of about $43 billion, the last I heard, on its drug war and not much good has been done. The money would have been much better spent on rehabilitation and education programs. The fact is that drugs are not really the major problem in this society, but they are using drugs as a justification for increasing the power of police forces and trampling on the Bill of Rights. Asset forfeiture laws make it possible for the police to kick in your door and do physical harm to you and take your house, car, boat, airplane, funds that you might use to hire an attorney to defend yourself without really accusing you of anything. All they need is a DEA officer's signature and a sympathetic judge and your property is gone. The police get to keep the money to use for more drug raids. I see the drug war as part of a constant layering of control at the expense of freedom, democracy, and basic rights. Part of this is the logic of a police society. It is like moving westward or going to the moon. You just extend police powers because the frontier is out there. We do have real problems that could be addressed but no one seems interested in them because resolving them—like poverty, illiteracy, or homelessness—would not produce the kind of society the ruling class here wants to see–that is, a police state.

Audience: I feel like I need to take exception to that. I feel that it is important to say that drugs are a tremendous problem in this country. They are not a problem for people who have a lot of money to hire a lawyer or have a boat that can be taken away from them. But for ghetto communities, for black communities, for Indian communities, for poor white communities, drugs are one of the ways that people are kept ignorant, down, and incapable of challenging the status quo. So drugs are a weapon, a terrorist weapon directed against the less socially advantaged who do not have the resources to fight drugs and the criminal implications of drug use. I understand your point and at some level I agree with you, but it makes me mad that we keep going to these statistics that suggest "ratio-wise" that it is worse for many people to die in car crashes than from drugs. I think the statistical approach is divisive. It moved me tremendously when Ward Churchill urged us at the end of his presentation to see our problems as very similar. I think it is important to see links between problems people suffer, such as apartheid in South Africa and the way Indians are treated here. Or the way Indian lands have been taken and sold and the treatment of Palestinians. Or the way AIDS is handled. It is terrorism, and I think drugs fall under this term. There is a way of talking about these things which although it holds a piece of truth can be dangerous. I just wanted to bring attention to that.

Merrill: Yes, I fully agree. African-American communities are targeted for drug policing in ways that white communities are not, in spite of the fact that middle-class whites consume the vast majority of illegal drugs. Policing makes drugs a double problem for African-Americans. I am tired of seeing young black men lying face down on the sidewalk being humiliated by police. And if you add the violence of the business end of drug trade, the problem is tripled. I still think the money would be better spent on rehabilitation and education programs than on police, but that would not be the kind of program anyone in high levels of government would want to run. Think of William Bennet, from Education Secretary to drug tsar. What I am struck by is how useful the drug war is to the whole covert operations industry of the U.S. government. The U.S. government has cooperated with cartels that have been responsible for the drug trade from the French Connection, to the Golden Triangle, to the Golden Crescent, to the Medellin. Every one of these had major support from the U.S. government, especially the CIA providing airplanes to transport the drugs. They also provided money and other resources so that certain people could gain a monopoly over drug trade in certain areas. Drug dealing was part of the Iran/Contra scandal and went right into the White House: the protection, the arrangements for airplanes, and the laundering of money. Profits from the drug business helps fund covert operations of the CIA. Oliver North took $10 million from Jorge Ochoa of the Medellin cartel to support the contras. While the government is helping the flow of drugs into this country, government officials are using that fact to justify a war in which they are absolutely changing fundamentally the nature of this society. It is becoming a police state or a police world. Maybe legalizing drugs would be a relief for many communities in this country.

Audience: Absolutely, and that is terrorism against a tremendous number of people who suffer both from the drugs and the repression. This hits black communities and poor people in general doubly hard since they do not have any protection from the drugs or from the government's police powers.

Cockburn: It was recently my misfortune to be a journalist observing the Democratic candidates debate in Manchester, New Hampshire, last weekend. Almost the entire space on crime was spent on the coercive aspect of the drug problem. Tom Harkin, who is supposed to be a liberal, promised to invade Peru and Colombia. Almost every other candidate said much the same thing. Paul Tsongas said he would like to execute drug lords. You can see that the way the issue is approached immediately crushes any real debate; it is just a contest to see who can be the most vicious in meting out punishment.

Schaap: I want to say that one of the biggest frauds in the drug war campaign is the notion that it is a supply-driven industry when in fact it is very clearly a demand-driven industry. Virtually all the experts know that. The fact is that there is no such thing as eliminating the supply of drugs. Most drugs just grow and require very simple methods to refine them. If they put the money that is supposedly spent fighting the drug war into trying to alleviate the conditions in this country that cause people to want to use drugs, they would have vastly more success. There is more to it, though, as Bob says. If you look at the places in the world where they are fighting the drug war and where vast sums of money are going—Peru, Bolivia, Colombia—they are all areas where there happen to be large insurgent political movements, separate and apart from any drug trade. In fact, most of this police aid—if you know people in the countries involved who are able to be on the air fields to watch the stuff being unloaded—is really military aid for the armies to fight the rebels. It is not police aid to fight the drugs because you can't fight it. There is just no way to stop the stuff from growing. You have to stop the demand for drugs.

Audience: I would like to address the points raised about the failure of the media to cover terrorism of states. I would like the panel to address the concept of national security in the context of terrorism. How national security is used as an excuse not to talk about certain kinds of terrorism.

Cockburn: I think all of the panel members have pretty strong views on national security. Who wants to go first? Angela.

Sanbrano: The national security state came about as a result of the cold war. The whole rationale of the national security state was to protect us from the enemy, mainly the Soviet Union. That is why they are having to redefine national security. They no longer have communism to protect us from, so now they are looking for new enemies. The terms will have to be re-defined: terrorism, subversive, anticommunism, counterinsurgency, counterrevolutionary, counter-this and counter-that. These are the terms that made up the national security state. Since we no longer have the threat from communism, we should do away with the national security apparatus. We don't need it. Abolish it and all its apparatuses.

Churchill: In a weird way I think that a line that was attributed to Jim Garrison in the film *JFK* applies here: "We are through the looking glass here." National security is a way of turning reality upside down, making the victims into victimizers, the oppressed into oppressors. Oppression becomes instinctively justifiable in the name of self-defense. In the process is created a repository of things that need to be kept secret in order to maintain the mythology of national security. That area of secrecy is now rather larger than the area of access—in order to maintain freedom and openness. It is a perfect rubric which a centralized state or an increasingly centralizing state needs in order to be able to function with ever-increasing efficiency in terms of imposing order and thus the rational capacity in itself. I think I will stop right there. We could go on for a long time on this one.

Audience: When we talk about terrorism sponsored by the state in these various contexts that have been mentioned, it seems to me that the real culprit is kind of hiding in the shadows. As we see the U.S. decline in global economic importance, we see it becoming a mercenary state. It may have been up front in the attack on Iraq, but it is behind in economics. I am wondering if there isn't a broader context in which this kind of state-sponsored activity should be discussed. Now that the communist pretext has ceased to exist and the Soviet Union is no longer a threat, cannot we now name that system and stop denying what it is and what it means for each of us down to the personal level? We are talking about a global system called capitalism, and apparently it is a system of wealth accumulation which requires that there be this intervention in the affairs of Native American people on reservations for their resources, it requires the kind of system that we see in South Africa, and it requires intervention in Grenada and other places for whatever reason. I would like someone to put state terrorism in the context of international private corporate interests. I would like to see what your perceptions are on the role of the state as an agent of private interests.

Merrill: I think you have hit it right on the head. In spite of the sentimental appeals to "the people," the U.S. government serves the interests of large corporations which are increasingly multinational and increasingly require "favorable" conditions in countries where they want to do business. Ed Herman's reference to the case of United Fruit Company and Guatemala this morning is a classic case. He did not mention that CIA Director Bedell Smith who initiated the overthrow of the Guatemalan government with something called "Operation Fortune" was a partner in United Fruit's law firm, Sullivan & Cromwell, along with brothers John Foster and Allan Dulles. Later under Eisenhower, John Foster Dulles became Secretary of State and his brother Allen Dulles took over as Director of the CIA. Bedell moved on to the Board of Directors of United Fruit. The rise of Bechtel Corporation in the 1980s has to be linked to Shultz, Weinberger, and some others who moved from the corporation into high levels of government. Now we have a huge and unimaginably powerful military which has to destroy nations like Iraq so that our corporations can control the world's oil supply. You are right: capitalism is a system of ownership and control of the world's resources by an elite few. And there is no reasonable end to what the capitalist wants to own or control. Somehow capitalism has to be stopped because it has shown that it cannot control or limit itself. I think your point is important because it says honestly what the root of the problem is. It is not complex; capitalism is just an evil ideology and it has taken over a government that was supposed to belong to all the people.

Robinson: At least in the African context it can be demonstrated that we are not in the least interested in democracy. Just looking at some figures, in the last aid request for three countries, Malawi, Kenya, and Zaire—none in the least democratic—we requested about $134 million in foreign assistance. Then if you look at three democracies like Benin, Namibia, and Botswana, we requested about $34 million in foreign aid. The first Bush request for Namibia, which put in place a constitution as democratic as our own, was for $500,000. If you look at Angola, you will see an exception to what was implied in your question. Angola has endured a war in which in excess of 400,000 of its nine million people have been lost. It has the highest amputee rate on earth. Everybody in the world was in Angola doing business but the United States. All of the companies from these countries enjoyed the support of their governments, including Margaret Thatcher. The Angolans have even left an empty spot overlooking the ocean on which they hope some day to see the American Embassy built. When I was last there I met with the British ambassador, who couldn't understand the lunacy of American policy in its support of Jonas Savimbi. We've got no further use for Mobutu in Zaire but we haven't pulled the rug yet. I don't think it is always a relationship between business and government. Our government simply doesn't want Third World countries, particularly African countries, to run themselves. The U.S. government just doesn't want it. And there is no indication that the U.S. government is prepared to tolerate autonomy and democracy in any Third World country. In the Middle East, Jordan has perhaps the most democratic of Middle Eastern governments, but when the Jordanians say something we don't like, we snatch their aid away. The Algerians democratically elected a fundamentalist group—I am concerned about how minorities would be treated—we don't like that. We don't like democracies to get cheeky. And nobody can tell you more about this than Michael Manley during his first term as Prime Minister of Jamaica. We are much more comfortable with obedient tyrannies than we are with free wheeling independent democracies in the world.

Audience: Recently the Justice Department announced that three hundred FBI counterintelligence agents would be dispersed throughout the United States. What is your analysis of that? The cover story is that they are going to combat street gangs, but what is your analysis?

Merrill: In a manner similar to counterterrorism and anticommunism, there is now ample momentum for increased antigang measures. It is hard for me to believe that the FBI is at all interested in stopping crime or gang violence because if you think about the history of the FBI, you see that its crime fighting is always political. For years, under Hoover, the FBI would not even admit that organized crime existed in the United States. It was too busy tracking down communists. In a manner similar to what Randall described with regard to South Africa, violence really serves the interests of the status quo. The more violence, the more powerful the FBI. What these counterintelligence agents will really do is make sure that these gang members don't become politically conscious in the way so many African-American groups like the Black Panthers did. The FBI will infiltrate gangs and attempt to keep them focused on small crimes, drug dealing, and fighting each other. In other words, containment and maintenance of the status quo is most likely.

Audience: I don't see how a counterintelligence agent for the FBI is going to have any impact on the domestic drug thing. What is their expertise in regard to that?

Merrill: It won't. The FBI doesn't want to control drugs. It sure hasn't done anything for the last thirty years. You have to go back to the FBI's use of counterintelligence agents in its wars against political dissidents in the 1960s and 1970s. Ward spoke about the program earlier: COINTELPRO they called it. The Counterintelligence Program. It was used to infiltrate, disrupt, and ultimately destroy political groups, especially the Black Panthers and the American Indian Movement. You will see some of that in a video later on called *Framing the Panthers in Black and White*. Angela's presentation shows what FBI counterintelligence agents do; they try to destroy groups like CISPES. I am sure that they will do the same thing with gangs. One of the things that COINTELPRO did was actually promote violence between rival groups, such as in Los Angeles where a gun fight broke out between the United Slaves and the Black Panthers. Actually, the fight was instigated by FBI undercover agents feeding false information to both sides about the hostile intentions of the other group. This sort of provocation would work well with gangs who already are suspicious of each other, and the result would be enhanced violence in cities. That violence would create a tremendous public call for even more policing. More young African-American men will be stigmatized as a criminal class. I don't trust the FBI counterintelligence efforts at all. They would like more than anything to see gang members kill each other off. This is essentially what counterintelligence does in the Third World; it keeps civil wars going because unstable societies can be exploited for their material resources. Stable societies are what our national security state must prevent at all costs. I am afraid that inner city gangs are already so fully infiltrated with FBI infiltrators that everything they do is in one way or another controlled by the FBI, like puppets on a string.

Audience: I agree with Randall Robinson's comment that this society is highly uneducated. This in turn leads to very simplistic answers to very complicated issues. I think all of the panelists have done an excellent job in defining some of the mis-information and dis-information that we face. What I would like to ask them is to discuss strategies that we in our communities can use to change the situation.

Robinson: May I raise a question pertaining to the previous point before we go on to the next item? I was interested in the comment about legalizing drugs. Those of you here from Baltimore probably know that Mayor Kurt Schmoke has supported the legalization of drugs. I don't know if that is still his position, but he was vigorously opposed by Charlie Rangel in the Congress. I initially opposed it too, but in our communities, particularly the black communities, we suffer more from the crime surrounding this enterprise than we do from the drug itself. I am not sure that if we can put alcohol and cigarettes on the shelf, we shouldn't sit heroin, crack, and all that other stuff up there too. At least it would do something to help ensure the safety of people who don't use drugs. As things stand now, non-users are as threatened in our communities as are the users. Is there an alternative to the violence that is only escalating in our communities?

Merrill: In spite of what I said, I have always been skeptical of legalization proposals because at worst we would have another alcohol with all the advertising and promotions for increased use, and at best we would have an open, low-priced, low-profit drug market which would nonetheless keep dealers on the streets. But the real problems go deeper in this society and they have to do with why people feel such a need to take drugs. This is the most drug-addicted society in the world. Something is missing in our lives that drives us to use chemicals to compensate for it. Mentally healthy people don't become addicts or abusers of chemicals. They may get high on occasion for fun, but they don't destroy themselves or others with their drug use. Many people, especially teenagers, have such a bad self-image that they do things to destroy themselves. Why are we raising our children this way? We need to take drug use out of the criminal system and put it into a mental health system. I would favor decriminalizing drugs. Don't send anyone to prison for drug possession or use. Give them something like a parking ticket. The problem is that we just don't have a mental health system that can handle the load. Another point is the dismal economy. If there were better futures for people to believe in, I am sure that many of them would not use drugs for escape, or at least drugs would just be a minor phase they passed through. I agree with your concern for drug-related violence. Which is a greater threat: drug-related violence or international terrorism? Unfortunately, both are used to terrorize ordinary Americans and make them demand from the government ever greater levels of policing.

Cockburn: We had a question about agendas for change. That is a big subject to embark upon a few minutes before the end of a panel.

Audience: That is why we are here. . . !

Cockburn: Yes, would the panel members like to discuss agendas for change. I would give them—you know how we are on the left, we like to keep these things pretty short—maybe ten seconds or so. . . .

Schaap: Everyone has their own field where they work and struggle. We try with our publications not to change what the *New York Times* writes but to change what you think when you read it. Educate and organize are probably the two most important things. Within everyone's field there are ways to educate yourself more and ways to organize yourself and your community more effectively.

Robinson: Very quickly, I think we ought to democratize public television. We ought to give a great deal more public support to public television. There is not, at least as I can think now, a single public television show on foreign policy in the Third World or even on foreign policy from a left-of-center point of view. There is *American Interest* which is a right-wing look at foreign policy. Generally, public television doesn't look at foreign policy at all. I think we have to become more aware about how decisions are made at the Corporation for Public Broadcasting, how PBS is run and where the money comes from. We need to have genuine national debates through public television. I say this because we are a television-driven country and we have to respond to that reality. Americans read less and watch more. Public television should have the capacity to advertise. We really have left it to die in this country.

Sanbrano: I wanted to say that some of the things we did when we discovered that the FBI was carrying out its illegal investigation of CISPES were very effective. We formed coalitions that forced the media to come to press conferences where they could hear our point of view. We forced Congress to investigate, and the whole thing became a scandal. You can organize to get specific things done, and in this way you can get the media to show your point of view.

Churchill: For me a very high priority would be to educate yourselves as to the nature of the agreements that the government entered into with American Indians in acquiring title to its land base. Do this whether you think the government represents you or not. You will discover the existence of areas that the government did not acquire title to. Push that point in the context of the sort of principles that the government generally propounds. Educating people about this might lead to an agenda of real wins for Native people. Understand that every inch of territory in North America that returns to Native control is one more inch that the United States government cannot rely upon to do what it is doing to you and everyone else in the world. That is a real political agenda. But it will take some time and a massive shift of consciousness in this country. It could begin right here in this room.

Merrill: I agree with everyone about education, especially with Ward's comment about a massive shift in consciousness. Unfortunately, I am uncertain that it can be done. The problem we face is a government that is out of control. It is run by a bunch of people who think they can run around the world killing, destroying, and stealing as much as they please. The Reagan-Bush years have seen a tremendous escalation of this capitalist looting. I hope it can't last forever. The government is broke and massively in debt. In the next few years, we will be asked for huge tax increases to keep it running. I say, let it fall. Resist those new taxes with all your might, no matter how good the programs sound. You know it will be just another swindle. Let the government go broke and we can pick up the pieces later on. The important thing is to work locally and regionally to create strong communities and local businesses that can sustain themselves when the mammoth in Washington collapses. These communities can link up with one another and form new regional governments which will be oriented to resolving real problems people face, not inventing problems in order to call out responses that only build up the military/industrial complex. The problem with the left is that it has always been focused on the central government. The reasons were valid; local and state governments tended to be in the hands of the most regressive and racist people, while the central government was at least committed to a somewhat progressive rhetoric. Things have changed. The central government has absolutely no commitment to resolving real problems. In the vacuum, cities, local governments, and sometimes states have had to become more responsive and responsible. The only real governing going on now is on the state and local level.

Audience: I was struck by Ramsey Clark's comment last night that terrorism is the use of fear to control behavior. And also struck by the absence in this panel or in the exhibit of the fact that as a class women in general are controlled by men through the use of fear. The controversy over abortion rights now is a good example. Women are afraid to walk on the streets at night or even to enter a parking garage by themselves to get their cars. It is disturbing but not at all surprising that the terrorization of women is the issue closest to home for all of us but it was not mentioned or discussed by the panel.

Cockburn: Your point is very well taken as a criticism of the limits each speaker imposed upon himself or herself. I think your question invites its own answer; terrorism at home is obviously the most overlooked terrorism, especially when it occurs, as we have all pointed out, for the benefit of the privileged group of people in this country—in this case men. Your question is also the perfect segue into this afternoon's panel. Someone must have planted it in the audience. Margaret Randall will be speaking on precisely that issue when we look more generally at terrorism and how it infiltrates systems of oppression just like this.

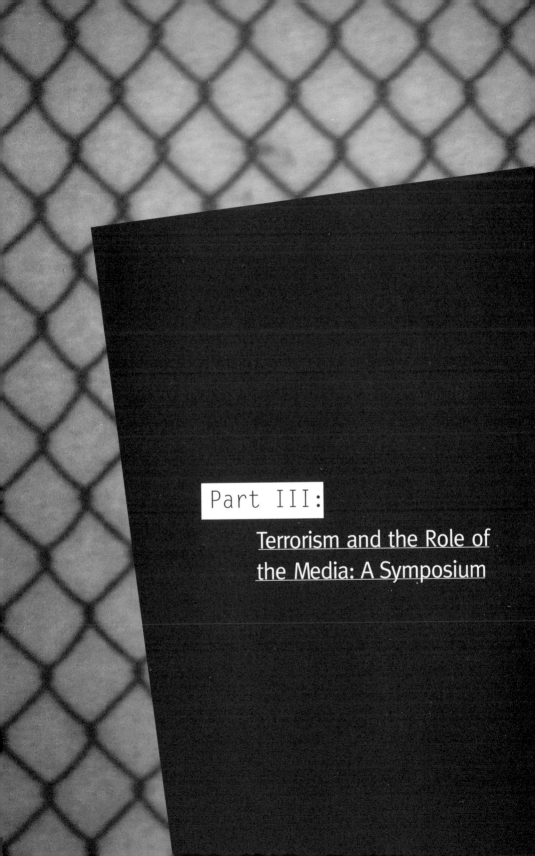

Part III:

Terrorism and the Role of
the Media: A Symposium

Terrorism and the Role of the Media: A Symposium

Annie Goldson
Chris Bratton
Margaret Randall
Michael Parenti
Alexander Cockburn
Robert Merrill, moderator

Merrill: To set the tone for this discussion, I want to mention two very brief anecdotes. The first picks up on something that was mentioned by Randall Robinson in the preceding panel. If you have ever watched *ABC World News Tonight* with Peter Jennings, you have probably seen the claim that more people get their news from ABC than from any other source. That is probably wonderful for ABC's sponsors, but it is bad news for us as people who depend upon ABC—and the other news producing corporations—for information. As people in a nation that is supposedly democratic, we are supposed to be able to deliberate over the issues that face us and as we make decisions empower our representatives in government to do something about them. Terrorism is one such issue, an important one. We need to be able to understand it well enough to decide what must be done and then authorize our government to carry out policies derived from the consent of the governed. If it works that way, then we live in a democracy where the consent of the governed or the will of the people drives the government's policies.

But of course if you think about the findings of a study on TV news watchers conducted by the Department of Communications at the University of Massachusetts during the U.S. war against Iraq, then you realize that it really works in the opposite way. The study concluded that the more people watch TV news, the less they actually know about the basic issues and facts of what is going on. Newspaper readers came out somewhat better, but certainly not good enough in order to have discussions and deliberate about the issues in a way that

ABC claims that more Americans get their news from ABC's *World News Tonight with Peter Jennings* than from any other source. Such news organizations constantly produce special reports defining terrorism but always carefully exclude Western state-sponsored terrorism and focus on exotic images of the relatively minor incidents of insurgent terrorism. The use of stereotyped images is one way that discourse about much broader uses of terrorism is contained.

would lead them to make any decisions other than what the government had already decided to do. What I think we are facing with the rise of television journalism and the following along of newspaper journalism in the same mode is the "dumbing down" of this society. Randall Robinson mentioned earlier that people don't seem to know very much in this society. This trend is becoming alarming. To borrow a phrase that was mentioned by Alex Cockburn this morning and also to allude to a book by Edward Herman and Noam Chomsky, what we are seeing is the "manufacturing of consent." News these days is so much involved with the manufacture of consent for policies that have nothing to do with the interests of most of the people. This isn't democracy; it's fascism purely and simply, although that is a very unfashionable word. How long it can last is the only question, in my mind, at least.

The second anecdote has to do with a personal experience. In July of 1985, I was in Washington and I came upon a very large and significant media event. It was Ronald Reagan giving a speech on international terrorism before the national convention of the American Bar Association. I tried to get in to listen to the speech, but I couldn't, so I hung around outside with the press crews to see what was being said. I watched them tape their feeds after the event and some reporter from ITN (International Television News) was speaking into the camera and telling about the speech, repeating the things Reagan said. He repeated certain key lines or sound bites about an international terrorist conspiracy extending from Moscow to Managua. He called it "the new international version of Murder Incorporated" and cited the usual list of suspect nations: Nicaragua, Iran, Cuba, North Korea, Libya, Northern Ireland, etc. The reporter was very serious and had a sense of urgency—almost fear— in his voice when he reported this new global terrorist threat. I am sure that ordinary people who watched his report that night felt threatened by some new terror offensive, just as people across the United States bought gas masks during the Gulf war. Then the camera stopped and the reporter, cameraman, and helper broke out in laughter. They said that this was the most lunatic speech they had ever heard. Reagan was an idiot. There aren't any Baader-Meinhof people working in Nicaragua, they said. I went on with them and joked with them for a while. Then I asked what I thought was an obvious question, "Why didn't you say all of that into the TV camera? Why didn't you question Reagan's obvious self-serving propaganda?" Their faces perceptibly fell. They explained to me that their job was to report on what Reagan said, report the event. They explained that the people who see the broadcast will have to make up their own minds about the truth or falsity of Reagan's claims.

I went away thinking that here is a staged event, a high-profile big lie told to the assembled lawyers of the United States who ought to have asked for evidence of Baader-Meinhof, ETA, Tupamaros, IRA, Sandinistas, PLO, Red Brigades, and many others working in coordination to destroy the United States. And the media acted simply as purveyor or an apparatus for disseminating a clear pack of lies. The reporters knew them to be lies.

Of course, people can't make up their own minds if they never get the opposite view or a critical analysis of these events. How can there ever be informed deliberation in this country with this amount of cynicism in the media? This is exactly the reason we are here today. Terrorism is certainly one of the crucial issues of our time, not because as Americans we are terrified victims of terrorism as Reagan said, but because as Americans we are the terror network, the "new international version of Murder Incorporated." How can we understand that truth, given the way terrorism is represented to us by all levels of media?

So let's begin our discussion today. We have a very distinguished panel of speakers. First will be Chris Bratton and Annie Goldson who are independent video makers. Annie is from Brown University and Chris now teaches at the Art Institute of Chicago. They are in the process of producing a four-part video documentary series called *Counterterror*, which examines how the term "terrorism" has been used by politicians and the media. The two completed videos in the series have been widely distributed throughout the country in the progressive and arts community as well as airing on PBS. Today they are going to show us selections from *Framing the Panthers in Black and White*, a documentary on the FBI's covert campaign against the Black Panther Party and from *Counterterror: The North of Ireland* which looks at the British "shoot-to-kill" policy in that region.

Goldson: The idea for the documentary series *Counterterror* grew in reaction to the Reagan years. Although one can hardly say things have dramatically improved since then, it was during those dark days that "terrorism" became an obsession in the United States. "Counterterrorism" formed, as that administration said itself, "the cornerstone of foreign policy," but also had significant impact on domestic policies too. In fact, the discourse that emerged around "terrorism" slotted neatly into that old American binarism, the "enemy without, and the taint within," which had also formed the basis of the ideology of anticommunism. Therefore, as many of us witnessed, the term or label "terrorism" was used both to justify a violent and interventionist foreign policy, as well as to tighten the screws on certain communities within the United States.

With lavish assistance from the mainstream media, the Reagan/Bush administrations used the term "terrorism" to gain public consent for their policies. The counterterror teams, using a blend of racism, hysteria and a-historicism, managed to take the fear and outrage people felt at the very few, very well-publicized incidents—hijackings, car bombings and the like— and generalize them beyond any proportion. This fear of "terrorism" could then be marshalled and redirected at any target the team chose, that is, wherever their perceived enemies were lurking, regardless of the real political circumstances.

This is not to deny that there have been incidents in which innocent civilians have been hurt or killed. These indeed are individual tragedies for relatives of the victims. But I think it has to be underscored that the numbers that have suffered through such incidents are minuscule in the greater scheme of things. This, I know, cannot ameliorate the immediate pain of those involved. But such incidents are tragic, too, because they are generally borne out of desperate circumstances. Armed action is most often a response to tremendous violence and injustice inflicted on members of certain communities by powers who are frequently aided and abetted by Western economic, military, and political interests. And it is precisely these circumstances that are obscured in the flurries of sensationalist demonizations that quickly follow in the wake of these rare incidents—a fact which ensures their repetition.

Therefore, the Reagan/Bush administrations achieved a double goal through invoking the label "terrorist." On the one hand, they were able to deny the context (and usual U.S. involvement) behind political conflict, and, on the other, they managed to use the fear generated through sensationalism to justify their agenda of political and military repression wherever they deemed it necessary. As a result, hundreds of thousands of people in Latin America, the Middle East, Asia, and Africa have been dispossessed, tortured, and murdered.

Of course, ultimately, Reagan and Bush were merely the voices for the interests that lay behind them. One only has to compare the instance when Daniel Ortega, who was at the time the elected president of Nicaragua, called Reagan a "terrorist" because of his sponsorship and promotion of the contras. Lacking Reagan's powerful backers, Ortega's speech could have little resonance internationally no matter how true the charges were. This is why the simple reversal contained in the phrase, "One person's terrorist, is another's freedom fighter" is incorrect. People speak *differently*, depending on what authority and threat lie behind their words.

As Robert Merrill suggested in his introduction, the mainstream media have been complicit in this use of the term "terrorism." Not because there are government-media conspiracies being hatched in a corporate office somewhere, but rather, as his anecdote tells us, because journalists have internalized the codes and conventions of the media, which instruct them to "objectively report," not to critique or editorialize. But "objective" reporting in this instance, with its refusal to examine the contradictions and ideological functioning of the administration's use of the term "terrorism," directly endorses the violent policies that marked the 1980s. In this way, I think it has to be argued that "objectivity" in the news is a bias that merely covers over its own tracks.

Looking through news reports from the period, for instance, one sees the media negotiate the problem of defining "terrorism." A definition had to perform many contradictory tasks. First, it had to include lists of "our enemies" while excluding allies of the United States, and of course, the United States itself. This meant generally avoiding consideration of what actions actually constituted "terrorism"; the grim record of the contras, the Israeli government, and the Salvadoran military amongst many others had to be exempted. Second, a definition had to be sufficiently fixed to be credible to an audience, yet at the same time, it had to be flexible. Both the Reagan and Bush administrations, as ever keeping their political interests uppermost, were constantly reformulating these lists. Finally, a definition of "terrorism" had to quickstep after the administration around questions of international law. This meant glossing over World Court hearings and United Nations resolutions when convenient, while at the same time, invoking the "community of nations" precept of "non-interference in a country's affairs," if any international condemnation of key allies was threatening to emerge.

While all three networks regularly offered up definitions of the term, there was an ambiguity and defensiveness about these definitions, betraying, I think, a calculated cynicism in their attitude. Similar, perhaps, to the attitude that Walter Laqueur, that well-known "theorist of terrorism," expressed in an interview we did with him. "Terrorism is like pornography," he chuckled in a burst of male camaraderie, "No one can really define it, but everyone recognizes it when they see it." So used was Laqueur to sharing this slice of wit with his male colleagues, he failed to consider, obviously, that my position on pornography might not be entirely consistent with his.

Despite the media's implicit acknowledgment of the ambiguities of the term, "terrorism" still worked. Discussions on "terrorism and the media" were limited to the fruitless but well-exercised debate around the legitimacy of coverage per se. Audiences were, and still are on occasion, subject to endless talk shows on whether or not the media should give the "terrorists" their "lifeblood," that is, the publicity they crave, or whether they should simply ignore terrorists. This pseudo-debate replaced any analysis of the ambiguity and political uses of the term. Almost without exception, then, media coverage assisted in naturalizing the dominant use of the term "terrorism," thereby gaining public consent for the notorious interventions that marked the Reagan/Bush years.

This is the context in which we began to produce the series, *Counterterror*. The premise of the works was an examination of the label "terrorism" from the perspective of communities/countries that had been described and treated as such. In addition to the two completed programs that will be showing today, we are just finishing the third and fourth hour-long programs. The third, *A Small War: The United States in Puerto Rico*, examines the treatment of advocates for Puerto Rican independence, while the fourth, *Up to the South*, which is being produced by Jayce Salloum and Walid Ra'ad, looks at questions of resistance and occupation in South Lebanon.

In producing a series of programs that could stand alone, yet also could be linked into a series, we wanted to challenge—but also use—the concept of a network that has informed the chief ideologists of "terrorism." As the friend of the Reagan years, Claire Sterling, mythologizes in her opus, *The Terror Network*, all terrorists fought under the direct command of the then-Soviet Union, which used these cells to further its nefarious ends. This version of "terrorism" linked together very disparate struggles and political histories, draining them of their specificity and collapsing them into pure evil. In opposition to Sterling, the *Counterterror* series attempts to provide a context for political conflicts as well as to historicize resistance and struggle. However, in a sneaky reversal, the series also borrows from Sterling. It too proposes a network, this time a "counterterror network" of Western military and economic interests that are determined to squash movements for national liberation around the world.

Speaking of networks, I wanted finally to discuss *Counterterror*'s relation to television. The series is an "independent production," that is, we have had no major media institution underwriting our expenses, but rather have relied on borrowed equipment, donated skills, and on smaller grants from arts and humanities organizations. Although I do not want to diminish the economic problems of producing independent programming, gaining access to audiences is perhaps now the bigger challenge. The commercial networks are virtually sealed against independents, while even PBS and the more innovative commercial cable stations, the only real venues for independent work, show very little commitment to alternative production.

How then, despite good intentions, can one contest the commonsense meaning of "terrorism" as it is (ill)-defined in the mainstream media? The unsatisfactory answer is that one distributes work where one can, and although the two completed works in the series have been broadcast on PBS, probably as important are venues in the closed circuit: the alternative distribution networks, the art world, universities, community groups, festivals, and so on. The cause for most optimism in the distribution field is the developments occurring in public access television, which in its use of satellite technology, has the potential to transmit alternative programming to a mass audience.

Finally, and this is always a point that is linked to questions of reception and audience, I wanted to talk about the formal strategies we've taken up within the tapes. Generally, the work manifests the point made in contemporary media criticism, that it is not only *what* is said within a work that constructs meaning, but also *how* it is said. Our challenge to mass media, then, necessarily functions at the level of form. Documentary and the news are constructed through codes that are largely read as "real"—this is the source of their persuasion. This is not to say, of course, that *Counterterror*, in challenging formal conventions, shows the "unvarnished truth" of reality. All representation is ultimately just that—a representation. But by foregrounding documentary convention, we hope to constantly remind all of us that every time we watch anything, we are ultimately watching a construction.

Now, Chris will make a few comments about the tapes themselves.

Bratton: The first tape we will be looking at here is *Framing the Panthers in Black and White.* This is one of the two programs that examine how the "discourse of terrorism" has functioned within the United States, and I would like to begin by making a few remarks about why we came to focus on the Black Panther Party as its subject.

We traced the label "terrorism" as emanating from three basic institutions within the United States: first, conservative academia—clustered around think tanks such as the Center for Strategic and International Studies, the Rand Corporation, and the Hoover Institute for War, Peace, and Revolution; second, the government itself; and third, the mainstream media. Of course, the interconnections among these three institutions are plentiful. A think tank functions for a government as an employee training ground, a retirement center, and as a pool of advisors. Think-tank members are often used as "terrorism experts" by the mainstream media. And the mainstream media is heavily dependent on government spokespeople as a major source of news. As a result few reporters bother or dare to interrogate the official use of the term "terrorism" for fear of alienating important sources of "fresh news."

Our initial approach to the exploration of the label "terrorism" was to interview those from the first category, conservative academics such as Walter Laqueur, Brian Jenkins, and Robert Kupperman, three of the standard "terrorism experts" used on television. I also pursued Claire Sterling around the world but never managed to track her down. As Annie describes, we asked all of our "experts" to define "terrorism," a task they ultimately failed. Indeed, several displayed noticeable irritation at being asked to explain the logical inconsistencies contained in their definitions of "terrorism."

After dealing with the "terrorism experts," we selected the FBI, deemed the lead enforcement agency for "counterterrorism strategy" to speak for the government. At FBI headquarters in Washington,

D.C., we interviewed Steven Pomerantz, who was appointed the "czar of counterterrorism" during the 1980s. Clearly, Pomerantz was more prepared to deal with media crews that whipped in for a quick sound bite than with our more in-depth approach. Nevertheless, he was obliging throughout our two-hour interview. Among other things, he gave us an FBI publication that described the "terrorism" threat within the United States, as well as listing the supposed "terrorist" groups themselves.

Therefore, after asking (but not really finding out) what "terrorism" was from the so-called academics, and after consulting the list in our FBI guide, we went in search of the "terrorists" themselves. The major groups included in the list were Puerto Rican *independentistas*, various factions of the Black liberation movement, Native Americans, and members of the white left generally called white anti-imperialists.

A number of things bound all of our interviewees together—first, they were all in prison; second, despite the clear political dimension of their cases, their status as political prisoners was consistently and absolutely denied by the government; and finally, the FBI had clearly been involved in all of their cases. So our research led us in a circle—exploring the "discourse of terrorism" led us to our interviews with certain prisoners, whose stories directed us back to the FBI itself. They all spoke of one program in particular, called COINTELPRO. This illegal and covert counterintelligence program was intended, in the FBI's words, to "disrupt" and "neutralize" the New Left movements of the late 1960s and early 1970s. A concise definition from no less than the Senate Intelligence Committee, which investigated COINTELPRO after most of the damage was done, states that it was "a sophisticated vigilante operation aimed squarely at preventing the exercise of first amendment rights of speech and association." I would just add that its efforts to destroy all movements for progressive social change in this country included everything up to and including murder.

In summary then we felt that COINTELPRO was the secret history of the United States. Without ever managing to become common knowledge, it still managed to completely deform political life here. We returned to the FBI because we felt that to understand what was called domestic "terrorism" in the 1980s, one had to investigate the history of FBI activities from the 1960s onward. Henceforth, our focus shifted to COINTELPRO.

Our first interview was with Dhoruba Bin Wahad, a former leader of the New York Black Panther Party, who had been one of the original Panther 21 defendants. At the time of our interview in 1989, he had been in prison for over nineteen years, serving a twenty-five-year to life sentence for the attempted murder of two police officers. He had claimed throughout his incarceration that he was innocent. During the long course of legal proceedings, Dhoruba had "liberated" 300,000 FBI COINTELPRO documents relevant to his case.

After our first interview, Dhoruba's case began to unwind. Much to everyone's surprise, his conviction was overturned and he was released from prison on bail in March of 1990.

The following is from *Framing the Panthers*. As you will see, we use the COINTELPRO documents themselves to structure the tape both visually and narratively, making the covert historical narrative into the overt narrative of the tape. This selection also includes a tour of the FBI's headquarters in Washington, D.C. Aside from being the national political police force, the FBI has always been excellent at public relations—as the following tour indicates.

From *Framing the Panthers in Black and White*

{For accuracy, the tapes have been transcribed word for word. Sometimes the transcription will not read as smoothly as a written text. Deletions are not marked.}

Dhoruba Bin Wahad: I know people ask me, "Well, are you bitter, that you spent nineteen years in prison?" And I think bitterness would be ah, the inappropriate word. I have mixed feelings about it, but it was something that came as a consequence of taking a position, and taking positions as a black man, in a racist society, and I had to accept that.

Robert Boyle (lawyer, voice over image of COINTELPRO documents from Dhoruba's case): This stack of papers I'm holding is a compilation of documents from the FBI's files on their efforts to destroy black organizations in the

1960s and early 1970s. That program of destruction was known as COINTELPRO; and according to this document, from August 1967, the purpose of COINTELPRO was to "expose, disrupt, discredit, or otherwise neutralize" the activities of Black Nationalist organizations.

Dhoruba: My name is Dhoruba Bin Wahad, formerly Dhoruba Moore, and I've been in prison for nineteen years. Knowing that I was innocent of the charges that I was convicted of, I've always maintained that the only reason that I was indicted for the attempted murder of two policemen was because of my active role in the Black Panther Party in New York, because of my vocal opposition to the criminal justice system in New York. . . .

Boyle (voice over images of documents): By mid-1968, the Black Panther Party became COINTELPRO's chief target. And according to this document, from December of 1968, all FBI field officers were instructed to submit hard-hitting counterintelligence measures aimed at crippling the Black Panther Party.

Dhoruba: One doesn't understand how young the average member of the Black Panther party was, in a lot of ways. We were very, very young. And I was like an old man, practically, at twenty-three, you know. I got caught up in the struggle in that way, and, yes my idealism, coupled with the energy of the times—these were very energetic times. It was the atmosphere in the African-American community that I had never seen before, and haven't seen since.

[Archival images of the Panthers from 1960s/1970s]

Chant: Power to the people! Power to the people!

Kathleen Cleaver: All power to the people is becoming a reality!

Dhoruba (voice over archives): The Black Panther Party was founded in 1966 in Oakland California, and in two years it had grown from a small local organization to a national organization, with chapters in every major city; thousands of members, and hundreds of thousands of sympathizers in the African-American community.

Boyle (voice over documents): This particular document is from Dhoruba's FBI file, and as you see, one whole paragraph has been blacked out. These deletions were put on this document by the FBI when it was released, and it's information which they do not want to publicly disclose. We believe it shows the true reasons why they targeted Dhoruba; namely because of his political activism, and his leadership qualities.

Dhoruba (voice over archives): So that type of work that we did, at that time, revolved around trying to better the conditions of African-American people in the inner city. In housing, in school, in welfare, in terms of drugs—drug rehabilitation.

Huey Newton (archives from the period): In America, black people are treated very much as the Vietnamese people, or any other colonized people, because we're used, we're brutalized, the police in our community occupy our area, our community, as a foreign troop occupies territory.

Dhoruba (voice over archives): We opened free health clinics; we opened up free breakfast programs to feed children during the school months.

Bobby Seale (archives from the period): We want some socialistic programs implemented in the black community so we can survive and be free. They have never let the Black Panther Party, we want some community control of police.

Dhoruba (voice over archives): And of course we also organized self-defense patrols in the black community, and we advocated that black people arm themselves from racist attack. That seems to be the part of our agenda that got the most attention!

Chant: People are tired of the bullshit!

Chris Bratton and **Annie Goldson** stills from the video *Framing the Panthers in Black and White*, 1991 courtesy of the artists (see accompanying text).

Chant: No more brothers in jail!

Leader: I am!

Crowd: I am!

Leader: A revolutionary!

Crowd: A revolutionary!

Chant: Pigs are gonna catch hell!
Off the pig!
No more brothers in jail!
Off the pig!

Dhoruba: It was the *idea* that had to be destroyed, you see. It didn't matter that the individuals may not have represented a significant physical threat to the United States government. What mattered was the idea: that black people had a right to defend themselves against white aggression.

[Montage of high school students]

Rebecca: My name's Rebecca Anthony, and I'm a junior here at Martin Luther King High School. Well, as far as I know that they [Black Panthers] had some, um, some of them was arrested, and, some of them fled the country. They had rivalry among their leaders and then they just got separated and went their separate ways.

Terrence: My name is Terrence L. Newell, I'm in the tenth grade, I'm fifteen years old. I know that it was a group in the sixties. They didn't have the same ideals as Dr. King, to an extent, you know, they believed in arming themselves.

[Archives from the 1960s]

Chant: Liberating power!

Leader: Power!

Crowd: Power!

Leader: Power to the people!

Crowd: Power to the people!

Chant: Free the Panther 21! Power to the people!

Boyle (voice over images of documents): The Panther 21 indictment was an attempt by local authorities to incapacitate the leadership of the Panther Party in New York by incarcerating them on trumped-up charges. The case was also used by the FBI as a means to intensify their covert campaign to destroy the Black Panther Party from within. The FBI instituted a plethora of counterintelligence activities, including the use of informants, and anonymous and spurious letters. For example, the FBI prepared this anonymous note, which was sent to Panther Leader Huey Newton's brother, instructing him to warn Huey that Dhoruba was going to kill him. Dhoruba became a pawn in this FBI plan. . . .

Dhoruba: You see, when I was acquitted, in the 21 case, I was a fugitive, and the reason why I was a fugitive was because the Counterintelligence Program had devised a plot by the leadership, to incite the leadership of the Black Panther Party to assassinate me. And in order to protect ourselves, we had to flee the jurisdiction of the court during the course of trial. . . .

Boyle (over documents): The acquittal of the Panther 21 on all charges was an enormous embarrassment to the New

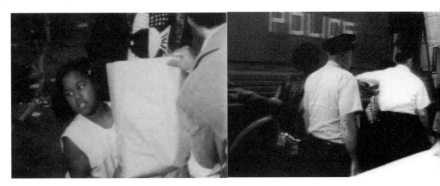

York City Police Department, to the District Attorney, and to the FBI. In a document dated May 24, 1971, J. Edgar Hoover ordered his New York field office to intensify investigations of Panther 21 members. And in sum, an all-out effort was undertaken to put acquitted Panther 21 members back in jail.

Elizabeth Fink (lawyer): In June of 1971, Mr. Bin Wahad was arrested and charged with the attempted murder of two police officers. And he was convicted.

Dhoruba: And I maintained then and I maintain now that I was innocent of that shooting. And subsequently, over the years, as a result of me filing, as a result of my filing a suit, I obtained approximately 300,000 pages of federal FBI documents. On the Black Panther Party, on myself, and on the Counterintelligence Program.

Boyle (over documents): The primary evidence against Dhoruba was the testimony of a woman named Pauline Joseph, a woman who was a diagnosed paranoid schizo-phrenic, and who was held as a material witness in the old Commodore Hotel in New York City for two years, while her testimony was fabricated. Withheld from the defense were approximately 25 prior statements of Pauline Jo-seph, which totally contradict her trial testimony, and would show, indeed, that Dhoruba was framed. She states: "The four men you are holding" (and Dhoruba was one of the four men) "are not suspects. They did not do it."

[Montage of high school students]

Ray: My name is Ray McEaddy, I attend Martin Luther King, and I'm in the tenth grade. I believe that they [Black

Panthers] just broke up, and they just never reformed again.

Question: Have you ever heard of something called COINTELPRO, or the Counterintelligence Program.

Ray: No.

[Title: Tour of FBI Headquarters]

FBI Headquarters Tour Guide: If you focus your attention to the monitors, you're about to see a brief introductory tape about your FBI.

FBI Narrator: Welcome to the headquarters of the Federal Bureau of Investigation. Since 1908, the FBI has been an investigative arm of the Department of Justice, working to preserve the safety and freedom of all Americans.

Boyle: COINTELPRO was a wide-spread campaign, and it operated on a lot of fronts. The Black Panther Party, of course, was the major target in the late 1960s, but Martin Luther King was a target; the Student Nonviolent Coordinating Committee was a target. Basically in any city in the United States where there was any kind of civil rights activity, or organized activity on behalf of black people, there was an FBI program to destroy that. And they memorialized it in their documents.

Dhoruba: The counterintelligence programs, COINTELPRO, utilized all types of tactics. They had a letter that was called, "Dear Irving." A "Dear Irving letter"—this is what they called it. And this letter was written, the FBI would write this Dear Irving letter to various Jewish organizations, and this Irving character, would purportedly be a disgruntled communist. He would talk about the Black Panther Party. That he was privy to information that the Black Panthers were anti-Semitic. That they were talking about killing all the Jews. What did that do between the alliance between liberal Jews and blacks?

FBI Narrator: Director Sessions is actually the fourth director of the FBI. A director cannot serve for more than ten years, and he cannot be reappointed. That law was passed in June of 1968; it did not go into effect until after Mr. Hoover's term. Mr. Hoover served as director of the FBI for forty-eight years.

Clarence Kelley (Hoover's successor, voice over images from the FBI tour): Because of the violent actions of the leadership of the New Left, FBI officials concluded that some additional effort must be made to neutralize and disrupt this revolutionary movement.

Boyle: The FBI always publicly maintains that the purpose of COINTELPRO was to prevent violence. But COINTELPRO itself was an exceedingly violent program. Law enforcement agencies throughout the country—with the FBI—raided numerous offices of the Black Panther Party. Fred Hampton and Mark Clark, Black Panther Party leaders in Chicago, were murdered while they slept in their beds. In the split in the party, which the FBI caused, and which forced Dhoruba to go underground, that split resulted in factional violence, leading to the deaths of many members of the Black Panther Party. And in this document we see that the FBI actually takes credit for the death of Robert Webb, who was killed during factional violence in March of 1971.

Dhoruba: There was nothing haphazard or incidental about COINTELPRO. OK? When we read the documents, we'll see that J. Edgar Hoover talks about the standards of moral conduct that hold sway in the African-American community. Being a racist he said that these standards are essentially low-life standards and they are different than white standards, you see. You know, they're not like us. It's the same thing that they did to the Vietnamese people. We see that historically, going back to the Vietnam war, a lot of police officers got their initial training in counterinsurgency and counterintelligence in Vietnam. These techniques were brought home. The war was brought home to the United States, and when we used to say that the war was being fought in our community at home, the peace movement, which was predominantly white, which was predominantly liberal, ignored us. They didn't want to confront and deal with their racism. It was all right to talk about "stop the war in Vietnam" because that threatened their future, you see? They would be the ones to be drafted, OK? They didn't want to deal with the war in Harlem. They didn't want to deal with the war in Watts. They didn't want to deal with the war in Buttermilk Bottom in Atlanta. They didn't want to deal with the war on Hastings Street in Detroit. They didn't want to deal with that, you see? Because that was too close to home.

FBI Narrator: There are over 4,500 guns in this collection. All of the weapons are in very good working condition, they're not simply for display, because the agents will use some of the weapons for test firing and also for interchangeable parts.

Boyle (over archival photographs): And a result of the violence in the Party, and the confusion—many members of the Panther Party had to go underground, Dhoruba being one of them. And some of them who went underground had charges against them. They were forced into a situation of living underground, and then local police and the FBI embarked upon what were in reality, search-and-destroy missions. Hunting down missing Panthers on the streets, many of whom were shot and killed in confrontations with the police.

Dhoruba: The first thing you have to do in order to oppress a people, to repress them, is to denigrate their humanity. Reduce them to something less than human. Make them into an Other, a threatening Other, and you can do anything you want to them—you can lock them up and put them in prison, like they did me. You can murder them like they did Fred Hampton and Mark Clark or Twyman Myers or Zayd Malik Shakur, or you can exile them, like they did Michael Tabor or Assata Shakur. You see? That's what the system does. It first strips you of your humanity, reduces you to the level of a mad dog, and a depraved terrorist, and then it's open season on you. They can do anything they want to you.

Chant: Educating power! Liberating power!

[Montage of high school students]

Damian King: My name is Damian King, and I'm a junior at Martin Luther King High School.

Question: Were you ever taught about the Panthers in school?

King: No.

Question: What about in a history class?

Rebecca Anthony: No.

Question: No? And do you think that you should be taught about the Panthers in school?

King: Yes. Because it's all part of history, so why shouldn't we be taught about it?

[Harlem rally for Nelson Mandela after Dhoruba was released]

Chant: Amandla! Amandla! Power to our people! Power to our people!

Dhoruba: Brother, comrade, Nelson Mandela, the political prisoners of the United States, especially African-American political prisoners, have written this brief statement to you, and have asked me, as one of their former comrades in prison, to present it to you. There is a common thread and a common humanity that we all share. My brother, I have spent nineteen years in prison in the United States for my political beliefs, and you, sir, you, were the symbol that helped sustain me and other African-American political prisoners. Here in the United States, African-American people and their movements for liberation have been criminalized, just as the ANC was criminalized by the racist, fascist apartheid regime in South Africa. Our fighters and freedom-fighters have been slain in the streets of Harlem and Brooklyn. Our people who stand up for our freedom have been rail-roaded to prison by the same legal system that tries to protect you today and that tried to kill you yesterday. So on behalf of my brothers in prison, on behalf of the Puerto Rican Nationalistas who cannot sit up here, on behalf of the Native American political prisoners, and on behalf of the white American political prisoners, I say to you brother, we love you and we will not give up the fight! We will not give up the fight! We will not give up the fight! We will not give up the fight! Amandla! Amandla!

Bratton: One update on Dhoruba's case: the New York State Supreme Court reinstated his conviction on December 16, 1991. He could face re-imprisonment.

The second excerpt we will be looking at is from *Counterterror: North of Ireland*, which we produced in collaboration with Derry-based video makers, Anne Crilly and Brendan MacMenamin. The program deals with a British strategy that up to that time had received little publicity—a policy of planned assassination known as "shoot-to-kill." Through this policy, the British security forces select, frame, and kill individuals that they consider to be leading members of the Irish Republican Army or the Irish National Liberation Army.

We structured this program around a short BBC report on a particular "shoot-to-kill" incident that occurred in a small border town called Strabane. In juxtaposing a "community history" with the BBC report, we attempted to reveal the way the mainstream media evacuate history and context from their coverage. We purposefully chose an incident in which the victims were armed. If we had concentrated on a situation in which "innocent" people got killed by the British—and there are plenty of them, too—we felt that the fact that there is a guerrilla war being fought in the North would be sidestepped. Through the program, we wanted to raise questions not only about British colonial domination, but also about organized resistance as well.

In this program, we attempted to show how notions of media "objectivity" and "neutrality" are impossible in what is fundamentally a colonial context. The Derry journalist, Eamonn McCann makes a point about this, as you will see. The visual component of the segment is composed entirely of a string of photographs, all of shoot-to-kill victims. We chose this formal strategy because the memorial photograph is part of cultural life of the Nationalist community in the North. Most of the photographs are cropped from family snapshots, enlarged, and framed, which gives them a particularly blurred, haunting look. The information accompanying each photo comes from Amnesty International reports.

From *Counterterror: The North of Ireland*

Eamonn McCann (text and voice-over on black): Even if the notions of objectivity and balance had meaning, they still wouldn't produce a fair account of what is happening here . . . for the very simple reason what is happening here is not itself fair.

BBC Anchor-woman (voice-over on black): It's led to renewed anger and complaints in Republican quarters that security forces are more intent on killing terrorists than taking them prisoner. . . .

[Peaceful image of Strabane neighborhood, with prominent Ché mural painted on wall. Title: Innisfree Gardens, 1988]

BBC Anchor-woman: The dead all came from Strabane where the shooting happened early this morning. The police said. . . .

[Images from VHS documentation of same neighborhood during a funeral, clashes between local people and British security forces very evident. Title: Innisfree Gardens, 1985]

Mary Breslin: Heavy gun fire . . . we didn't know what was happening. The shooting was all over the place. The first thing I said to Joe was it can't be shooting, it must be explosions. At 5 minutes to 5:00, we were awakened at 5 minutes to 5:00 by the heavy shooting.

Question: How did the police treat your family on that day?

Joseph Breslin: They raided us about 10 past 7:00.

Mary Breslin: 10 minutes past 7:00 that's right. They came out to the house. There was a policeman just stood in that doorway. He never moved away from the doorway. He just seemed to be sneering in.

Karina Breslin: We were nervous because we saw a priest driving up and all, we didn't know what had happened. We knew somebody was dead.

William Devine: I got up that morning about 8:30. I looked out of the window, and there were police Landrovers everywhere. I knew then something was wrong. I had another cup of tea while the police—the RUC [Royal Ulster Constabulary]—were searching the house. I remember one of them looking up at the display cabinet and saying who owns the trophies? [Pan of trophy display and memorial photos.] I said they were my son's, Michael's, he was a snooker champion. And he said, he must of been a good snooker player. That's all I remember from that morning.

BBC Anchor-woman: No shots were fired at the security forces. Two of the dead were brothers, one aged only sixteen. It's led to renewed anger and complaints in the Republican quarters that security forces are more intent on killing terrorists than taking them prisoner. The dead all came from Strabane where the shooting happened early this morning. The police say three rifles and two rocket launchers were found near the bodies. Neil Bennett has been to the scene.

Bennett (stand-up, in field, 1988): The shooting happened before dawn this morning in a field on the outskirts of Strabane. A uniformed army patrol obviously acting on information was ready and waiting. And the IRA men didn't have a chance to fire their weapons. The shootings were next to a strongly Republican housing estate. . . .

Mark Tinney (eyewitness): There was three, four, different camera crews, in this actual room filming.

Question: Did you feel they gave a fair representation of what you had said?

Tinney: Roughly . . . bits of it, just. They didn't say about me hearing the helicopter, or about the six men lying shooting in the field or that there was so many army about, and that the men shooting in the field had masks on their faces.

Question: So were you standing at the window at the time?

Gerry Stephenson (eyewitness): I was indeed. I had the curtains pulled back and looking out. Mostly at this

Chris **Bratton** and Annie **Goldson** stills from the video *Counter-terror: The North of Ireland*, 1991 courtesy of the artists (see accompanying text).

There was a local voice shouting,

"Don't shoot, don't shoot."

fella that was shooting down there, you know.

Question: Did any members of the security forces see you looking out?

Stephenson: Oh yes, this boy that was down the road saw us, because he turned around and looked up, and he shouted, "Get your head out of the window or I'll blow your fucking head off." And he pointed the rifle directly up towards us. Then he turned around and commenced firing again. At that point, I took the kids into the backroom with me and the wife.

Tinney: There was about fifty army men from here to the back of the houses.

Question: Was this at the time of the shooting or directly after it?

Tinney: The first couple of Landrovers pulled up about ten seconds from when that gun had started shooting.

Bennett (BBC News Report, 1985, at the scene of shooting): One of the men killed is believed by security sources to be a member of the provisional IRA. There were also two brothers.

Question: So all in all, it seems that it was a very well organized and set up situation?

John Fahey (lawyer for the Breslin family in field where shootings occurred): Well, certainly it would seem to be a well organized operation because within a very, very short period of time—within less than 2 or 3 minutes, the area was saturated with police officers and military.

Bennett: Following incidents like this there are inevitable criticisms that the security forces shot first and asked questions afterwards. But at the end of a week in which the IRA have gunned down. . . .

Tinney: Where I was, I could see over the boundary that they had put around the three bodies, and could see the three people but I couldn't identify them. They just kept walking up and down. They had the bodies lying there for about seven hours.

Question: Do you think there was any reason for doing that?

Tinney: In my view about it, I think they were just trophies.

Fahey: This case here hasn't been formally examined or investigated. But if it were to have the benefit of an independent inquiry, it will reveal that they were meant to be killed and that there were no other instructions given.

Question: So these killings were not isolated killings of their type, they were a part of a pattern?

Fahey: Yes. Part of the pattern, the shooting of these three is part of a pattern.

Bennett: There are many people in Northern Ireland who will say that the ends justify the means.

Joe Breslin (voice-over): This is Strabane, this is the town that I come from. I was born in Strabane. I left Strabane and moved to the United States shortly after my brother and his two comrades were killed. Their deaths and my exile are tied up with what's happening back there. [Cut to check point.] Strabane is located north of

INCIDENT 30
5.8.87
TONY GORMLEY
AFFILIATION: IRA

INCIDENT 20
12.2.84
TONY McBRIDE
AFFILIATION: IRA

and that was to shoot them.

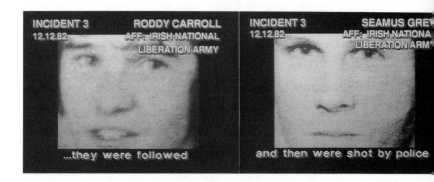

INCIDENT 3
12.12.82
RODDY CARROLL
AFF: IRISH NATIONAL
LIBERATION ARMY
...they were followed

INCIDENT 3
12.12.82
SEAMUS GRE...
AFF: IRISH NATIONA
LIBERATION ARM...
and then were shot by police

the border. The border which was set up in 1922 which
partitioned the six counties from the twenty-six counties. The six counties became a Unionist state, which was
controlled by Britain. The Unionists were a section
within the Protestant community who were loyal to Britain. The British gave the Protestants privileges—land
like this land here, good jobs, better houses. The
Catholics were discriminated against. In fact, the
Catholics got nothing. [Cut to images of Super-8 home
movies from the 1960s, shot by local Strabane filmmaker.]
In 1968 the Civil Rights Association took to the streets.
They were demanding better jobs, better education,
housing, and an end to discrimination. This didn't suit
the Unionists who feared they would lose their privileges. And there was a backlash. The Unionists wanted the
police to beat the people off the streets. The Catholic
people were under a great threat. They had no protection
whatsoever. So when this was going on, the IRA re-emerged
as a defensive force and started to reorganize to defend
Nationalist areas, where most of the Catholics lived.
[Cut to security forces in field at time of the Strabane
shootings.] This was when the British troops were sent in
to reinforce the police, and they've occupied the six
counties ever since. [Cut to Breslin house, U.S.] The
security forces accused me of being a leading member of
the IRA in Strabane. They issued me with numerous death
threats. They told me that they wished I was in the field
the morning they killed my brother and two comrades. They
don't make idle threats, because previous to the killing
of my brother and the two comrades, I know that they
received many threats too.

Karina Breslin: His decision to take up arms—we didn't know about it when he was living, we only found out about it when he died—the morning he died. It was a shock for us because even though you support the IRA—and I always have done—even though you support the IRA, you still can't get used to the idea of them having a mask on, having a gun. And I've never seen Charlie with a gun, never seen him with a mask. To me, he was just my big brother Charlie, big easy-going Charlie. . . . And we have to say, "Look, this is the IRA." They're not men with masks, they're not men with guns. They're young fellas who've taken just about all they can take. They've taken torture, they've taken seeing their own countrymen lying, languishing and being allowed to die of hunger, through the want of justice. They've seen their friends being taken away and imprisoned, themselves or their friends being beaten up by the RUC and UDR. They've seen foreign armies coming into their country. Shooting people dead. Shooting six year olds, seven year olds, twelve year olds, children, girls and boys, with plastic bullets.

Question: Did you know your sons were in the IRA?

William Devine: No, at no time. As a matter of fact, that was one of the questions, when I went to identify the lads, that was one of the questions one of the policemen asked me, "Did you know that your sons was in the IRA?" I couldn't answer that.

Patricia Devine: Michael was the biggest shock to everybody. Michael thought only of his snooker. I think it was a shock to everybody in Strabane.

William Devine: I mean after all David was only sixteen years of age, he hadn't even left school.

Pat Devine: David was still in school.

William Devine: He was still in school.

Joe Breslin (over images of Strabane housing, security forces): I don't think there is any family or home in Strabane who are not affected by the presence of British rule in Ireland. Unemployment is still the highest in Western Europe. Housing is very poor. This is typical of the Catholic area, houses boarded like this. Nationalist areas, which are mostly Catholic, are under surveillance twenty-four hours a day. The police and army occupy Strabane, and harass the residents, constantly beating them, raiding their homes, arresting them and putting them in jail.

William Devine (over Devine's house): And if there's such a thing as terrorism, there's something wrong somewhere with a setup that has to have terrorists. And until people like the government get down and thrash all that out, and define what a terrorist is. I mean let's face it, there are no bigger terrorists than the British themselves.

Joe Breslin (over photos of the funerals): The British try to make it look like there is no war going on. They say that the IRA are terrorists and criminals and that the British are here to keep the Catholics and Protestants from killing each other. But basically it's not religious war, it's a colonial war between Ireland and Britain. And until Britain pulls out, it's going to continue.

John Stalker (former Deputy Chief Inspector, Manchester Police): I was in Northern Ireland investigating what had become known internationally as a shoot-to-kill policy. I was fully intending to do a meticulous and careful re-investigation of what had happened when six men were shot dead over a period of five weeks. Of the six people, none of them were armed when they were killed. They were followed, surveyed over a long period, and then were shot by police. My job was to investigate wrong-doing, if there was any, by policemen. I believe that there was wrong-doing by policemen and I investigated it thoroughly up until the point that I was removed.

Question: And the rationalization for that was that you were involved with some people who were allegedly involved with criminal activity?

Stalker: Well it was an absolute lie. I mean it was a smear campaign by whom I don't know, but it just wasn't true. That was the reason given, because, in my view, some hasty reason had to be found to remove me from the investigation and that was the best anybody could do.

Fahey: As I understand the shoot-to-kill policy, it has been another weapon used by the government in an attempt to defeat what they describe as terrorism. The shoot-to-kill policy was one whereby the government selected targets, usually people that they believed to be very high in the ranks of paramilitary organizations but had failed to gain any admission of involvement. So then it was based on the idea that this was the only way they could defeat these people and that was to shoot them. That was the ultimate because in addition to taking out men they believed to be dangerous, it was also acting as a threat or intimidation to other people who may have been considering becoming involved in what they described as terrorism.

Question: Do you think that the killing of your sons was a continuation of the shoot-to-kill policy?

William Devine: That was a shoot-to-kill policy, and their lives could have been saved. I mean even in time of war, you take prisoners. Their lives need not have been taken, no bother.

Elaine McNicholl: I heard a local voice—they were mostly English voices. And the local voice was shouting, "Don't shoot, don't shoot!" And um, after that it was sort of quiet for a while and you know there was another flash again.

Devine: Michael had twenty-eight bullets in his body. David had seven. . . . And young Charles had thirteen.

Question: Even though the three men were carrying arms, had the soldiers a legal right to shoot them?

Fahey: I don't believe soldiers have a legal right to kill anyone just simply because they are carrying arms. And I don't think their own directives would entitle them to kill someone just because they are carrying arms. In a situation where soldiers are confronted by people who are armed, their first duty would be to call upon them to halt and to throw down their guns. I also believe that soldiers would not have the right to open up indiscriminately against people armed or otherwise, unless they believed that life, either their own, a comrade, or someone else, was in imminent danger.

Question: And do you not believe that was the case?

Fahey: Well, there is no evidence of that.

Devine: Their lives wasn't in danger because the simple reason why: the safety catches was all on. So the guns was unfireable. They were just shot in cold blood. I mean, every one of them was shot in the back.

Fahey: The media and indeed the British government have waged a very successful war against the IRA and the other paramilitary organizations on the Republican side. Those organizations are held to be the only people who engage in violence whereas the incidents I have given you are equally as violent as the violence of those organizations.

BBC Report, Strabane: . . . There were scuffles and stones thrown before order was restored. Following incidents like this . . .

Question (Beslin house, Strabane): Why do you think the term terrorism and international terrorism are used by the British media?

Karina Breslin: Because it justifies their attack on our people. Their attacks on the Irish people. Their attacks on the most vulnerable section. Not the middle class not the clerics, but the working class. . . .

Mary Breslin: The ordinary people in England. . . . I don't blame them for that they're here, the Brits, to fight against terrorists. I don't blame them for thinking that, because they don't even know what's going on.

Question: Why is that?

Mary Breslin: They were told what the Brits can do here and the police can do and get away with it against the people, there's no way that they could believe that this is actually happening.

[Cut to image of media surrounding the Breslin's the day of the funeral, filmed by local resident on VHS.]

McCann: Language is very important. The word "terrorist" immediately slots someone into a particular category beyond the pale of ordinary human discourse. Perhaps less intensely value-laden words, like "the IRA guns people down."

BBC News: But at the end of a week when the IRA gunned down a prison officer and a community policeman . . .

McCann: You would never hear on a report on the television news, saying the British army "gunned people down two people from Derry, or something," they never "gun down people," in fact, it's not just the words used, even the tense used is passive. You will find that civilians tend to "get killed." When something like the Strabane killings happens, the first source of information is the RUC press office. Now that's quite simple and in the mind of the journalist doing the story he or she will go to the RUC press office not because they're consciously biased in favor of the RUC, but simply because you've got a phone number for there, there'll be someone on duty, and that someone will give you up-to-date information. Of course it's the information which the RUC wants to give you.

BBC News: Three loaded rifles were found at the scene as well as two homemade grenade launchers. . . .

McCann: If you want to get a balanced account and assuming that balance is possible, it's enormously more difficult. Who are your other witnesses? Who are you going to present again? It's usually someone who has got no experience with making a statement to the media. Usually someone who will be interviewed, while standing in the street with the wind blowing through her hair.

BBC Interviewee: I did hear someone shouting, "Don't shoot, don't shoot me"— and there was another burst of fire.

Devine: One lady came and she said it was a very, very good story. And the next thing was nine policeman were killed—God rest them—and that overshadowed any events that took place from Strabane.

BBC News: Also in Northern Ireland . . .

Karina Breslin (watching BBC report, Breslin house): Jan Leming was the first to use the word "terrorist" in relation to Charlie, Davey, and Micky. First of all, she couldn't possibly have known the three boys. She had no understanding, nor does any of her colleagues have any understanding of who they are, what the IRA are, what they're doing, what they're fighting for. They don't feel it's necessary to justify the use of the word "terrorist" and it isn't really, because people will just accept whatever they see on television as being fact unless they know otherwise. And most of them wouldn't have known Charlie or Davey or Micky. And most people in England don't know what the IRA are about. So they're content to keep people ignorant, to play their part in the British propaganda machine. And I suppose they're getting well paid for it so why rock the boat?

Merrill: Thanks very much Chris and Annie. Maybe during the question-and-answer period we can talk some more about independent networks for videos and film but also magazines and books and things of that sort. I want to make one connection with what you said in the tape to Ward Churchill, since he is here today. Ward is the author of three books on COINTELPRO. The first is *Agents of Repression*, a very detailed study of the activities of the FBI against the American Indian Movement and the Black Panthers. The second is *The COINTELPRO Papers*, in which are reprinted hundreds of internal FBI memoranda, and you can read their own instructions for carrying out these repressions, just as Dhoruba and Bob Boyle describe. There is also a third book, *Cages of Steel*, which tells about the current whereabouts of many of these victims of FBI terror—many are in prison and much of the book is written by the political prisoners themselves.

Our next speaker is Margaret Randall, who is a poet, a novelist, a publisher, a journalist, a translator, and a great many more things. Currently she teaches at Trinity College and she has taught also at the University of New Mexico. Probably the most important reason she is here is her life experiences. In the early 1960s she moved to Central America and spent a long time in Cuba working as a free-lance journalist and later for the Cuban Book Institute. Later, in the 1980s,

T.O.D.T.
Bike Bomb, 1987
mixed media
60"x84"x51"
courtesy of the
Chris Middendorf
Gallery, Washing-
ton, D.C.

she moved to Nicaragua and worked for the Foreign Press Center and the Ministry of Culture. In the mid-1980s she decided to return to the United States, but the State Department refused to return her U.S. citizenship and sought to have her deported. She has since resolved that problem through a lawsuit. But her experiences in countries that have been labelled by the U.S. government as terrorist countries, such as Nicaragua and Cuba, are invaluable for those of us who haven't visited those countries.

Randall: I will begin with a public event which I am sure is still fresh in our minds, although each of us may view it differently, placing the emphasis in different ways according to who we are and what we are able to remember of our own lives. In October of 1991, in the midst of what might otherwise have been a rather ordinary Senate confirmation hearing, a woman stepped forward and accused a man about to become an associate justice on the U.S. Supreme Court of gross sexual misconduct.

For at least four days, millions were glued to our television sets or radios; later we continued to pore over the written commentary. Anita Hill is a law professor. She is African-American. She had made it to one of the most prestigious law schools in the country and on to high-level Washington jobs from the same impoverished beginnings as those suffered by the man she said sexually terrorized her when she worked as his legal advisor. As she gave her testimony, Hill's demeanor was impeccable. She was clear and concise and never showed undue emotion (which might have permitted her inquisitors to characterize her as a *hysterical woman*). She was always respectful, never strident, even when faced with the disrespect, condescension, and rudeness of the fourteen white men who questioned her for hours.

In an effort to explain away her accusations, those men looked to every reason but the real one. They asked why she had waited so long to come forward with the information that she had been harassed by Judge Clarence Thomas (he was routinely referred to as Judge; she was often addressed by her first name only). They asked if she had been duped by feminists, if she was a "woman scorned," if she had plans to write a book, if she was given to fantasy.

Hill's dignity and her testimony itself were unshakable. Thomas, on the other hand, refused even to address the accusations against him. He belligerently grandstanded his way through a passionate denial (showing emotions that would have been termed *hysteria* had they been indulged in by Hill). Yet, predictably, Hill was accused by at least one of the senators of having perjured herself, and ultimately dismissed by the lot. Thomas was confirmed—to a chorus of lamentations about how horrible it had been that a judge and his family be forced to endure such outrage. Some senators and media commentators even implied that the way the hearings had been handled threatened our very institutions of government!

I am struck, particularly, by one aspect of these events. Many of those who were impressed by Hill's testimony, even some who were inclined to believe that what she said happened did indeed happen, continually repeated a question that was also meant as an indictment: "Why did Anita Hill follow Clarence Thomas from the Department of Education to the Equal Employment Opportunities Commission? Why," these people asked, "would a woman who had suffered that type of abuse continue to work for the man who harassed her? Why did she wait ten years to come forward?"

People who ask these questions do not know that torture psychologically conditions the victim even as it damages and destroys the body. The reason Hill followed Thomas even when he had abused her confidence and her integrity is transparent to those who understand the nature of terrorism and the role of memory. It is obscure for those who do not. This is relevant to what I want to talk about today.

In an atmosphere of terror, terrorism itself becomes ordinary, expected, acceptable. In such an atmosphere, memory bends to make room for what is most heinous. We are accustomed to hearing the word "terrorist" used to describe an Arab driving a car of explosives into a U.S. embassy compound in Beirut. Frequent TV images reinforce the connection. We are not so used to thinking of the perpetrators of incest, rape, or sexual harassment as terrorists, although these acts affect their victims for the rest of our lives. When terrorism is an everyday occurrence, victims do not feel encouraged, or even able, to complain.

Before going any further, I want to make very clear that what we call sexual harassment or sexual abuse, any abuse perpetrated against someone who is vulnerable by someone who has power, is in fact a form of terrorism. When these practices are widespread, as they are in our society, what we have is a reign of terror, made more insidious by the fact that it is ignored or trivialized.

The *Random House Dictionary of the English Language* defines "terrorism" as " 1. the use of violence and threats to intimidate or coerce, especially for political purposes." In the same dictionary, the first and second definitions for "terrorist" are "1. a person, usually a member of a group, who uses or advocates terrorism" and "2. a person who terrorizes or frightens others." The verb, "terrorize," is defined as "1. to fill or overcome with terror" or "2. to dominate or coerce by intimidation."

When we talk about the concentration camps or dungeons of some far-off place, when we speak about a time historically distant from our own, there isn't likely to be much disagreement regarding these definitions. But when it comes to what constitutes terrorism in our own lives, in our family and/or social relationships, the defining gets much more complicated. For example, most of us have no trouble calling Hitler's systematic capture, torture, and murder of six million Jews a reign of terror. Yet among the many who acknowledge this as a terrorist act without precedent in human history, few refer to the homosexuals, gypsies, and political dissidents who suffered the same fate in the German camps. Some even work to erase the holocaust from our collective memory, claiming it never happened.

Massive campaigns of political terrorism, ranging from centuries of genocide against the American Indians to the continuing campaigns of violence, torture, disappearance, and mass extermination of peoples in Indonesia, Cambodia, Latin America, South Africa, Palestine, our own inner-city streets, and within our families and workplaces, have been met with a range of responses. Depending upon our particular quota of ignorance, racism, xenophobia, or homophobia, we may claim that these histories are "political propaganda," "exaggerations," "maybe true but don't have anything to do with us," or "just the way things are." For most it seems too painful, overwhelming really, to have to confront these events as having something to do with our own lives. Much less are we able to speak out, break the chain of abuse, and contribute to changing this state of affairs.

I believe that the reason for this can be found in the relations of domination—political and/or of our most intimate lives—through which we are conditioned not to see things as they are but instead to accept them as they are not. Those with the power to impose this lie present us with a false picture that becomes our central point of reference. This is where memory becomes dangerous—to the perpetrator of abuse.

Severe trauma damages memory, can destroy it entirely. A process of reclaiming memory can help us to face and work through the trauma. Memory and healing are the only ways to break the chain of abuse.

In cases of unextirpated damage, we come to believe that the terrorist tactics used to control us are *for our own good*. We cannot *remember* or *re-member* the abuse (literally re-assemble it, make ourselves whole). If we feel uncomfortable or crazy, it is our fault. And the vow of silence, which may have been a survival tool at the moment we first suffered the abuse, becomes the protective curtain behind which the perpetrator conserves the necessary anonymity and power to continue his work of terror. Like the iron or bamboo curtains, this curtain of silence separates us from ourselves.

Today we have the vivid testimony of Rigoberta Menchu, a Quiché Indian woman who tells us in simple, straightforward, almost transparent language how her younger brother and her mother were tortured to death.[1] How the Guatemalan soldiers refused to let her bury her mother's body, leaving it exposed to dogs and buzzards as a way of further terrorizing an entire community. Today, in forums as dissimilar as the U.S. Senate and a people's tribunal, we can listen to the words of women and men who have been tortured at the hands of experts. Many if not most of these experts are trained by specialists in centers run and funded by the United States military or State Department. They are called psychological operations or "psy-ops," and they range from mild harassment to outright torture.

A form of terrorism peculiar to our times is that which we call *disappearance*. In Guatemala, Uruguay, Argentina, Chile, and elsewhere in Latin America, political dissidents are taken from their homes or workplaces, sometimes even picked up off the street, and are never seen or heard from again. They literally disappear. Acknowledged torture and death (often with a body we can mourn) are preferable to the agony of not knowing—whether a loved one may be alive, hidden away in some torture center, utterly dependent upon the efforts of family and colleagues who continue to hope and work tirelessly for his or her release. This form of terror was refined by paramilitary forces, beginning in the 1970s. It damages the collective memory of entire populations, perhaps altering for generations its functionality.

Why is it so difficult for many people to believe that terrorism is a political fact of life, waged against the weak by the strong, who misuse their power in so many different arenas? Why, even when some acknowledge this reality—perhaps because we have been touched by it in our own social milieu or in the person of someone we know—do we continue to think of it as an exception, a perversion, something utterly unconnected with our lives?

I can still hear Senator Alan Simpson (R-Wyoming), responding to Anita Hill's testimony by musing that a man who committed the acts of which she accused Thomas would surely be in a prison or a mental institution! The implication seemed to be that since Thomas was not locked up, he couldn't be guilty. Amazing reverse reasoning. Lip service, at best, was paid to the recognition that sexual harassment and abuse of women is commonplace in our society. In keeping the secret, the white male establishment defends what it perceives are its own interests. Memory is essential here.

Nevertheless, over the past several decades women and some men have come to understand that large groups of people are routinely terrorized, not only in the concentration camps and political prisons of foreign countries we have never visited, but in our daily lives, our families, our relationships, the most intimate corners of our being.[2]

Victims of rape have begun to accuse our rapists. Battered women have begun to tell our stories of hidden agony. Survivors of incest and other terrorist acts are remembering and speaking out. Molested children are beginning to be listened to. As a nation, we can no longer turn our backs (although many still do) on the human communities—women, minorities, lesbians and gays, the homeless, people with AIDS, and others—who are routinely victimized by terrorist tactics, *a campaign of terror that is considered "natural" and defended as acceptable social behavior by dominant segments of the population.*

Some of us have begun to make the connection between the patriarchal ideology that encourages (and hides) woman and child abuse and the political ideologies that encourage the abuse of masses

Willie Doherty
Same Difference,
1991
On opposite sides
of the room were
projected images
of the face of
Donna McQuire, a
woman accused of
collaborating with
the IRA. Words
were projected
across her face
in a changing
sequence. On one
face positive
words described
her, while the
other image
received the
opposite.
McQuire's trial
found her not
guilty.
20'x20'
courtesy of the
artist through the
Tom Cugliani
Gallery, New York.

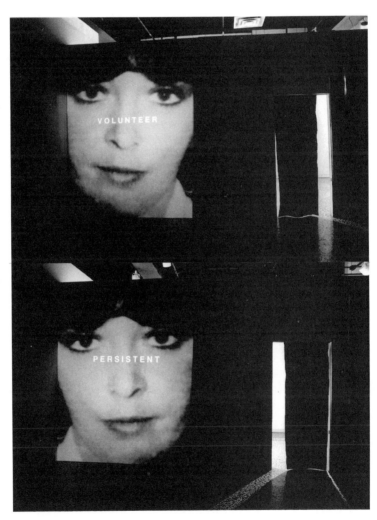

of people in the interests of a ruling few. Still, every day we hear questions—often asked in honest good faith—like "Why did Anita Hill follow Clarence Thomas to the EEOC? Why did she wait ten years to speak out?" *As a society*, it still seems difficult for us to understand the links between terrorism as an accepted practice and those patterns of behavior that result from the fact that our innate survival instinct has been dulled by memory which is altered in its struggle to survive.

Do I need to point out that Anita Hill followed Clarence Thomas from the Department of Education to the EEOC because he was a man and a rising star in the civil rights bureaucracy, while she was a woman, someone whose career depended upon the power he wielded over her? Is it necessary to explain, again, that if Anita Hill was not believed when she came forward in October 1991—supported by her professional position, a panel of extraordinarily credible character witnesses, and her own exemplary presence—much less would she have been believed ten years earlier, when she was nothing more than a young African-American woman whose abuser, also her boss, was the man in charge of implementing sexual harassment legislation at the national level?

For how much longer must women who are raped have to answer questions like "What did you do to bring this on?" or "Why were you dressed like that?" How many times do women, who show the physical wounds of their husbands' battering, find that police officers and social workers and judges and the public at large accept the man's version of what happened? How many times, in the numerous recent cases of preschool child abuse, has it been said that the children "made it all up"? How often do we hear fundamentalist Christians and members of other conservative groups express the opinion that AIDS is God's way of punishing homosexuals, drug addicts, or other "deviants"? One of the corollaries of memory damage is the blame-the-victim mentality affecting abused and perpetrator alike.

If not stopped, this phenomenon reproduces itself from one generation to the next. We have not yet been able to interrupt it, with any degree of success. Judith Lewis Herman explains how society periodically approaches and then retreats from dealing with endemic violence against women, because confronting it would necessitate confronting patriarchy itself.[3] Unfortunately, almost independent of political ideologies or other social imperatives, the ongoing protection of the abusers enables each succeeding generation of men (and the women who internalize their patriarchal values) to continue to misuse their power to batter women (and the males who for one reason or another are not in a position to take control).

Wilhelm Reich, in his classic *The Mass Psychology of Fascism*, tells us that "The question of the 'how' of a new social order is identical with the question of what is the character structure of the *broad* masses, of the unpolitical, irrationally influenced working population. The failure of a genuine social revolution, then, is the indication of the failure of the masses of people: they reproduce the ideology and the forms of living of political reaction, in themselves and in every new generation."[4]

In fact, *it is the very same power inequity and the very same resistance to challenging the status quo* that enables a superpower to invade the territory and integrity of a smaller nation, with no fear of reprisal, as that which permits, indeed encourages, rich white men to continue to invade the bodies and minds of women, people of other races, or of other sexual orientations, children, and all those with less power than they. I say rich white men because they hold the most power. But of course other men also commit these acts, and male-identified women often do too.

The psychotherapist Alice Miller has written starkly and admirably about this chain of action and reaction. Her first books address the issue of child abuse, and its effect upon the life of the adult who was once that child.[5] A disciple of Freud's, Miller acknowledges the father of psychoanalysis for his discovery that "the survival of childhood experiences in the adult unconscious and . . . the phenomenon of repression"[6] inform all later human activity. But she reexamines, questions, and ultimately discards Freud's conclusions, his theories of infantile sexuality, Oedipus complex, and death wish.[7] She goes to Freud's own life to find the reasons he could not deal with this reality. And she examines the terrible damage that Freudian analysis has done to subsequent generations of victims. In fact, Alice Miller ends up rejecting psychoanalysis altogether, quitting the International Psychoanalytic Association in 1988.

Of course, as I've mentioned, men are not the only perpetrators of abuse. In *Pictures of a Childhood*, Miller explores her own childhood with a distant and repressive mother, by taking us through a series of

sixty paintings and their accompanying text.[8] These trace her
discovery of the abuse memories as well as the beginnings of her
process of healing. In a more recent book she talks about the lives and
thought and art of Pablo Picasso, Käthe Kollwitz, Chaim Soutine,
Buster Keaton, and Friedrich Nietzsche.[9] This is where Miller begins
to apply her theories to well-known cases of extraordinary creativity.
She shows us what was done to these artists in their childhoods, and
how their responses (memory or lack of same) inform the kind of art
they produced.

Miller continues to discuss Nietzsche in her most recent book,
Breaking Down the Wall of Silence.[10] Some critics have accused her of
repetition, but I am struck by how often these truths must be spoken
before they make the slightest impression upon contemporary schools
of psychology, sociology, anthropology, and other of the disciplines
that attempt to explain human behavior. Power is not easily relin-
quished.

Speaking about Nietzsche's personal damage and the way it
colored his life and thought, Miller asks: "Is it possible that . . . a
person who became a professor of philosophy at the age of twenty-five
and dared as no one before him to expose the hypocrisy of our culture,
did not see through his helpers' power play?" And she responds, "In
fact, it is quite possible. Were he to live today, Nietzsche would
probably dutifully swallow his pills, say 'thank you very much,' and
look forward to being helped by—of all people—these learned
gentlemen who are not only unable to help him face his own truth
but, in fact, have a vested interest in his not being able to do so. As a
result, they employ dangerous drugs to destroy the very thing that
has the potential to heal him: namely, his memory."[11]

Memory. That's what it's all about. When a child is abused by
someone she or he is supposed to be able to trust, and further, when
the abuser threatens his young victim with the horror of retaliation
should s/he resist, tell, accuse, then that child's memory is blocked by
trauma. Sometimes forever. At the moment of the abuse, survival
may depend upon forgetting. Powerless, too young to recognize the
act for what it is, the child may fixate on something else. She may
block the abuse by being unable to remember or by transferring the
memory and transforming it into something easier to handle. Some
victims have what has been described as out-of-body experiences.[12]

Some develop phobias that take the place of an act impossible to acknowledge (remember). In extreme cases victims may acquire multiple personalities to aid them in dealing with what in reality is no more nor less than torture.

Recent therapeutic experience shows us that recovering the painful memory, as an adult capable of understanding what was done, who did it, and why, is the single road to healing. Alice Miller and others have shown us how religion, "corrective" therapies, drugs, psychoanalysis, and other palliatives only make things worse for the person who must remember in order to live. Feminist theory and therapies have been invaluable in pointing to the retrieval of memory as the necessary point of departure in any process of recovery.

Statistics which are obviously very partial tell us that three out of every four women will be sexually abused—incested, raped, or in some other way invaded–during our lifetimes. Most often the perpetrator will be someone we know and trust, often a father, mother, brother, grandfather, grandmother, neighbor, or friend of the family. Neither are men immune from this type of abuse. They, too, are sometimes among the victims. Sexual and of course other forms of abuse cross lines of class, race, gender, and culture.

Myth to the contrary, incest has not been a taboo in our society. Only *talking* about it has been a taboo. I want to emphasize, in case it is still not clear to some, that sexual abuse, especially against women and children, is rampant among us; that it is a pervasive form of social terror.

From this terrorism within the family, from this status quo so obviously protected by church, state, school, and family structure, the leap to state terrorism, terrorism against a particular group, or international terrorism is only a matter of numbers. The chain that leads from abused to abuser, or to one who permits abuse, has been well documented. Alice Miller writes:

It is in no way exaggerated to say that *every tyrant*, without exception, prefers to see thousands and even millions of people killed and tortured rather than undo the repression of his childhood mistreatment and humiliation, to feel his rage and helplessness in the face of his parents, to call them to account and condemn their actions. Not without reason, that is what he fears the most and what he is constantly seeking to avoid by all available means. Once we have understood the mechanisms by which repressed feelings are acted out, we *will* find a way to protect ourselves from their consequences—not by producing more weapons, but by fighting for more truthfulness and awareness. [13]

The road to truthfulness and awareness is memory, in the same way that it is the distortion of memory that enables, indeed encourages, us to remain blind and deaf to the acts of barbarism committed all the time, everywhere, and often in our names. In our homes. In our families. In our neighborhoods. In our institutions. In our country. And by our representatives in other parts of the world.

It is this distortion of memory, for example, that makes it possible for us to *see* newsreel evidence of the destruction we wrought upon Iraq, and not link that destruction to the lives of men, women, and children not very different from ourselves. It is this same distortion of memory that enables us to ask Anita Hill: "Why did you follow Clarence Thomas from one agency to another?" Racism, sexism, homophobia, anticommunism, and the newly coined "anti-terrorism" are invaluable in effecting this distortion of collective memory.

In a recent *New York Times* review, someone looking at a biography of George Orwell speaks of the fact that 1984 came and went, and with it went the demise of the Soviet State that was the model for Orwell's prophetic book. [14] The reviewer tells us that "The global totalitarianism that Orwell feared and warned against is not going to happen, at least not for a while." Only a failure of memory can possibly account for such an affirmation, and the many like it that abound in today's world. What of South Africa, El Salvador, Guatemala, Northern Ireland, Haiti, Palestine's occupied territories, and the millions of perfectly respectable middle-class families in "the best neighborhoods," appearing to lead the most protected lives?

Totalitarianism is alive and well, in its one-on-one manifestations as well as in its broadest and most complex scenarios. Totalitarianism is a way of naming an ongoing state of terrorism, no matter what the arena. As long as we refuse to recognize this, in our home or in the world, we will lack the individual and collective memory needed to fulfill our creative potential.

Daniel Martinez
Ignore Dominant Culture, 1990
four-color offset
on opaline in
fabricated lightbox
40" x 78" x 6"
courtesy of the
artist.

Memory is an ingredient absolutely necessary to life. Perhaps it is *the* essential ingredient, right up there with air, sustenance, shelter. The damaging or destruction of our memory robs us of our points of reference, our experience, the connective tissue that enables us to appropriately claim both time and place. "Amnesia is the silence of the unconscious," the poet Adrienne Rich has said.[15] Terrorism, in all its variety of forms, reduces our ability to live first of all by attacking memory, fragmenting it, blocking it, and/or replacing it with the lie of fantasy.

The lie which is superimposed soon weaves an alternate "reality," one designed to enlist our cooperation in the very war waged against us. This destructive pattern is described by Rich when she explains that "in lying to others we end up lying to ourselves. We deny the importance of an event, or a person, and thus deprive ourselves of a part of our lives. Or we use one piece of the past or present to screen out another. Thus we lose faith in our own lives."[16]

Another poet, Minnie Bruce Pratt, writes a great deal about the hypocrisy of a society that presents things as they are not, in order to hide how and what they are. Elegantly, passionately, she evokes the explosive tensions between silence and memory. In a recent essay, she speaks in this way about her youth in the American South:

There was in the silence a fear that to let out the pain and anger would bring chaos, anarchy. Inequality between men and women, rich and poor, Black and white, was ordained; there was the curse of Ham in the Bible, and of Adam and Eve, too.[17]

Pratt says, "I forgot this moment very quickly, but I remembered it later, when I began to *practice memory*" (my emphasis).

For memory is something we are born into, that can be interrupted or damaged by abuse. We *can* bring it back. It takes knowledge, courage, and requires risk. And we must practice—hard.

The three great social movements of the 1960s and 1970s in the United States—civil rights, the antiwar movement, and feminism—all reclaimed or reexamined history, and so redefined the role of memory in our lives. Feminism, particularly, also provides us with some of the tools we need in order to reengage what fear and pain kept inaccessible. If terrorism is the unspoken (often unacknowledged) status quo, then memory is the route to healing, wholeness, and a reclamation of identity.

Merrill: Thank you very much, Margaret. I think your point about the unequal distribution of power that we accept all around us in the places we work, our families, and other institutions is such an important one as we try to consider ways to end terrorism. Ramsey Clark spoke to that point very eloquently and cogently last night, and your paper today addressed it very powerfully. Tomorrow, some hundreds of millions of people will watch the Super Bowl and, again, relegitimize the mythology of power. The people sitting in the boxes will be having their power lunches with their power ties on. We live in a time when power has been fetishized so much so that Bush can massacre a quarter of a million people in Iraq and in this country people celebrate the re-masculinization of America, as if a football game had been won. Those parades and wild celebrations are etched in my memory.

Margaret Randall's presentation leads in very well to our next speaker, Michael Parenti, because for people who study the media there are two books Parenti has written that I think are absolutely essential. The first is called *Inventing Reality: The Politics of Mass Media*, available in a recently published second edition. So much of the problem is that in our own individualized imaginations we hold ideas, structures, images, that are in fact constructions given to us by mass media. This book is followed by another book called *Make Believe Media: The Politics of Entertainment* in which Parenti examines ordinary TV sit-coms, drama, or popular movies and talks about the relations of power and the kinds of economic groups that one sees in these shows. They all go to reinforce the world view of Thomas Hobbes, as if unequal positions of power are the natural condition of human beings. Of course, the kind of inequality we are really talking about is not natural at all; it is social and therefore human con-structed.

Parenti: Thank you. It is very nice to be here. Terrorism is defined and treated in the media exactly as the state defines and treats terrorism. In other words, terrorism is treated no differently from every other policy and propaganda issue that emanates from the White House. That means that state-supported, right-wing terrorism, as exists in U.S. client states, is never defined as terrorism. My son Christian just returned from Guatemala. He filed a story for Pacifica Radio and KPFA about how in Guatemala the terror and repression are so thorough that people are actually becoming conservative. In their desperation, they are beginning to believe what the government is telling them. He told me about riding on a bus which was stopped by the army. The soldiers walked down the aisle and shoved guns in people's faces and asked for their identification papers. The people responded, "*Sí, con mucho gusto,*" and smiled and did whatever the soldiers asked. They were totally terrorized because they knew that any one of them could have been yanked off the bus arbitrarily and shot.

That systemic terrorism, a total, all-permeating terror, is not just something that comes along because there is a bunch of bad guys in the army. It·is a function of a deliberate counterinsurgency policy that is supported by the U.S. national security state. But it is not news, for it is never mentioned in the press here. Only occasionally do the major newspapers, news weeklies, and TV networks talk about repression or about someone famous who gets shot by government assassins. When this happens, the reporter who writes the story often gets transferred to some obscure assignment, as happened to Ray Bonner when he tried to file stories to the *New York Times* about the massacre of some six hundred people, mostly women and children, at El Mozote. His reports were flatly denied by the State Department's Assistant Secretary for Inter-American Affairs, Thomas Enders, who claimed to have ordered an official State Department investigation. Bonner was attacked by *Time*, the *Wall Street Journal*, and many other major media who took the State Department's story at face value, so much so that the *New York Times* pulled him out of El Salvador. We learned much later on that the two investigators sent by the State Department never actually went to the village of El Mozote. Even so, the reports they did file indicated that something along the lines of a massacre had occurred. Higher-ups at the State Department, Thomas Enders and Deane Hinton, simply lied to Congress and the media about what their investigation produced. Or rather, the investigators were sent to El Salvador as a part of the cover-up in the first place.

The mass media never make the link between what is happening out there and the policy that is made in Washington. And the question is never asked "why?" Why is Washington supporting this kind of terrorism? What interests, what class and economic interests are thereby supported and what interests are being held back when a whole village of women and children is openly murdered by a military which is totally financed by the U.S. government, trained at U.S. military bases, and under direct control of U.S. military advisors in the field?

The media define terrorism as the lone gunman or the individual who plants a bomb on a plane. The media faithfully follow all the twists and turns that state policy goes through reflecting, as stenographers of power, the state. Take the case of the bombing of Pan Am Flight 103. Very strong signs pointed to terrorist groups in Syria or Iran as being involved in the blowing up of the plane. However, during the Gulf war, Syria was seen as a friend in lining up with U.S. imperialism. Iran cooperated in the release of the last hostages in Lebanon. So Libya was targeted and two Libyan intelligence agents—as the press calls them; actually they are just Libyan airline employees—have been named in the U.S. media as having committed the act of terrorism. The *New York Times* in an editorial said they should be handed over to face justice. It seems like the idea of innocence until proven guilty does not apply. The editorial went on to say that the Libyan government, particularly Mummar el-Qaddafi, should be held accountable. The Libyans, understandably, are refusing to hand over the two intelligence agents because they say no evidence has been presented linking any Libyans to the Pan Am bombing.

Libya has been targeted before. In 1981 and 1985, U.S. planes attacked Libya; in the first case shooting down two Libyan jets and in the second bombing two cities. Why? Is U.S. policy just stupid or mean? It turns out to be a very rational thing to attack Libya because Libya is one of those very few countries that has refused "client state status," as with Iraq on oil, or Nicaragua under the Sandinistas, or Cuba. There are some countries which do not want to be U.S. client states; that is, they do not want to open their land, labor, resources and capital to American corporate foreign investment and say, in effect, "Come on in, it is all yours, there are no occupational safety regulations, no environmental protections, no minimum wage, no real labor unions. And if there were and they got out of line, our police and military can take care of them. You give me and my friends our money and the rest is all yours." There are some countries that refuse to say this and these countries are then targeted as terrorist states.

Colonel Qaddafi took over in Libya in 1969 in a colonels' revolution. He transformed a country which had a social structure like Saudi Arabia, a kingdom, literally, where a few filthy rich families with more money than they ever could know what to do with controlled the oil for their own benefit and the benefit of U.S. oil corporations. Before Qaddafi's revolution, U.S. companies actually owned Libyan oil and there was mass poverty. The colonels' revolution was a populist nationalist rebellion which did all sorts of things like plant millions of trees, put up public health centers, open free public schools for everyone for the first time ever in Libya. Thousands of Libyan students were sent to universities in Europe and the United States to study things like engineering or TV broadcasting. The government nationalized the oil fields; that is, they started to take control of the land, labor, resources, capital, and use it for the development of their own people instead of remaining a client-state cow that is milked by foreign interests. And that was Qaddafi's unforgiveable sin. From then on, he has been targeted for diplomatic isolation and branded as a terrorist. And the faithful media in lockstep has done its part in portraying Qaddafi as a mad murderer. A nut. Think of the stern, threatening pictures of Qaddafi on the covers of *Time*, *Newsweek*, or *U.S. News and World Report*.

In late November 1981—let me give you this brief case history—the White House issued a statement that under orders from Colonel Qaddafi Libyan assassination teams, assisted by "East German terror experts," had entered the United States armed with surface-to-air missiles. Their objective was to kill President Reagan and ten or so top officials, including cabinet members such as the Secretary of State and the Secretary of Defense. Now, I knew this story was false immediately because it was too good to be true. The way the media responded to this extraordinary White House statement was something to behold. ABC newsman Frank Reynolds said on November 26 that "it is known that Libyan agents are in this

Alan Belcher
Guns, 1988
photographs
on fiberboard
fabricated into
suitcases,
dimensions
variable,
courtesy of a
private collector
through the Josh
Baer Gallery,
New York

country for the purpose of assassinating the highest officials of the U.S. government." That same evening CBS and NBC asked, "Is it true?" They then promptly treated the story as if it were true. An NBC correspondent asked President Reagan if he was worried about the assassination plot. Reagan answered, "Well, yes, of course." Then the camera cut to Secret Service men leaping out of cars, racing along beside the President's limousine, pacing rooftops with machine guns, searching the skies for incoming missiles. Here was a collage of images that suggested that the President was under imminent attack.

A week later, on December 4, ABC's *Nightline* presented a show called "Libyan Assassination Plot" featuring Ray Cline, a former deputy director of the CIA, who claimed that Libyan and other Arab terrorist groups were organized "basically and initially by the Soviet Union." He went on to surmise that "in our open society our officials are sitting ducks because we have been busy handcuffing the FBI and CIA for a number of years." He was somewhat relieved that President Reagan was trying to give FBI and CIA counterterrorism operations a little more operating power to deal with these threats. Cline was followed by right-wing journalist Arnaud de Borchgrave, editor of the Moonie-owned *Washington Times*, who was introduced as a "terrorist expert" when actually all he has done is write a novel about terrorism. He assured viewers that the Libyans were working for the Soviet Union and that Qaddafi, whom de Borchgrave claimed to have interviewed five times, was a pathological liar. The image of de Borchgrave calling anyone a pathological liar presents a delicious irony. Inversion is the *modus operandi* of the media here. The third guest was Marvin Zonis, described as a Mid-East expert but who is really a Likud cheerleader. He said, "Colonel Qaddafi had a conversation with another Middle Eastern leader"—he acted as if he knew this for a fact—"in which he discussed very coolly and in a rational way how he intended to go about assassinating President Reagan." Nobody questioned Zonis about his source or why the head of one country would openly discuss his plans to assassinate the President of the United States with the leader of another nation—over a few drinks—who might impart this information to others. No one appeared on the show to inject a skeptical or cautionary note or question the rather remarkable statements of three right-wing cold warriors. That is the balance we get on television: from far right to moderate right.

AHMAT ABASS   ALI CHAFIC   LUITZ SCHEWS?.N

AHMED JOOMA   IBRAHIM EL HAYA   IBRAHIM EL HAYA
(glasses)

Composite sketches
of alleged Libyan
"hit team" which
Jack Anderson
distributed to press
and TV networks.
Later Anderson
wrote that he had
been set up by an
unnamed intel-
ligence agency.

In the weeks that followed, twenty-four stories about the hit teams were carried on the network evening news. They told viewers that there were three, then five, then ten, twelve, or thirteen hit men. After a while there was not one team, but there were "teams"—plural. "The assassins had entered the U.S. from Canada," said ABC and CBS. "They entered from Mexico," said NBC. "Not from Mexico," said ABC. "The hit squads were composed of three Libyans," said ABC and NBC. "Three Iranians," said CBS and NBC. "Two Iranians," ABC. "Three Syrians," NBC. But all three networks agreed that there were two Palestinians, one Lebanese, and one East German. Never before had a team of assassins received such advance billing. This media attention alone would be enough to deter all but the wildest, craziest publicity hounds in the terrorist ranks.

It remained for *TV Guide* six months later to come up with an article admitting that the Libyan hit teams never existed. The assassination story was a complete fabrication. *TV Guide*'s cover story was titled, "Why American TV Is so Vulnerable to Foreign Propaganda" (June 12, 1982). The assassination plot was nothing but wild conjectures, *TV Guide* noted. It then told its millions of readers that the whole thing was probably a KGB campaign "to destabilize public opinion in the West with alarmist rumors." Talk about wild conjectures! "Or perhaps the story had been planted by Qaddafi himself," *TV Guide* went on, "who is no madman but a shrewd Bedouin sitting back laughing at all this." Imagine this, they are accusing Qaddafi of planting stories that he is planning to assassinate the President of the United States. They imply that he likes to get bombed in retaliation. In any case, *TV Guide* suggested regretfully that "in our open society where anything can get reported, the press should be more wary of the diabolically clever stories floated by Soviet intelligence sources."

TV Guide's assertion is as outlandish as the original story itself. The charge against Soviet intelligence could be made only by ignoring the fact that the White House itself was clearly the instigator of the original disinformation campaign about a plot to assassinate Reagan.

Let me turn very briefly to the treatment of Father Jean-Bertrand Aristide, the president of Haiti, who was thrown out of office by a military coup led by General Raul Cedras in September 1991. If you read the stories in the *New York Times* and the *Washing-*

ton Post, you begin to realize that this Aristide was a terrorist and with the horrible, lethal power of his words provoked a helpless, quivering, and frightened army into acting. The army had to do something after all, as the *Times* and *Post* surmise, because Aristide had rhetoric. No one has ever traced down the speech in which he is reported to have said he supported terrorism and the use of violence against Haitians who opposed his policies. In his speeches, he actually repeatedly admonishes people not to take the road to violence. But the *Washington Post* said, "Independent observers and diplomats"— usually the CIA operatives in the U.S. embassy, but known here by our press only as "Western or independent diplomats"—"were troubled because Aristide had used implicit and explicit threats of mob violence." So the *New York Times* headline said, "Haitian General Says Misdeeds Prompted the Coup." The army, with shades of Pinochet in Chile, had to act. Aristide was pilloried in the press because he was only mildly critical of the mob violence that crushed the violent military coup that first threw him out of office. Remember, when he first took office there was a military coup, and large masses of people stopped that coup. The U.S. press criticized him for not attacking the citizens who rose up against the military violence that attempted to kill him and his administration—the only popularly elected president Haiti has ever known. It really gets kind of twisted and weird, but the Haitian aristocracy, the small group of extremely wealthy families who own the Haitian economy, has very close connections with the United States, and it is clear that the Haitian military exists to protect their privileges. The U.S. media follow along to protect the image of the Haitian aristocracy.

Let me end by saying that the media is not stupid or misled, and they are not confused. They know what they are doing. They are instruments of state policy. You know this when you look at the lock-step support and the way they fell in line in support of the war against Iraq with a uniformity and a celebration that would be called totalitarian if observed in some other countries. The media are that way not because they are cowards or are dependent upon government officials so they have to do what officialdom says. They toe the official line because they are owned and controlled by the same people who own and control just about everything in the U.S. and throughout the Third World. They do that because they are part of that same overall class interest.

Antonio Gramsci said—and this gives us a little shred of hope—that there is dual consciousness in people; that is, they have that one level of consciousness wherein they believe the things that are told them and fed to them, but they also have some other level of consciousness which comes from their experience of the everyday and which leads them to wonder and question why things are the way they are. And that is the level of consciousness we have to keep working on and supporting. I said during the height of the Gulf war that the American people will eventually drift off into reality. They have this bad habit of drifting into reality now and again. Mankind cannot live on yellow ribbons alone. After all, people have to pay the rent, hold on to a job, and feed the kids. It is our job to show people that this government and this media work methodically, systematically, and consciously against their interests in very bad ways and against the interests of everyone else in the world.

Merrill: Thank you very much, Michael. Our final speaker is Alex Cockburn, who is no doubt well known to you from his columns in the *Nation*, the *Wall Street Journal*, *Village Voice*, or *LA Weekly*. He is a native of Ireland who came to the United States in 1972, as he noted once, at the exact moment that Nixon's Plumbers were breaking into the Watergate. I guess he got here not a moment too soon. We are certainly glad to have him here. But perhaps he is best known because he is simply the most vigilant and vigorous critic of the commercial media at work today. He was the one who first showed that the reports about Iraqi soldiers throwing Kuwaiti babies out of their incubators were complete fabrications. He was the only one at the time who said, "Let's check the sources of this story." Now, a year later when it doesn't matter any more, you can read in the *New York Times* that the story was fabricated by the public relations firm Hill and Knowlton, who had been hired by the Kuwaiti ambassador to rouse public opinion in the United States to support the war. But when the story did count, Alex checked the sources. I want to mention one other thing. If you haven't followed Alex Cockburn's writings for the last ten years or so, many of the columns have been collected in a book called *Corruptions of Empire: Life Studies and the Reagan Era*. Edward Said has said that Cockburn's province is the

Gregory Green
Assault, 1989
12 saw blade floor
sculpture with
electric motor.
The bottom four
blades lift the base
off the ground.
24" x 13 1/2" x 13 1/2"
courtesy of the artist
through Randy
Alexander.

consciousness industry, and I think this book may turn out to be one of the best histories of consciousness in the 1980s. His interests are wide ranging. He has recently co-authored a book with Susan Hecht called *The Fate of the Forest: Developers, Destroyers, and Defenders of the Amazon*.

Cockburn: I will try and keep my remarks pretty short since I know a lot of you will have comments to make before this panel draws to a close. My introducer was nice enough to say I check sources, and this business of the incubator atrocity story which was used to demonize the Iraqis as the United States moved toward war shows that you don't have to check very hard. Those stories initially disseminated from the testimony of the daughter of the Iraqi ambassador, a fact known to the congressman who put her on the witness stand but who did not divulge even to his colleagues in Congress that she was an interested party, so to speak. What she said was that fifteen babies had been taken out of incubators and thrown on the floor as the Iraqi soldiers made off with the incubators. You don't need to check very much. You just need to think for about ten seconds. This is a hospital. Doctors and nurses are walking up and down. Is it likely that when the babies were put on the floor they all ran away? Very often when you are looking at these stories, you don't even need to go to the library. You just need to think, how likely is it? In that incubator story, the main charge was made by a doctor in the Red Crescent who is employed by the emir of Kuwait—thus ensuring his absolute objectivity—who was living in the Taif Sheraton, the emir's hotel in Saudi Arabia. He said that in the main episode 312 babies were taken from their incubators in the maternity hospital in Kuwait.

Now, if you want to check that on a simple reality test, all you have to do is ring up the leading maternity hospital in your own town and ask how many incubators they have. Out of interest, I did this for New York and Los Angeles. In New York, I called the largest maternity hospital and I think the answer was that there were seventeen incubators. And in Los Angeles, a place hardly without medical resources, there were fifteen. So what this shows is that when people look back and say, "How could I have believed this incredible drivel," is that in the regimentation of emotion, in the engineering of consent, there is a moment when the most elementary principles of common sense get thrown over the side. That is an extremely dangerous moment. The engineers of consent or the manipulators of opinion in this country are extremely sophisticated and know very well what they are doing. The most important thing to do at such moments of intense emotional appeal when they are bombarding you with horrific stories about babies being thrown on the cold floor is to stop yourself and with whatever means one has available, whatever access one has, call for a reality check. If it doesn't match, say that this is absolutely not true, there is no conceivable way it could be true, and try and push against it. If one can gain access, exploding these fabrications is not such a difficult thing to do.

I think what we can see in these discussions is a number of ways one can look at terrorism as an overall concept, a way of perceiving repression in society. One can see it as a long-term way of demonizing the enemy. I grew up in Ireland, and if you go back and look at nineteenth century English publications like *Punch Magazine*, you will see demonization of the Irish people. The caricatures are very similar to what you now see for Arabs, what you used to see for Jews: the same feral *untermensch* depicted day after day after day. That is the long-term caricature of the opponents of power. I think we have also seen in these discussions the rather shorter term, what might be called the "terrorism boom," as cataloged and chronicled by Edward Herman in particular.

The terrorism industry developed from two prime sources in the late 1970s and early 1980s. One was the aim of the Israelis to denude Palestinians of identity. It was Golda Meir, after all, who said that there is no such thing as a Palestinian. And hand in hand went the common usage of the term "terrorist" to describe Palestinian Arabs. This was a very deliberate policy. Along with it went the ambition of the Reagan team as it moved toward power in the late 1970s. It defined a conveyor-belt image of terrorism as originating in Moscow and then spreading out over the globe. Some of you may remember the rather exciting terrorism maps that used to appear on the evening news, with huge arrows that would lunge down from Moscow toward the Gulf. The width of the arrows would cover thousands of miles on the map. This was arrow politics; flows could wash through national borders as if nothing stood in the way. Another particularly exciting arrow would lunge down towards the Basque country of Spain.

The prime articulator, although he didn't speak English particularly well, was General Alexander Haig. His aim was to do two things. The first was to attribute all political struggle or all disturbance in the world to the sponsorship of the Soviet Union. And the other was to present the idea of international politics as a question of civilization against barbarism. Of course, the press was an integral part of all this. People often ask how all this works. Does a message go out? Does the telephone ring at the desk of the publisher of the *New York Times*? Is the program articulated or barked over the telephone? It doesn't need to be so obvious. Power has a number of conveyor belts or venues in which the change of a policy or the framing of debate is discussed. It can happen in an endless series of conferences. People sometimes get obsessed by particular conferences that are going on, let's say the Trilateral conferences or the Builderburg conferences. It doesn't mean that the world is run by the Builderburgs or the Trilateral Committee; it just means that at that time those are the preferred venues at which the usual villains are developing, formulating, and justifying their policies. Of course, publishers of newspapers or owners of other media are major players in our society in terms of property, ownership, or financial influence. They are part of the process of policy development, not just reporters of it.

Do these people in turn summon in their subordinates and tell them that they must take a particular line on a certain story or must report something like the incubator baby fabrication? They do sometimes, as a matter of fact, rather clearly, extremely clearly. But if you work in any form of news organization, you will learn that it takes only about a second for any employee to learn what the policy is and what the outlook of the boss is. Everybody knows what the boss wants; in journalism it is the same as everywhere else. A lot of the ways that it actually works after that is self-censorship. There is an old British rhyme that some of you may know which goes: "You can never hope to bribe or twist, thank God, the British journalist. But seeing what the man will do unpaid, there is no occasion to."

Journalists and members of the media work in what are in effect some of the most authoritarian organizations in the world, in terms of the inability of subordinates to challenge instructions. If an editor removes a paragraph in a story which has set some event in context—such as that social services in Iraq during the period of rule of the Baath Party were rather improved as compared to other Middle Eastern nations—there is no recourse or redress at all. We are talking about extremely totalitarian institutions. And in today's markets, journalists tend to be rather insecure people, like everyone else. There are a lot of people willing to take the job of the journalist who does not cooperate. So when you end up in Managua, Havana, Tripoli, Beirut, or elsewhere as a reporter in the field, you are going to be extremely careful of the way you frame things. If you are incautious enough or courageous enough, as Ray Bonner was at one point in his career, to report what you actually see, you will simply be removed. Ray Bonner went to El Salvador and looked around and came to the exciting and novel conclusion that the people fighting the civil war were not Russians and Cubans, as Haig's State Department had suggested as the source for all disruptions in the world. Bonner's challenging thesis was met with outrage by many conservatives in the United States, particularly Reed Irvine and his Accuracy in the Media. He was speedily recalled and put on the night rewrite financial desk. It was a demonstration punishment and was well noted by his colleagues.

I think now the agenda is changing. One of the things you may notice about the media is the rapidity with which the conversation can be changed. One minute you open your newspaper or you turn on *Nightline* or you watch *MacNeil/Lehrer* and you think that the whole world revolves around the issue of terrorism, that it is dangerous to drive on an interstate or go to an airport without the risk of being blown to bits. The most wonderful example of that was indeed the famous terror team coming down to murder President Reagan, as Michael just mentioned. I remember vividly being in Detroit when the great terror scare was going on and the hit teams were coming down from Canada, proceeding, I suppose by Greyhound or whatever, toward Washington. I was giving a talk, and a chap who works on the border post between Windsor, Ontario, and Detroit came up and told me that he thought that on the day that the scare began he would receive orders about whom to look out for. He expected security to be at the highest level and to be warned to look out for people with conspicuous bulges in their coats or someone who fits the conventional terror profile in the media. But he got not a single word. They did not even bother to pretend it was real, as Michael just pointed out. But I think the subject is changing. The narrow usage of the terror network has had its day. It behooves us to keep with the times and see how power is redefining the issues and restate the debate.

The reality being faced now is one in which substantial parts of the world are getting rapidly poorer and more desperate. This is the absolutely central reality of our time: that as power and money are devolving to fewer and fewer elites in the core capitalist countries, the rest of the world is starving and dying at rates that cannot escape the notice of even the most oblivious cheerleaders for the American way. I was looking the other day at some economic figures compiled about the time Walt Rostow wrote his famous book *Stages of Economic Growth: An Anti-Communist Manifesto*. That was 1960, and Rostow said the capitalist way will sweep over the earth, and he laid out the way a developing nation or an underdeveloped country could proceed toward the happy state of developed capitalism. If you look at the figures now, never has a manifesto been more thoroughly negated by reality. We are looking at countries that have lost more than 50 percent of their national income. We are looking at levels of economic deprivation that are unprecedented in this century. It is also clear that this situation will continue to accelerate. The economic strangulation of the developing world is manifestly a form of terrorism. When the International Monetary Fund (IMF) imposes an austerity policy on a country in order to ensure that the country's debts to the developed world can continue to be repaid, they don't proceed to the armory, remove the guns, and fire on the people. Sometimes the program has to be enforced by guardsmen and soldiers who do use guns to quell the protests of the people. But more often, the program simply removes more and more wealth from the people and ships it north to the United States, Europe, or Japan. Often, vital natural resources are deeded over to foreign corporations.

We are looking at huge terror. How does the media deal with this? They are inventing a new language, a new language based on terms from free market policies or entrepreneurship. The language of so-called economic liberation or free markets is contrasted with the old ways of the past. The economic terrorism we see in the developing

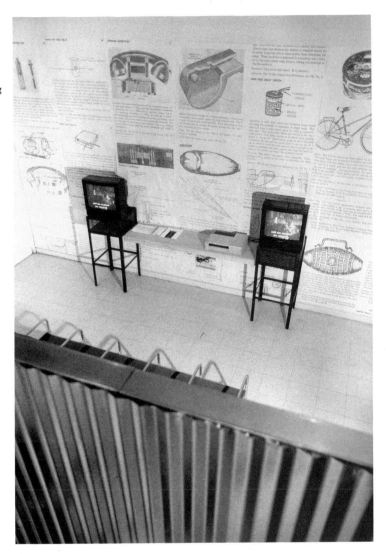

Detail of the exhibition's video and film screening room, Meyerhoff Gallery, Maryland Institute, College of Art.

world, we are told, is nothing more than a process of economic liberation, and the risks associated with entrepreneurship and the transfer of economic resources into private hands are called nothing more than a temporary period of adjustment. In a way, the real process is the same as it was in the 1960s of Rostow's manifesto. We are led to believe that the course of events in developing nations is still the path toward the happy state of capitalism and the free market. In this way the suffering and terror inflicted for the profit of multinational corporations is erased under the language of economic progress and independence.

I will conclude with one final thought about what I think to be a central relationship between media indifference and state terror— this is the embargo against Iraq. It was the embargo that really brought the situation in Nicaragua to the level where the UNO coalition was able to get an advantage at the polls. It was the embargo that bore down on the people of Cambodia, still bears down on the people in Vietnam, and, of course, as we speak exacts a savage toll in Iraq. The embargo is in a way a part of reality, ongoing reality, the denial of resources to the poorest people in society. It is a symbol of what the economic relations in the world at large are now. It is also a profoundly violent form of terrorism and one that is hardly addressed by the media that surround us today.

Merrill: Thank you very much, Alex. Last night, Ramsey Clark reminded us that the embargo has doubled the infant mortality rate in Iraq. We have some time for questions, so I will just open the discussion to the whole group.

Audience: Chris and Annie, when you were in Ireland could you tell us what kind of censorship you ran into there or what problems you ran into as you did your film work.

Goldson: Basically, we did face a form of low-level harassment from the British security forces. They would tell us to stop, get out of the car, and unload our equipment. They would rifle through our production bags and then we would all stand around on a grass verge for fifteen minutes, while the security forces would call up their bosses. After about another twenty minutes of waiting, they would suddenly receive word, and say cheerfully, "Have a great holiday" as if they hadn't detained us for an hour. Off we would go until next time. It was process of continuous intimidation really, but I have to stress it was nothing compared to the daily harassment meted out to the Nationalist community in the North.

I think that the security forces found it difficult to place us. Clearly, we didn't look like "real" television, yet we seemed to have enough legitimacy to prevent them bullying us too much. They have to remember that the North of Ireland, despite all the special emergency laws, is supposedly part of democratic Britain, which enjoys a "free press." This may have made them more cautious. In addition, I had a British passport, so they tended to regard me (if they could place my accent) as a New Zealand colonial.

The reality is, of course, that the security forces are mostly young, scared, working-class men, who are ill-informed about the situation. Few, I imagine, want to be in the North. The whole place is extraordinarily tense.

Bratton: You have to remember that outside of Ireland there is a virtual media blackout on reporting the North. No major international media currently maintain an office in the North. What little does trickle out is framed and released by the British authorities. Since 1971, the British put together an effective system of interlocking press offices to control how the conflict is represented. These include the Northern Ireland Press Office, the Royal Ulster Constabulary—the "police"—press office, and the army press office, all of whom work closely with the British broadcast media themselves, the BBC and ITV (Independent Television). Despite this bleak picture, there are important alternative sources for information such as the Republican newspaper *An Phoblacht*, and The Derry Film and Video Group, the group of film and video makers we collaborated with to produce *Counterterror*.

Audience: I wonder if someone could comment on the story in the back pages of the "Style" section of the *Washington Post* about a film critic for the *Washingtonian Magazine* who was fired for writing a favorable review of *JFK*. She was an award-winning film critic, but the editor was supposed to have said that such a review would reflect badly on our nation.

Parenti: There is someone back there who knows something about the story.

Audience: Actually she resigned because the story was killed. She offered to make some changes in the review, but the editor still wouldn't run the review. When she threatened to resign, the editor accepted her resignation.

Parenti: The editor also told her as she left that he hoped she would keep "calling 'em like it is." She replied, "What's the use of 'calling 'em like it is' if you won't print what I call?"

Audience: This is a question to everyone. It goes to Randall Robinson's point that we are a literate people but not an intelligent people. Sometimes the presentation of the news is more important than the content of the news. The ability to present the true facts in a way that no one will take notice of them is, I think, an important strategy. The press often gives you the information, but they know where to put it. Knowing that we are passive people conditioned by television, we end up debating what is in the headlines. The press can cover itself by saying that they did print that information. It is just that no one saw it.

Parenti: I can give you an example. The accepted view is that the Holocaust was ignored in the West while millions of Jews, gypsies, homosexuals, and others were being rounded up. That is not true. There were stories from the mid-1930s onward in major newspapers like the *Chicago Tribune*, the *New York Journal-American*, the *New York Times*, *Herald Tribune*. But they appeared as two-inch stories on page eight, next to an obituary column or a cooking recipe. Placement and framing is very important. The stories were there but not noticed. The sources were often from Jews who were treated as unreliable or over emotional. The way you frame a story matters. You have said it very well and it is what I have been struggling with in my book. Much media distortion comes from framing, placement, toning, emphasis, and context. CBS did an hour story on the Pittston coal miners' strike. In the whole hour you heard management saying that they wanted to get back to work if the union would just come to its senses. You heard the police saying that they were just neutral. You saw scabs saying that "we just want to work and don't want the union telling us what to do." And then in a show of balance you saw the strikers rallying, sitting down blocking the mine entrance, saying that they would keep fighting until they got all they wanted. What they didn't do in the whole hour is tell what the strike was all about in the first place—why the miners were striking at all. They didn't mention that Pittston Mine was up on charges of violating the National Labor Relations Act, that Pittston wanted to cut wages, that Pittston was cutting back on benefits. None of that was mentioned. So what you got was an image of rather stubborn and perhaps foolish striking miners who put up a noisy and shrill fight against a measured management. In sum, the best propaganda is not a lie. The best propaganda gives you a show of the truth and slants it in a certain way.

Randall: I just want to remind you of a line from an Alice Walker poem: "We know that your newscasters do not cast the news." The misconception is thinking that the establishment media is there to inform us. It is not there to inform but to protect certain interests. That's why it produces two-inch stories on important things. Or why it stops an important story at mid-point and you never hear of it again.

Goldson: In all of the situations covered in the *Counterterror* series, it has been necessary to address some of the complexity of media representation. The progressive community, it seems to me, is too ready to publicly label the media as right-wing, as the "tool of capitalism." In a reversal, the right, of course, does the same, labelling the media as the "tool of liberals." As a consequence, the media can smugly point to "extremists on both sides" and assume a position that appears like moderation, neutrality or balance, which gives it credibility with its audience. Thus analyses of the institutional and financial basis for the media, their development under commodity capitalism, their role within the same, their dependency on selling audiences to sponsors for their survival, can be avoided. This is where their interests and ideological biases are formed, and this is where exploration and analysis are needed.

Audience: If you want to find out about progressive journalism worldwide, you can go to the Progressive Action Center in Baltimore. The number is 410-467-9388.

Merrill: I think centers like this are very important. Every city has a center or bookstore like this. Sometimes it is hard to find sources of alternative news and if there are bookstores or centers that carry alternative publications we should support them.

Audience: I want to follow up on that and then ask a question. You should read Tom Chalkley's article in the latest issue of the city paper on the break-ins at the Progressive Action Center targeting the Cuban activists. My question is that on January 8, 1992, I heard the first report of Bill Arkin of Greenpeace who was just back from Iraq and who said that 70,000 to 90,000 civilians were killed. The U.S. Census Bureau confirms that, saying that about 70,000 civilians were killed since the bombing. The next day in the *Baltimore Sun* a story appeared saying that the Pentagon is very upset with the Census Bureau for releasing this information. On January 10, *Nightline* ran a show which was a promo for the Pentagon, featuring the two 5,000-pound bombs that were dropped on Saddam Hussein's underground headquarters. They talked about how the military was humanitarian—that was Ted Koppel's word— because it really didn't kill all that many people. When they looked at the destroyed vehicles on the highway of death, there were no bodies to be found in the burned-out trucks and cars.

Merrill: Right, I saw that. It was a one-hour ad for a book published by *U.S. News and World Report*. It is called *Triumph without Victory: The History of the Persian Gulf War*. This book is being promoted with the line that it is based on secret Pentagon information. I might note what struck me as cynicism to the last degree. The book is dedicated "To the Victims"; since it claims there were very, very few Iraqi casualties, I wonder which victims it has in mind. If there is any doubt, the next page of the book is all black except for a small quotation from Norman Schwarzkopf. It reads, "Any soldier worth his salt should be antiwar." It makes you wonder what the value of salt is these days! What a production! Just how cynical is this

Helen Altman
Frost Queen, 1991
This electric
freezer housed
a number of
anatomically
correct human
hearts made of
ice in both adult
and children
sizes.
36 1/2" x 22" x 22"
courtesy of the
artist.

Schwarzkopf? The *Nightline* film did not show any bodies in those trucks on the highway of death because the Saudi mortuary brigades were the first on the scene and the bodies were all dumped in mass graves. But photos do exist. I have seen some and there are plenty of bodies burned to cinders. *Nightline* was a whitewash; the Pentagon means to keep the images of this war clean. It is a war for images now. Whose images will, as Margaret Randall suggested, persist in memory. Also, the researcher for the Census Bureau was fired for producing that report on deaths in Iraq. It was, of course, just part of her job to produce annual reports on demographic changes in the Middle East. She has successfully sued to get her job back.

Audience: Yes, and it is my suspicion that this *Nightline* was an intentional plant to counter the Census Bureau story. The whole show featured Pentagon spokespersons. There were no other views presented at all. It appeared as if the Pentagon contacted *Nightline* and asked for an opportunity to present its story on the numbers killed in the war.

Parenti: Could I just interrupt for a moment. Why would you say that "it is your suspicion that this was an intentional plant"? The Pentagon has a propaganda machine that is larger than any major network. They have hundreds and hundreds of people working on public relations. They have squads who are consciously planting stories and leaking information hundreds of times every week. You don't have to be so tentative about it.

Merrill: But you would love to have the smoking gun in the form of a taped phone call to the producer of *Nightline*.

Parenti: You get the smoking gun every day. The Secretary of State gets up every day and says "black is white, green is red, blah, blah, blah." And tomorrow you read in the papers, "black is white, green is red, blah, blah, blah." You see the process every day. There is no conspiracy. He says it and the press goes out and reports it.

Audience: I have a question for the video producers. You did not touch on the pacifist left in the United States. Was this intentional on your part? I know that Helen Woodson has been in prison for twenty-one years for civil disobedience and there are others like that. Was there a reason why they weren't part of your focus?

Parenti: The list of atrocities is so huge. There are any number of cases of oppression that we didn't touch.

Goldson: That was part of the problem. Our project could, unfortunately, be endless. There are endless situations both domestic and international that we could take on. I think, however, that we were interested in issues of self-determination. In the four choices we made, there are glaring omissions and the choices often had to do with the connections we had in communities or in the previous work we'd done. I am often very sorry for the situations that we haven't been able to cover.

Bratton: There is much to be covered but given the conditions of independent production in this country, I don't think we are going to see an explosion of that which should be covered.

Goldson: But on the other hand, there is reason for optimism. There is a steady group of committed media makers that often can be seen through these alternative channels and are consistently working on these issues.

Audience: Some things I have been reading recently have reminded me how much everything I have heard today sounds more like Orwell than Huxley. I have to say that surprises me a little bit. I have heard the word "they" used an awful lot. I am getting the sense that although everyone is too sophisticated to talk about conspiracy theories, that is the tenor of it, the Orwellian sense that there is a very well-organized group out there or up there which talks to each other a lot, rather than Huxley's sense of our being a lobotomized population that more or less brought it on ourselves. I am wondering if any of you in private moments in the middle of the night ever entertain the notion that maybe it is more random than you have made it seem today.

Randall: I would like to say that there's been some talk here about conspiracies. I don't agree that conspiracy theories are unsophisticated. They may not work in the Donald Duck way some people would like us to believe. But there certainly are conspiracies. I also want to address your comment on the use of "they." I do talk about "we" and "they" because I refuse to identify with the "they." I demand the right to be "we," "me," "center," "I." Not "other." I think this is an important part of the process of recovering our memories, to see ourselves as actor, as protagonist in a situation. Not simply the pawn of some "they" over whom we have no control.

Cockburn: There is a slight propensity to see everything linked in a conspiracy and I think that is not always useful. There are, however, clear projects to engineer opinion. You can look at the whipping up of emotions before the outbreak of the war against Iraq. People talk about sophistication, but it wasn't really. You could see people trying different strategies. It wasn't that difficult to detect. First they said the war was for oil and no one wanted into that. Then they said it was for freedom in Kuwait. No one particularly bought that one. They said it was for jobs and the American way of life, and the response was, basically, give me a break. All the time they were taking polls, the White House pollsters, that is. And then they got to Saddam is a madman with a nuclear bomb and there was a big jump in the opinion polls. It happened right away; people seemed not to like the idea of that. Then you could chart the speeches from there on. First they said he is five years away, then he is a year away, then he is six months away, then he is a week away. Then, on the second day of the war, they bombed the Tuwaitha research reactor, which is a breach of international law. Fortunately, the Iraqis had turned it off or you would have had a mini-Chernobyl right there. But your point about randomness has a lot of truth to it. A lot of reporters don't need to know the basic agenda. There is a certain instinctive knee-jerk of just following the agenda without even knowing what it is at all, or knowing a "they" exists at all, because of the saturation of idiotic lies and stupidities has happened already before. People just move within that overall context.

Parenti: I wanted to say I never used the word "they." I said ABC, NBC, the White House, the CIA. I was very specific; I named reporters and government officials. Specific human agency is always actively involved. Specific agencies of government are involved. Their job is to maintain the conditions of political and economic dominance. They work at that all the time; that is what they are paid big salaries to do. As for this other thing about us all being lobotomized and us bringing it all on ourselves. I don't see any lobotomized people here. The people who are misled are misled through a process of misinformation or limited information, or missing information, or idiot puffery in the media. That is a necessary condition. You are confusing a necessary condition with a sufficient cause. It is necessary to lobotomize—if you want to use that term—portions of the population to have them respond in a knee-jerk fashion and say Noriega is a demon, Saddam is a demon, and so on. Since they have no alternative information, it is hard to disbelieve the President and think he is a liar. That is a necessary condition, but not a sufficient cause. That doesn't bring on the bombing in Iraq. The public just doesn't get out there one day and say, "Let's have a war with Iraq." There were individuals consciously planning that war for conscious goals and defending interests they were conscious of. Why not? You consciously organize your life. You consciously make decisions about where you are going to live, how you are going to work, and so on. School teachers organize themselves, farmers organize, blue-collar workers organize. The minute you suggest that the people who own the banks, the factories, the media, or occupy the positions of Secretary of the Department of Defense and Secretary of State and so on consciously consider their own interests, you start getting all this flack about a conspiracy theory. Are we supposed to think they just float from one thing to the next? The alternative is the somnambulist, lobotomized, or coincidence theory.

Audience: I would like to submit that the ordinary Joe in the street is not all that stupid.

Parenti: I didn't want to say stupid—just ill-informed.

Audience: I see people wearing T-shirts saying "Don't Vote" and that doesn't suggest that they are stupid but that they understand how corrupt the government is and they don't like it. But they feel helpless. We always have these conferences and when we get to the last five minutes we say what are we going to do about it. That is the part we seem to struggle with.

Merrill: People who don't vote are, in fact, voting with their feet. They are making perhaps the most conscientious choice of all because they are withholding their grant of legitimacy to a government whose legitimate power derives only from the expressed consent of the governed. When the number of people who participate in an election falls below 50 percent of adults, there is a real question about whether the government that takes office has any real democratic legitimacy at all. In cases like that, we should simply have a new election with a new slate of candidates or, more fundamentally, we should abolish the government entirely since it has failed to gain the consent of the people. I am saying that the people who don't vote are casting the most important vote of all. That's why there is so much effort spent on trying to get people to vote. This point is not yet generally understood in political theory—and practice—because our discourse on democratic government is all just cheerleading for the present government. Even academic political science is mostly cheerleading for the status quo. We need more analysis which would help us understand that democratic government is the result of a contract between people and government for certain services. If the contract is breached by those required to perform the services, that is, the government, it is null and void. The implications of that are that government does not legitimately exist when it fails in its contractual obligations. It is a serious mistake simply to vote for the lesser of two evils because what you are really doing is giving over your inherent rights to the institution of government; that is, you are ratifying a contract that you know will never be performed. Would anyone keep on paying a building contractor who never built anything but rather spent all of your money buying weapons to murder and terrorize people of other neighborhoods?

Audience: I submit that there is a conspiracy and it is right here in this room, a conspiracy of liberals and others who are not going to do

Luis Cruz Azaceta
*Latin American
Victims of Dictators:
Oppression, Torture
and Murder*
acrylic on
unstretched canvas
76 1/2" x 168"
courtesy of Frumkin-
Adams Gallery,
New York.

anything about what is going on except come back the next year and have another conference. You are not going to do anything about the homeless people on the street. When we come back next year, there will be more homeless. I would like to hear what we are going to do. Are we going to organize and do anything? Or are we just going to keep on talking while these things get worse and worse? I haven't heard anyone suggest any plans for an organization that will do something.

Cockburn: I think that is a very good point and it connects to the previous point about people raising the question of what to do in the last fifteen minutes of a conference. Actually, I think a lot of people are doing the best they can and I don't think people should lacerate themselves and feel guilty that they have done nothing for the homeless. A lot of people in this room are activists and are trying to change things. Last weekend I was in Burlington, Vermont, at a meeting of seven hundred people who were setting up the Progressive Party. They already have a socialist congressman, Bernie Sanders. That is Vermont, a small state. In New Hampshire, Ralph Nader is campaigning, not to be another candidate at the behest of business, but with a number of very specific suggestions about the way people can deal with power, ranging from access to the media and so forth. There is no secret recipe, no secret way that you can suddenly take on the possessor classes. The energies trying to create new political formations are this year very profound. So is the disillusion with the old parties. The political terrain this year is very rich in possibility. You are quite right; the years do pass, but I don't think they are entirely static.

Audience: One thing we are doing in Baltimore that has met with some success is the Baltimore Emergency Response Network, a nonviolent action group. We published a substitute front page for the *Baltimore Sun*. We replaced the front page of the *Sun* on all newspapers sold in vending machines. This was pretty well received and got a lot of response. The publisher of the *Sun* actually held a forum on TV. Then, too, we tacked a big poster-sized statement about the *Sun*'s coverage of Central America on the door of their offices. I think this may have made the *Sun* a little more conscious of how readers felt about their coverage. I would invite others to join in this kind of action, holding local papers responsible for their coverage of the news.

Merrill: It is a very frustrating thing, trying to hold big media organizations accountable for the stories they disseminate. I know I have written dozens of letters and op-ed articles to the *Washington Post* but they have ignored them all. I don't know what they do with them, actually. But I keep on writing. I am very frustrated.

Audience: After you write your letter, you can go to the paper and pass it out among the employees so they can at least read it.

Audience: This is a comment. Within the newspaper known as the *Chronicle* which serves the Baltimore area there is an insert called the "Sentinel" which deals with these issues of how the media covers stories. It is well worth seeing.

Merrill: There are very good media watch-dog organizations such as Fairness and Accuracy in Reporting (FAIR) which publishes a journal called *Extra!* or Bill Schaap and Ellen Ray's *Lies of Our Times*. I think there is a rising awareness to the level of lying that passes for news these days. Michael's comment about people drifting back into reality is a good one.

Audience: One of the things that Baltimore did was have a Save Our City March last fall to deal with the problems of crime, homelessness, and unemployment. This year the march is to be national. All the cities are going to participate. It will be May 16, 1992. That is something that began locally and people can work on. When I look around this room, I see many people I know who are working very hard and whose lives center around their work as activists. They do hold jobs because they have to pay bills, but their social activism is what really concerns them. We are in a real hard situation because we are people who read books but we live in a city where my neighbor comes to me and tells me that the TV coverage is too hard to understand because it has a lot of big words. He is twenty and he wonders if he will be drafted and sent to fight in Iraq. We haven't lobotomized him; he is an intelligent child, the son of Irish immigrants and American Indian parents. He has a fascinating history and he ought to want to know it. It is for people like him that we need to march on Washington to get funding for education.

Audience: This is a question for Alex Cockburn. The extreme right has a tendency to attack the media as being too liberal. Is this campaign orchestrated by the media itself? Or is it a legitimate commentary?

Cockburn: I think your question is a very important one. There is a campaign initiated by the right and accepted with pleasure by sections of the media. When Reed Irvine of Accuracy in Media began complaining of the liberal bias in the *New York Times*, he was received by the publisher of the *New York Times* in solemn conference who listened respectfully to a man whose views of the world are demonic in the extreme. Or demented. You would think after reading Irvine's stuff that the *Times* was written by Trotsky. But actually, their interests coincided there. This campaign began in the middle 1970s right after the eviction of Nixon when I think the country was in a radical state. A number of things happened. One was the inception of the *MacNeil/Lehrer* show. This was a moment when people had decided that Nixon was a crook and the country was in the hands of powerful and criminal corporate interests. All of these things had emerged during Watergate. Two things happened then. One was a liberal form of stabilizing dissent. *MacNeil/Lehrer* is devoted to the proposition that there are two sides to every question. Slavery— should we have free slavery or should we regulate it? That is the liberal track. The conservative track was a much more vigorous counterattack. The Mobil ads began to appear on the op-ed pages of newspapers. Editors said in effect, "We will take a substantial portion of our editorial page and sell it to an oil company. Twice or three times a week. We don't care what drivel they write. It's theirs. It is a free country. It's free speech and we are very good to give it to them." These two procedures went on and they both reinforced each other because what the publisher of the *Times* was doing was signaling to his reporters a warning shot against the turbulence of the 1960s. The implied premise was the idea that American newspapers somehow stabbed the country in the back over Vietnam. That is a preposterous premise because the first editorial against the war didn't appear until 1967 in the *Boston Globe*. But the message was that we have to regain our objectivity. In other words, we have to signal clearly the fact that we are against any further radical flowering in the 1970s. That's what all these complaints about the liberal bias are about.

Goldson: Could I add to that? I also think it is a good question because there is this insidious effect in the public mind. When they hear repeatedly that the media is controlled by left-wingers, somehow it comes down to the notion that there is the left and the right and those in the middle. The left is cast as conspiratorial. There is a mechanism in the popular imagination in which the left is seen as having control of the big institutions of power.

Parenti: May I say something? For extreme right-wingers, the media *is* too liberal. There are *things* that get in. It is as simple as that. For the media to carry out its function of class control, it must have a certain credibility with the public. To have credibility, it must at times make concessions to reality. So it carries stories about Pentagon waste, toxic dumps, environmental problems. If the right wing had its way, none of those stories would ever appear. Any time something comes in that mildly touches reality, the right wing screams about a leftist bias. But reality is very *leftist*; reality is about all these things like toxic dumps and the terrorism we have been talking about. When someone says you just gave a left-wing analysis, the truth is I just gave an analysis of what is happening. I can't help it if reality is leftist. An ideal right-wing newspaper would be one that just had stories on the glories of the free market, the horrors of communism, how affirmative action is so unfair to white people, and then cross-word puzzles, features, and cartoons. By the way, that description fits most newspapers in America, but the mainstream press does some-times get things in which the right wing does find very upsetting. When that happens, they are convinced that it is a left-wing con-spiracy to control the news.

Bratton: I think that it is a mistake to focus all of our energies on making corporate media more "responsive." These institutions are an integral part of the overall social formation and as such will change only to the degree that the entire society changes. I'm not saying we should ignore corporate media. We need to develop analyses and strategies to challenge them. These efforts, however, must take place within a wider effort: to change this society through political struggle. Now, an aspect of any struggle involves defining the field of representations by a particular political movement. You see, for example, a commitment to alternative media production by the guerrilla coalition in El Salvador, the FMLN, by setting up *Radio Venceremos* or more recently here in the United States, by ACT UP. In both cases, the major emphasis was not simply to make the corporate media more truthful, but more important, to create real and living alternatives to broadcast media. What I mean by "alternative," then, is that our work must find new forms, produce new meanings, be produced by and through new processes—and we must find new ways to involve and reach audiences. In short, the task is to invent the means to represent and reimagine the history, politics, and possibility of ourselves and our communities.

Merrill: That is a good point and there is something to the economy of scale. Even alternative magazines that are fairly well known, like the *Nation*, have only a circulation of about 95,000. That is ludicrous. How many people read the *New York Times?* Several million? Or *Time* or *Newsweek*, which have four or five million subscribers? Everyone should subscribe to the alternative press so that it can begin to build an institutional base that can compete with the big commercial press. Commonsense judgments about credibility have a lot to do with scale, whether we like it or not. Bigness or how often something is repeated confers a kind of legitimacy on information or ideas. That is, of course, what the Nazi "big lie" tactic held; but why can't the truth sometimes take advantage of scale?

Audience: I have a comment, not a question. The people who write for the local media are just people too. As members of the left we tend to be a little purist and not want to get involved with messy local issues. The fact is that we have to exercise influence. I want to speak directly to the man who raised the point about homelessness a few moments ago. On these local, close-to-the-street issues, sometimes you have to

Lynne Cohen
War Games, undated
silver print
28 1/2" x 36"
courtesy of
P.P.O.W. Gallery,
New York.

hold your nose and get to know the reporters. One of the reasons reporters write the way they do is a lack of time and energy to get another viewpoint. They look at what else is written in other papers and they are influenced by that. They don't want to be the discordant note. Maybe it is laziness and cowardice. We have to be part of the community of influence that affects them. Just as people on the left who write try to influence the climate of ideas, those of us on the left who are not writers also have to influence the climate of ideas by influencing the climate of the writers. You have to get to know the reporters themselves, particularly on a local level. On a national level you can't have as much influence, but on the local level we have to be constantly in their faces and in their ears, sending them press releases and influencing the way they see the world. Eventually, if they get fired, that is not our problem. At least they told the truth. If they don't know the truth, that is our problem. This is something that on a local level we can have some influence over. National movements and change, I am convinced, start on a local level.

Merrill: Along those lines, you can be sure that right-wing organizations like the Heritage Foundation, the American Enterprise Institute, or any of the various Pat Robertson-type fundamentalist Christian political parties send press releases by the stacks and work very hard to hound or cultivate reporters. They can work up phone calls or letters to newspapers or congresspeople on a massive scale. This idea of creating the climate in which a writer works is very important. Edward Herman's statistical studies of the terrorism industry prove how important it is. If we on the left cannot have access to the actual pages of a newspaper or television time, we must be sure that those who do have access also have access to our view of the world. Ultimately, capitalism and the increasing monopoly of resources and production by an elite class must be imposed by force, since in truth capitalist economics liberates only a few people and enslaves the rest. The spread of Western capitalism over the face of the earth has been accomplished only by a reign of terror, murder, and suffering of unimaginable proportions. The history of capitalism is really the history of colonialism and now neocolonialism. In this country where so many people have prospered at the expense of the native peoples, Africans, Asians, and others brought in to do the heaviest labor, and the land itself, the terror remains hidden a bit longer. But it can't remain hidden forever. Perhaps the amount of effort expended in the 1980s in constructing this myth of terrorism truly indicates how difficult it is becoming to keep the people quiet and unaware.

Afterword:

Women and Children First–
Terrorism on the
Home Front

Afterword: Women and Children First– Terrorism on the Home Front

Nina Felshin

Shortly after *Beyond Glory: Re-Presenting Terrorism* opened, I received a phone call from a journalist who was covering both the exhibition and the accompanying symposium, *The Politics and Imagery of Terrorism*. I was asked why no work in the exhibition addressed terrorism against women, as in domestic violence. I replied that we were interested in looking at acts of governments rather than individuals. By addressing global politics, we hoped to retain the kind of focus that might be lost if we expanded the definition of terrorism.

From the outset, we intended the exhibition to serve as a critical examination of the media's representation of terrorism and the issues surrounding it—hence the subtitle, "Re-Presenting Terrorism." Because the exhibition was dedicated to two Maryland Institute, College of Art students who died in the tragic bombing of Pan Am Flight 103 in 1988, it became even more important to demonstrate that state or "wholesale terrorism" (as Edward Herman has named it) is more consequential, quantitatively speaking, though certainly no more tragic for those involved, than so-called "retail terrorism." The latter usually refers to terrorist acts carried out by individuals or small organizations, who are virtually powerless, against individuals or organizations who are perceived as their oppressors. It is these acts that are usually presented by the media as terrorism.

Although it was the phone call that forced me to rethink our omission, two of the symposium's participants, keynote speaker and former Attorney General Ramsey Clark and author/poet Margaret Randall, had planted the seeds. Clark compared "battering a woman or threatening to, threatening a child, beating it once in a while so it knows for sure that you will really do it" to "acts of a police state." "If we want to end all terrorism," Clark concluded, "we have to stop practicing terrorism in our lives, in our families, in everything we do." Randall's feminist perspective on the subject called for a definition of terrorism that would include domestic violence, child abuse, incest, rape, and sexual harassment. She referred to the latter as "low-intensity terrorism," a phrase which recalls the Pentagon's official name for its own terrorist campaigns, "low-intensity warfare." In Randall's view, terrorism against women, like state terrorism, is about the abuse of patriarchal power. Like Clark, she reminded us that "from terrorism within the family . . . the leap to state terrorism . . . often seems to be a problem of numbers."

Domestic violence, child abuse, rape, sexual harassment, and the escalating violence of the anti-abortion movement all meet the requirements of Ramsey Clark's definition of terrorism as "the use of fear to cause or compel the conduct of other people." The importance of placing terrorist acts against women *within* the broader discourse of international terrorism has become very clear.

Since the summer of 1991, when I was invited to co-curate the exhibition, various media events have brought greater attention to issues affecting women. The most pivotal was the Clarence Thomas hearings in October 1991.[1] Not only did Anita Hill's testimony bring sexual harassment out of the closet, the fact that it took place before an all-white, all-male Senate Judiciary Committee greatly contributed to the political mobilization of women in the upcoming presidential election year as well as encouraged women to run for office.

The Thomas hearings were also instrumental in the formation of the Women's Action Coalition (WAC) in January 1992 in New York City. WAC along with several other recently formed women's groups breathed new life into the feminist movement and brought greater public awareness to issues affecting women. From the start, violence against women was a major target against which WAC launched "a visible and remarkable resistance."[2] WAC Chapters have since been established in other cities, including Chicago, Los Angeles, San Francisco, San Diego, and Minneapolis.

The escalating campaign of terror and violence by anti-abortion extremists, which culminated in the murder of a Florida doctor in March 1993, has also focused greater attention on the fact that women's bodies are a frequent site of violent struggle. The rapes of

Rachel Lachowicz
Black and Blue,
1992
wood, pigment,
leather, metal
49 1/2" x 20 1/2"
(king), 6"x 20"
(queen).

thousands of Muslim women in the former Yugoslavia that began in the spring of 1992 have painfully literalized the female body/battleground analogy. Back in the USA, less visible but no less terrorized, is the woman who is battered every fifteen seconds,[3] the more than a third of female homicide victims who are killed by husbands, boyfriends, or live-in lovers,[4] and the woman who is raped every 1.3 minutes.[5]

The prevalence of terrorism against women and the accompanying explosion of media attention have not escaped the notice of contemporary artists. An exhibition like *Beyond Glory: Re-Presenting Terrorism* would have provided an interesting context for the work of some of them, including Ida Applebroog, Nan Goldin, Ilona Granet, Rachel Lachowicz, and Kiki Smith; and for excerpts and documentation of projects by others including Richard Bolton, Peggy Diggs, Donna Ferrato, the five artists (Deborah Small, Elizabeth Sisco, Carla Kirkwood, Scott Kessler, and Louis Hock) who produced the *NHI* project in San Diego in 1992, and the six artists (Barbara Kruger, Carrie Mae Weems, Margaret Crane, and John Winet, Susan Meiselas, and Diane Tani) who participated in the Women's Work project on domestic violence in San Francisco in 1992.[6]

Ida Applebroog's interest in the subject dates from the mid-1970s when she made her first text and image works on vellum that dealt with abusive domestic behavior in a poetically associative way. Although Applebroog has expanded her investigation of the abuse of power to the political arena, she continues to explore aberrant domestic behavior in her paintings and in a videotape, *Belladonna* (1989). A collaboration with her filmmaker daughter, Beth B, *Belladonna* seems like a summing up of her ongoing interest in asymmetrical power relations. Until the credits roll, the viewer is not aware that the intercut monologues spoken by a cast of male and female adults and one little boy are quoted from victims of the infamous Nazi doctor Josef Mengele, woman-batterer and child-murderer Joel Steinberg's trial testimony, and Freud's 1919 essay "A Child Is Being Beaten."

Like Applebroog's videotape, Rachel Lachowicz's sculpture *Black and Blue* (1992) conflates the abuse of patriarchal power on home and global fronts. King and queen chess forms are her cast of characters. In a symbolic evocation of male dominance and domestic

Sue Williams
A Funny Thing Happened, 1992
acrylic on canvas
48" x 42"

violence, a prone blue queen carved in relief on a blue poker chip is leashed to a four-foot-high black king.

At the other end of the spectrum from Lachowicz's ironically cool aesthetic lies the work of Kiki Smith, Sue Williams, and Nan Goldin. Smith's recent realistic cast wax and pigment sculptures include one of a woman curled up on the floor in a fetal position with her spinal column exposed, another woman with horrific red scratches on her back, and a third on all fours, animal-like, with a long tail-like extension that suggests excrement or entrails.[7]

Sue Williams and Nan Goldin draw on personal experience of abuse. In her cartoon-like text and image paintings, Williams launches an attack—not without humor!—on the battery and sexual assault of women. Goldin's self-portraits from the early 1980s were partly motivated by her need to "recall exactly what happened without nostalgia or revisionism memory often affords."[8] They represent part of her ongoing attempt to "demystify and deromanticize sexuality, to explore the power struggles and the mutability of sexual desire."[9]

The works cited above were made for presentation in an art context—museums, galleries, and other artworld venues. In an effort to reach beyond that rarefied context, a number of artists have undertaken public projects aimed at reaching a broader audience, heightening awareness, educating and providing hotline and other information.

Three projects should be mentioned first because they represent a bridge between the first and second groups by combining elements of each: Donna Ferrato's documentary photography project, *Living with the Enemy* (1991); Ilona Granet's sexual harassment poster project commissioned by media conglomerate Capitol Cities-ABC Inc. in 1989; and Richard Bolton's installation *Subject: Male Violence* (1992).

Ferrato's ambitious ten-year documentary project, *Living with the Enemy*, depicts battering within the context of the family and the community; men (including police officers) and children are very much in evidence in her photographs. She combines haunting images of domestic violence and its aftermath, including some optimistic signs of progress, with text drawn from interviews with battered women, their male batterers, activists, and reporters.[10] Ferrato, who is adamantly opposed to having her work aestheticized, was disturbed

Ilona Granet
Thinking Women's Wear, 1989
enamel on metal
48"x96"

that the book and an accompanying traveling exhibition were circulating exclusively within the fine art context without benefiting victims of domestic violence. So, under the auspices of the Domestic Abuse Awareness Project, the nonprofit organization she created to raise money for shelters, Ferrato organized a second tour of her own. Only galleries that agreed to raise money for shelters were allowed to present the exhibition. In one year, $150,000 was raised.

Granet's sexual harassment posters were intended for the corporate offices of Capitol Cities-ABC Inc. One of the proposed designs, *Thinking Women's Wear*, depicts a woman gradually donning a full suit of armor in the course of the workday as protection against verbal assaults from her male colleagues. In another, a woman is seated at a desk flanked by two men in suits, one with a wolf's head, the other with a snake's, and both with tongues hanging out. "Check Your Wildlife at the Door" warns the sign behind her. Unfortunately, the designs were rejected and the posters were never produced. Instead of the non-art context for which they were intended, they have been exhibited in an art gallery in the form of painted enamel metal signs. One wonders if they would have fared any better *after* the Clarence Thomas hearings.

Richard Bolton's *Subject: Male Violence* (1992) was conceived for presentation in an art institution and was shown in several on the West Coast. In order to attract a non-art audience, Bolton worked closely with the presenting institutions and local organizations to develop community outreach programs and to tailor the documentary contents of the installation to the specific locales. The installation was dominated by seventy-five stations—tables and stools—set up for visitors to examine a broad range of documentary material about domestic violence. Visitor participation was further encouraged with questions that asked: "Do you often accuse your partner of having affairs with other men? Do you insult your partner or try to embarrass or ridicule her? Do you throw or break objects when you are angry?" Domestic objects that are often transformed into weapons—candlesticks, a vase of roses, a coffee pot, and an iron—were placed around the room. An audio-visual component included clips from American films and slides of ads that conflate sex, violence, and male dominance. In a separate room, visitors were invited to record their own domestic violence experiences and tack them on the wall. They

Peggy Diggs, *Domestic Violence Milk Cartons*, 1991 distributed in New York Metropolitan area.

Photo: Ralph Leiberman

were also invited to use a telephone that was hooked up to a victim hotline. Like other projects by Bolton, this one succeeded in transforming an art space into one for community participation and education.

Bolton's installation demonstrated the media's complicity in perpetuating the national epidemic of male-perpetrated violence against women. Several fully public projects exploited the media by using its forms and conventions in order to heighten awareness and in some cases encourage victims to seek assistance.

Peggy Diggs's *Domestic Violence Project* utilized milk cartons and billboards to reach victims of domestic violence. In January 1992, with the support of Creative Time in New York City and Tuscan Dairy of New Jersey, 1.5 million Diggs-designed milk cartons were distributed in the Metropolitan New York area. A menacing silhouetted hand was accompanied by the question: "When you argue at home does it always get out of hand?" Below was the number of the National Domestic Violence Hotline. Diggs's inspiration came from interviews with women who told her that, except for grocery shopping, they were not allowed to leave home by themselves. The response was overwhelming, with calls coming in long after the milk cartons were gone from the shelves.

In a related project, Diggs designed a billboard for three economically divergent sites in western Massachusetts, where she lives. Sponsored by the New England Foundation for the Arts and a local sign company, the billboards were up for several months in the fall of 1991. A photographic image of a white, well-dressed, middle-class family of four, marred only by the woman's battered face, was accompanied by the question "Does he hurt you?" and the phone number for the Women's Services Center Hotline. The typography floated on red and black scribbles that evoked out-of-control violence. Diggs deliberately used the image of a stereotypical American family of four in order to undermine another stereotype, that of the economically and racially marginalized family as the exclusive site for domestic violence.

A similar violence project was undertaken in the San Francisco area in September 1992 under the corporate sponsorship of Liz Claiborne, Inc., the manufacturer of women's clothing. As a part of Women's Work, the company's community-based national marketing program, six artists were commissioned to design posters for bus shelters and billboards in the Bay Area. The artists included Barbara Kruger and Susan Meiselas from New York and Carrie Mae Weems, Diane Tani, and the collaborative team of Margaret Crane and John Winet from the Bay Area. Approaches varied greatly but all addressed the issue of domestic violence, all used photographic images combined with text, and all included the hotline number of the San Francisco Domestic Violence Consortium and the Liz Claiborne logo. Claiborne also provided seed money for a permanent twenty-four-hour multilingual hotline. Like Bolton and Diggs, the organizers of this project worked closely with local organizations.

Unlike any of the other projects, *NHI* addressed the issue of violence against women by focusing on some unfinished local history: the unsolved brutal murders of forty-five women that occurred in San Diego County between 1985 and 1991. Identified by local authorities as prostitutes, drug addicts, and transients, they were labelled "NHI" by the police—No Humans Involved—which is internal police shorthand for those accorded nonhuman or marginal status. Their deaths, therefore, were deemed unworthy of proper investigations. San Diego artists Deborah Small, Elizabeth Sisco, Carla Kirkwood, Scott Kessler, and Louis Hock produced *NHI*, a four-

TOP
Barbara Kruger
image from
Women's Work, Bay
Area billboard and
bus shelter project,
funded by Liz
Claiborne, Inc., 1992.
BOTTOM
Carrie Mae Weems
image from
Women's Work, Bay
Area billboard and
bus shelter project,
funded by Liz
Claiborne, Inc., 1992

ONE IN FOUR WOMEN IS A VICTIM OF DOMESTIC VIOLENCE

THE HOSTAGE CRISIS

To get help call: 415-864-4555 San Francisco Domestic Violence Consortium ▲ Liz claiborne

Margaret Crane and John Winet image from Women's Work, Bay Area billboard and bus shelter project, funded by Liz Claiborne, Inc., 1992.

faceted multimedia project in early 1992 to bring attention to the murders and the continuing cover-up. They did so through downtown billboards, an exhibition, a performance that addressed violence against women, and a public forum. Partly because these events unfolded over a period of a month, the artists, who are known for their ability to generate extensive media coverage, succeeded in focusing and sustaining a great deal of attention on the deaths and the official cover-up.

From the bedroom to the living room, the living room to the office, and from there into the streets and the community—these are the primary landscapes in which women are subject to fear and violence. These are the landscapes in which all of us encounter the misuse of power for the first time. And finally, these are the landscapes in which both Ramsey Clark and Margaret Randall are calling for some major changes in scenery. Until there is an end to patriarchal acts of coercion and violence against women and children, their broadened definition of terrorism must stand.

Notes

David J. Brown, Foreword: Difficult Religion

1. Michel Foucault, *Discipline and Punish: The Birth of the Prison* (New York: Vintage Books, 1979).

2. Matthew Yeomans, "Hell Is for Heroes," *Village Voice*, September 24, 1991: 156 and 197.

3. *Washington Post*, October 15, 1991: A20.

4. *Bulletin of Atomic Scientists*, September 1989.

5. Noam Chomsky, *The Culture of Terrorism* (Boston: South End Press, 1988).

Maurice Berger, Visual Terrorism

1. Frantz Fanon, *The Wretched of the Earth* (New York: Grove Press, 1968), p. 74. For more on Fanon and the political construction of violence, see Anthony M. Burton, *Urban Terrorism: Theory, Practice, and Response* (New York: The Free Press, 1975), pp. 120-21.

2. Concerning the collaborative, serial videotape project *Counterterror*, Annie Goldson and Chris Bratton (who wrote and produced the "United States" segment) write: "In *Counterterror*, we are proposing that the discourse of terrorism has been specifically designed to maintain repression within countries or communities whose labor, resources, and ideological alignment have sustained the wealth and privilege of the 'Free World.' In other words, we see the discourse as emanating from the advanced capitalist countries (led by the United States) that use as their object the Third World. This discourse, to use Antonio Gramsci's theory, is one mechanism through which the 'ruling class factions' can exercise 'political and cultural hegemony over the entire society' (or in this transnational example, over societies)." See Goldson and Bratton, "Counterterror," in Cynthia Schneider and Brian Wallis, eds., *Global Television* (Cambridge, Mass.: M.I.T. Press, 1988), pp. 148-49.

3. On the issue of terrorism's "legitimacy," see Martha Crenshaw, ed., "Introduction: Reflections on the Effects of Terrorism," in *Terrorism, Legitimacy, and Power: The Consequences of Political Violence* (Middletown, Conn.: Wesleyan University Press, 1983), pp. 1-5.

4. Ibid. p. 15.

5. Roland Gaucher, *The Terrorists: From Tsarist Russia to the O.A.S.* (London: Secker and Warburg, 1968), p. 268.

6. Brian Jenkins, *International Terrorism: A New Mode of Conflict* (California Arms Control and Foreign Policy Seminar, December 1975), p. 5. For a counter-

terrorist reading of political violence and the media, see H. H. A. Cooper, "Terrorism and the Media," in Yonah Alexander and Seymour Maxwell Finger, eds., *Terrorism: Interdisciplinary Perspectives* (New York: The John Jay Press, 1977), pp. 141-56.

7. As Roland Barthes writes, "the *punctum* shows no preference for morality or good taste; the *punctum* can be ill-bred." See *Camera Lucida*, trans. Richard Howard (New York: Hill and Wang, 1981), p. 23.

8. See, for example, Maurice Berger, "Broken Bodies, Dead Babies, and Other Weapons of War," in *How Art Becomes History: Essays on Art, Society, and Culture in Post-New Deal America* (New York: HarperCollins, 1992), pp. 63-77. On the tendency of the media to elide images of extreme violence, Kathy O'Dell has written: "By absenting the . . . gory core, news people believe that they evade sensationalism. . . . What began as a protest against the exploitative and manipulative use of language has been transmuted into a sort of photographic and televised conservatism. Out of an effort to protect us . . . from the potentially traumatic effect of violence, we are provided with references that, in their continual elision of the central act of violence, keep us ever mindful of its having ever taken place and ever searching for its manifestation." See Kathy O'Dell, "Images of Violence: Functions of Representation" (unpublished essay, 1982, p. 2).

9. Thierry de Duve, "Time Exposure and Snapshot: The Photograph as Paradox," *October*, 5 (Summer 1978): 119.

10. Ibid., pp. 119-20. For a detailed analysis of de Duve's arguments and the function of shock and trauma in propagandistic photographs, of which the above paragraphs are a condensation, see Maurice Berger, "F.S.A.: The Illiterate Eye," in *How Art Becomes History*, pp. 1-21.

11. Roman Jakobson has observed that personal pronouns are the last elements to be acquired in a child's speech and the first to be lost in aphasia. Thus, as O'Dell has observed, to "become aphasic before a photograph is to be effaced—to lose contact with the 'I' which would ordinarily begin any utterance made in response to the observed photo." For an important analysis of Jakobson's idea in relation to language, see Roland Barthes, *Elements of Semiology*, trans. Annette Lavers and Colin Smith (New York: Hill and Wang, 1967), pp. 22-23, and O'Dell, "Images of Violence," p. 6.

Robert Merrill, Simulations and Terrors of Our Time

1. Robert Kupperman and Jeff Kamen, *Final Warning: Averting Disaster in the New Age of Terrorism* (New York: Doubleday, 1989), p. 122.

2. Ibid., pp. 3-4.

3. Cornelius Castoriadis, *The Imaginary Institution of Society* (Cambridge, Mass.: MIT Press, 1987).

4. "Decade Shock," *Newsweek*, September 5, 1988: 14-21. The headline asks, "Will We Ever Get Over the 60s?" See also among many others, P. J. O'Rourke, "Let the Sixties Die," *Rolling Stone*, September 24, 1987: 114-16.

5. *Terrorist Group Profiles* (Washington, D.C.: U.S. Government Printing Office, 1988), pp. ii-iii.

6. Jean Baudrillard, *Simulations* (New York: Semiotext(e), 1983), p. 2.

7. *National Security Strategy of the United States* (Washington, D.C.: U.S. Government Printing Office, 1993).

8. Cited in Bob Woodward, *Veil: The Secret Wars of the CIA* (New York: Simon and Schuster, 1987), pp. 92-93.

9. Department of State, Current Policy, No. 1045, February 12, 1988.

10. Department of State, Current Policy, No. 1055, February 26, 1988.

11. Woodward, *Veil* pp. 124-26.

12. Ibid., pp. 125-29.

13. Department of State, Current Policy, No. 721, July 8, 1985.

14. Jay Shafritz, E. F. Gibbons, and Gregory Scott, *The Almanac of Modern Terrorism* (New York: Facts on File, 1991); Walter Laqueur and Yonah Alexander, *The Terrorism Reader* (New York: NAL Penguin, 1987).

15. Kishore Mahbubani, "Pol Pot: The Paradox of 'Moral Correctness,'" *Studies in Conflict and Terrorism* (January-March 1993): pp. 51-60.

16. Michel Foucault, *Discipline and Punish: The Birth of the Prison* (New York: Vintage Books, 1979), p. 78.

17. Elliot Abrams, Department of State, Current Policy, No. 792, February 10, 1986.

Edward S. Herman, Terrorism: Misrepresentations of Power

1. See, especially, Taylor Branch, *Parting the Waters: America in the King Years, 1954-1963* (New York: Simon and Schuster, 1988); Nelson Blackstock, *COINTELPRO: The FBI's Secret War on Political Freedom* (New York: Vintage, 1975).

2. On the Western model of terrorism and the North-South application of this model, see Edward S. Herman and Gerry O'Sullivan, *The "Terrorism" Industry: The Experts and Institutions That Shape Our View of Terror* (New York: Pantheon, 1990), chs. 2-3.

3. Ibid., pp. 25-29; see also Phyllis Johnson and David Martin, eds., *Frontline South Africa: Destructive Engagement* (New York: Four Walls Eight Windows, 1988).

4. See also Joan Dassin, ed., *Torture in Brazil: A Report by the Archdiocese of Sao Paulo* (New York: Vintage, 1986); Edward S. Herman, *The Real Terror Network* (Boston: South End Press, 1988), pp. 110-32.

5. See Johnson and Martin, eds., *Frontline South Africa*; Herman and O'Sullivan, *The "Terrorism" Industry,* pp. 25-29.

6. For an extensive discussion, see Peter Kornbluh, *Nicaragua: The Price of Intervention* (Washington, D.C.: Institute for Policy Studies, 1987); Noam Chomsky, *The Culture of Terrorism* (Boston: South End Press, 1988), chs. 3-5, 12.

7. See Herman and O'Sullivan *The "Terrorism" Industry*, pp. 113-15, 168-73, 180.

8. Bernard Weintraub, "President Accuses 5 'Outlaw States' of World Terror," *New York Times*, July 9, 1985: A1.

9. John Haiman and Anna Meigs, "Khaddafy: Man and Myth," *Africa Events*, February 1986. On Qaddafi as a condensation symbol, see next note.

10. Noam Chomsky, "Libya in U.S. Demonology," *Covert Action Information Bulletin*, Summer 1986.

11. *Sources for the numbers in Table 1 are as follows*:

a. H. J. Horchem, "Political Terrorism: The German Perspective," in Ariel Merari, ed., *On Terrorism and Combatting Terrorism* (Bethesda, Md.: University Publications of America, 1985), p. 63.

b. V. S. Pisano, Terrorism and Security: the Italian Experience, Report of the Subcommittee on Security and Terrorism, Senate Judiciary Committee, 98th Congress, 2nd. Session, November 1984, p. 63.

c. B. Michael, Ha'aretz, July 16, 1982. He cites police statistics. Some of the 282 were killed by Israeli forces in attempts to free hostages by force.

d. CIA, *Patterns of International Terrorism: 1980*, June 1981, p. vi.

e. M. McClintock, *The American Connection*, vol. 1, *State Terror and Popular Resistance in El Salvador* (Atlantic Highlands, N.J.: Zed Books, 1985), p. 306.

f. R. Leonard, *South Africa at War* (Brooklyn, N.Y.: Lawrence Hill, 1983), p. 67.

g. Amnesty International, Special Briefing, "Guatemala: Massive Extrajudicial Executions in Rural Areas under the Government of General Efrain Rios Montt," July 1982, p. x.

h. The Lebanese government claims that it recovered 762 bodies and 1,200 were privately buried by relatives: N. Chomsky, *The Fateful Triangle* (Boston: South End Press, 1983), p. 370. In a careful study, Amnon Kapeliok estimates 3,000-3,500 murdered; *Sabra and Shatila: An Inquiry into the Massacre* (Association of Arab-American University Graduates, 1984), pp. 62-63.

i. J. Simpson and J. Bennett, *The Disappeared and the Mothers of the Plaza* (New York: St. Martin's Press, 1985), p. 7.

j. Amnesty International, *Report on Torture* (New York: Farrar, Straus & Giroux, 1975), p. 252.

k. C. M. Guitérrez, *The Dominican Republic: Rebellion and Repression* (New York: Monthly Review Press, 1972), p. 11.

l. R. Armstrong and J. Shenk, *El Salvador: The Face of Revolution* (Boston: South End Press, 1982), p. 30.

m. Central America Historical Institute.

n. Amnesty International, "Guatemala: Massive Extrajudicial Executions," p. x.

o. "Bitter and Cruel . . ." report of a mission to Guatemala by the British Parliamentary Human Rights Group, October 1984. C. Kruger and K. Enge, "Without Security or Development: Guatemala Militarized," report submitted to the Washington Office on Latin America, June 6, 1985.

p. Amnesty International, *Political Killings by Governments* (Amnesty International, 1983), p. 34. This is a conservative estimate.

q. N. Chomsky, *Towards a New Cold War* (New York: Pantheon, 1982), p. 341 and 470, citing Father Leonardo Vierra do Rego and Father Francisco María Fernández.

r. Amnesty International, *Political Killings by Governments*, pp. 69- 77.

s. Ibid., p. 24.

t. H. Sklar, *Washington's War on Nicaragua* (Boston: South End Press, 1988), p. 393.

u. Johnson and Martin, eds., *Frontline South Africa*, p. 467 and sources used there.

12. On how this is done, see Edward S. Herman and Noam Chomsky, *Manufacturing Consent: The Political Economy of the Mass Media* (New York: Pantheon, 1988), preface and ch. 1; Mark Hertsgaard, *On Bended Knee: The Press and the Reagan Presidency* (New York: Farrar, Straus & Giroux, 1988).

13. See Noam Chomsky, *Pirates & Emperors: International Terrorism in the Real World* (New York: Claremont Research Publications, 1986).

14. For a discussion of this multinational structure of institutes, see Herman and O'Sullivan, *The "Terrorism" Industry*, ch. 5.

15. The "Media 16" is comprised of the 16 most often cited experts based on a representative sample of 135 mass media news items on terrorism. The "Big 32" includes the "Media 16" as well as eight additional experts cited in Alex P. Schmid's *Political Terrorism* (North-Holland Publishing Company, 1983; revised and updated with Albert J. Jongman, 1988) and eight more experts whose influence is pervasive. See Herman and O'Sullivan, *The "Terrorism" Industry*, pp. 143-45.

16. Christopher Dobson and Robert Payne, *The Terrorists: Their Weapons, Leaders, and Tactics* (New York: Facts on File, 1982); Walter Laqueur, *The Age of Terrorism* (Boston: Little, Brown, 1987); Paul Wilkinson, *Terrorism and the Liberal State* (New York: New York University Press, 1986); Claire Sterling, *The Terror Network* (New York: Holt, Rinehart, Winston/Reader's Digest, 1981).

17. In fact, Henze insisted that network news programs not mention his CIA connections. See Edward Herman and Frank Brodhead, *The Rise and Fall of the Bulgarian Connection* (New York: Sheridan Square Press, 1986), p. 147, n. 65.

Part II: Case Studies in Terrorism

Randall Robinson

1. During 1991 some sixty people were gunned down as they boarded or exited trains that carry black workers from the townships to industrial sites. See for example, "S. Africa 'Death Trains' to get Tighter Security," *Washington Times*, October 30, 1991: A2.

2. On the sources of Buthelesi's weapons, see Patrick Laurence, "Buthelesi's Gamble," *Africa Report*, November/December 1992: 13ff. On cultural weapons, see "Armed Marchers Defy S. Africa's Weapon Ban," *Washington Post*, October 18, 1992: A36.

3. John Battersby, "A Secret Network to Preserve White Power," *Christian Science Monitor*, August 24, 1992: 6ff.

4. Christopher S. Wren, "Pretoria's Police Admit Subsidizing Mandela's Rivals," *New York Times*, July 20, 1991: A1; David B. Ottaway, "South Africa Says It Covertly Funded Groups in Namibia," *Washington Post*, July 26, 1991: A1.

5. Paul A. Wellings and Michael O. Sutcliffe, "The Widening Rift: Buthelesi, Inkatha, and Anti-Apartheid Politics in South Africa," *TransAfrica Forum*, Summer 1986: 6ff.

1. See U.S. Senate, Select Committee on Indian Affairs, Indian Mineral Development, 97th Congress, 2nd Session (Washington, D.C.: U.S. Government Printing Office, 1982).

2. See Frank Kitson, *Low Intensity Operations: Subversion, Insurgency, and Peace-Keeping* (Harrisburg, Pa.: Stackpole Books, 1971). The FBI in the mid-1970s referred to AIM not as "militants," "radicals," or "political extremists," but as "insurgents"; see Ward Churchill and J. J. Vander Wall, *The COINTELPRO Papers: Documents from the FBI's Secret Wars against Dissent in the United States* (Boston: South End Press, 1990), p. 264.

3. See excerpts from an interview with an FBI Public Information Officer in Lan Brookes Ritz's documentary film, *Anna Mae: A Brave-Hearted Woman* (Los Angeles: Brown Bird Productions, 1979). Also Athan Theoharis, "Building a File: The Case against the FBI," *Washington Post*, October 30, 1988; and Alan Dershowitz, "Can Leonard Peltier Be the Andrei Sakarov of America?" *Denver Post*, October 21, 1984.

4. See Ward Churchill, "GOONs, G-Men, and AIM: At Last the Story Will Be Told," *The Progressive*, April 1990.

5. *The Spirit of Crazy Horse* was produced by Michel Dubois and Kevin McKiernan, and first aired on December 18, 1990. The author is in possession of a 125-page transcription of the Brewer interview from which the televised excerpts were drawn.

6. These are minimum figures, derived from reports collected by researcher Candy Hamilton, who resided on Pine Ridge throughout the period as an unpaid paralegal for the Wounded Knee Legal Offense/Defense committee (WKLD/OC).

7. Bruce Johansen and Roberto Maestas, *Wasi'chu: The Continuing Indian Wars* (New York: Monthly Review Press, 1979), p. 83.

8. Johansen and Maestas, relying on data from the FBI Uniform Crime Report (Washington, D.C.: U.S. Government Printing Office, 1975).

9. Johansen and Maestas, *Wasi'chu,* p. 84.

10. Ibid.

11. See *American Indian Policy Review Commission, Final Report, Task Force Nine: Law Consolidation, Revision, and Codification* (Washington, D.C.: U.S. Government Printing Office, 1977), pp. 173-74. Also see *U.S. Commission on Civil Rights, Indian Tribes: A Continuing Quest for Survival* (Washington, D.C.: U.S. Government Printing Office, 1981), p. 145.

12. This is incorporated into official findings: "[W]hen Indians complain about the lack of investigation and prosecution on reservation crime, they are usually told the Federal government does not have the resources to handle the work." See U.S. Department of Justice, *Report of the Task Force on Indian Matters* (Washington, D.C.: U.S. Government Printing Office, 1975), pp. 42-43.

13. *Report of the Task Force on Indian Matters*, pp. 42-43.

14. Interview with George O'Clock by Michel Dubois and Kevin Barry McKiernan, 1987; transcript on file.

15. Zigrossi explained to David Wier and Lowell Bergman in 1978 that the proper function of the Bureau on Indian reservations is to serve as a "colonial police force." See Wier and Bergman, "The Killing of Anna Mae Aquash," *Rolling Stone*, April 7, 1977: 5.

16. U.S. Senate Committee on the Judiciary, Subcommittee on Internal Security, *Revolutionary Activities within the United States: The American Indian Movement* (Washington, D.C.: U.S. Government Printing Office, 1975), p. 61.

17. U.S. v. Consolidated Wounded Knee Cases, CR 73-5019, U.S. District Court for Nebraska, Lincoln, 1974.

18. U.S. House of Representatives, Hearings before the Subcommittee on Civil and Constitutional Rights, 97th Congress, 1st Session on FBI Authorization, March 19, 24, 25; April 2, 18, 1981 (Washington, D.C.: U.S. Government Printing Office, 1981).

19. Quoted in Ward Churchill and J. J. Vander Wall, *Agents of Repression: The FBI's Secret Wars against the Black Panther Party and the American Indian Movement* (Boston: South End Press, 1988), p. 329.

20. Shirley Hill Witt and William Muldrow, *Monitoring of Events Related to the Shooting of Two FBI Agents on the Pine Ridge Reservation* (Denver: U.S. Commission on Civil Rights, Rocky Mountain Regional Office, July 9, 1975).

21. Churchill and Vander Wall, *Agents of Repression*, pp. 186-87.

22. Ibid., p. 185. This is hardly the only incident in which innocent bystanders were on the receiving end of GOON bullets.

23. The amount is from Wilson's testimony during congressional hearings on Pine Ridge violence excerpted in Saul Landau's documentary film *Voices from Wounded Knee* (Washington, D.C.: Institute for Policy Studies, 1974).

24. A 1974 GAO audit determined that the Wilson administration kept virtually no books on its expenditures of federal funds. See Johanna Brand, *The Life and Death of Anna Mae Aquash* (Toronto: Lorimar Publishers, 1978), p. 62. Also see U.S. Commission on Civil Rights, Report of Investigation: Oglala Sioux Tribe, General Election, 1974 (Denver: U.S. Commission on Civil Rights, Rocky Mountain Regional Office, October 1974); and Peter Matthiessen, *In the Spirit of Crazy Horse* (New York: Viking Press, 1984), p. 62.

25. At least $200,000 in tribal housing funds were spent in 1973 and 1974 to acquire house trailers used exclusively by members of the GOON squad and their families. See Brand, *The Life and Death of Anna Mae Aquash*.

26. The per capita annual income on Pine Ridge during this period was a little over $1,000. Wilson increased his pay from $5,500 to $15,500 per year, as well as a $30,000 annual "consultancy." See *Voices from Wounded Knee, 1973* (Mohawk Nation via Rooseveltown, N.Y.: Akwesasne Notes, 1974), p. 21; Cheryl McCall, "Life on Pine Ridge Bleak," *Colorado Daily*, May 16, 1975; and *New York Times*, April 22, 1975.

27. The percentage of BIA police who moonlighted as GOONs in the fashion of Latin American death squads is uncertain. Speculations have ranged from 25 to 50 percent.

28. The area, located in the northwestern quadrant of Pine Ridge, got its name when it was "borrowed" by the U.S. Army Air Corps in 1942 as a practice site for dive bombers and aerial gunners. By agreement, the government was to return the land to Oglala control at the end of World War II, but never did. Agitation among Oglala traditionals to recover the gunnery range had become pronounced by 1972, but, unknown to any of the Indians involved, a secret venture undertaken by NASA and the National Uranium Research and Evaluation Institute in 1970-71 had revealed rich uranium deposits inter-

mingled with molybdenum. See J. P. Greis, *Status of Mineral Resource Information on Pine Ridge Indian Reservation*, S.D., BIA Report No. 12 (Washington, D.C.: U.S. Department of Interior, 1976). The title transfer at issue was/is illegal under provision of the still binding 1868 Fort Laramie Treaty, a stipulation requiring three-quarters express consent of all adult male Lakotas before any lawful land cession may take place.

29. The traditionals formed the Oglala Sioux Civil Rights Organization (OSCRO), headed by Pedro Bissonette, in 1972 to pursue recovery of the gunnery range, continue broader land claims under the 1868 treaty, and resolve heirship problems with property owned by Pine Ridge residents but administered "in trust" by the BIA. OSCRO opposed Wilson's agenda and became the primary target of GOON terrorism. The traditionals then attempted to exercise their legal right of impeachment. The BIA named Wilson to head his own impeachment proceedings and requested a 60 member Special Operations Groups of SWAT-trained U.S. Marshals.

30. *Voices from Wounded Knee, 1973*, p. 123.

31. Concerning M-16s in the possession of GOONs during the Wounded Knee siege, consider the following excerpt from a federal radio monitoring radio traffic on the night of April 23, 1973: "Tribal Government [a euphemism for the GOONs] Roadblock to Tribal Roving Patrol: 'How many M-16s you guys got? Where are the other guys?' Tribal Patrol to Tribal Roadblock: 'We got eight M-16s and some men coming up on horseback.'"

32. For researchers' conclusions, see Johansen and Maestas, *Wasi'chu*; Matthiessen, *In the Spirit of Crazy Horse*; Churchill and Vander Wall, *Agents of Repression,* and *The COINTELPRO Papers*; and Brand, *The Life and Death of Anna Mae Aquash*. Also see Rex Weyler, *Blood of the Land: The Governmental and Corporate War against the American Indian Movement* (New York: Vintage Books, 1984), and Jim Messerschmidt, *The Trial of Leonard Peltier* (Boston: South End Press, 1983).

33. Chuck Richards is the eldest son in a clan so grotesquely violent it is collectively referred to on Pine Ridge as the "Manson Family." Chuck, predictably, is known as "Charlie Manson."

34. Brewer's reference to a "Treaty Convention up at Fort Yates," on the Standing Rock Sioux Reservation, concerns the founding conference of the International Indian Treaty Council, AIM's diplomatic arm, in June 1974. "Pine Ridge's little crew" was also on hand at Standing Rock on June 8, 1975, when AIM leader Russell Means was shot in the back and nearly killed by BIA police.

35. In fact, FBI were "around," at least on some occasions. For example, on February 26, 1973, AIM leader Russell Means, accompanied by Milo Goings and Pedro Bissonette, attempted to meet with Dick Wilson in a final effort to avert the confrontation which became the siege of Wounded Knee. They were assaulted in the parking lot of the tribal office building by five GOONs headed by Duane Brewer. At least two FBI agents were on hand as "observers." No further action was taken by the Bureau.

36. Finzel, Gordon, and James were members of the Wounded Knee Legal Defense/Offense Committee (WKLD/OC), a National Lawyers Guild project initiated during the 1973 Wounded Knee siege to provide legal counsel to AIM members and supporters.

37. Aside from Dick Wilson, the victims identified GOONs Duane, Brian, and

Vincent Brewer; Chuck, Cliff, Bennie, and Woody Richards; Mark and Greg Clifford; Lloyd and Toby Eagle Bull; Robert Escoffy, Johnson Hold Rock; Bennet "Tuffy" Sierra, John Hussman; Glenn Little Bird; Marvin Stolt; Glenn Three Stars; James Wedell; Michael Weston; Dale Janis; Charlie Winters; Salty Twiss; Manny and Billy Wilson; Fred Two Bulls; and Francis Randall.

38. Quoted in the *Rapid City Journal*, February 28, 1975.

39. A further perspective has been offered in an interview by former WKLD/OC coordinator Ken Tilsen: "Somebody had to tell Dick Wilson how to go about beating the rap on this one. He wasn't smart enough to figure out the double jeopardy ploy all by himself. And you can bet that that 'somebody' was in the U.S. Attorney's office or the FBI."

40. For instance, AIM supporter Philip Little Crow was beaten to death as part of a GOON "educational seminar" on November 10, 1973; AIM supporter Jim Little was stomped to death by four GOONs on September 10, 1975; AIM member Hobart Horse was beaten, shot and run over repeatedly by a car on March 1, 1976. No one went to trial on any of these murders.

41. The late Robert Burnette, at the time tribal president of the Rosebud Sioux, recounted how, "Frizzell . . . called me to request that I come to Wounded Knee with two FBI agents in an attempt to find eight graves that were around the perimeter. The activists who spoke of these graves believed they contained the bodies of Indians murdered by white ranchers or Wilson's men [or both]." See Robert Burnette with John Koster, *The Road to Wounded Knee* (New York: Bantam Books, 1974), p. 248. The Akwesasne Notes book, *Voices from Wounded Knee, 1973,* contains an excerpt from transcription of U.S. Marshal radio logs which report that a GOON roving patrol had captured a group of "13 hippies" attempting to backpack some supplies into Wounded Knee. A BIA police unit dispatched by the marshals to take custody of the prisoners was fired upon by the GOONs and retreated. None of the prisoners was ever seen again.

42. In late 1974, Young Bear requested that an AIM security unit be placed on his property in much the same fashion that the Northwest AIM group subsequently established its defensive encampment at the request of the Jumping Bull family, near Oglala. As a result, GOON violence directed at Young Bear's home "dropped off real fast," as he remembers it.

43. It is worth noting that there were no African-American gun dealers in Rapid City — or anywhere else in the region — in those days and still aren't. The individuals in question were therefore "imported" in order to serve as go-betweens for some one else — say, a federal agency — and compensated accordingly. The scenario fits well with the remainder of Brewer's commentary on arms transactions and with the known means by which the Bureau armed the Secret Army Organization in southern California at about the same time. See Michael Parenti, *Democracy for the Few* (New York: St. Martin's Press, 1982), p. 24.

44. This concerns the altercation outside the tribal office building in Pine Ridge village on February 26, 1973.

45. The cause of death listed in both the police report and the coroner's report in the Pedro Bissonette slaying is also suspect. See Churchill and Vander Wall, *Agents of Repression*, pp. 200-203 and 206-11.

46. DeSersa was hit in the left thigh by a bullet fired from one of four carloads of GOONs pursuing his own vehicle in a high speed chase outside Wanblee.

Charlie Winters, one of the assailants, was arrested for the crime by local police in nearby Martin, South Dakota. This led to a state (not federal) case in which Winters, Chuck Richards, Billy Wilson, and Dale Janis were charged. Despite the fact that DeSersa and his companions had been unarmed, charges were dismissed against Richards and Wilson on the basis of their having acted in "self-defense." Winters and Janis were then allowed to plea bargain to second degree manslaughter and served two years apiece. Neither the FBI nor the BIA police played any constructive role in obtaining even this minimal outcome.

47. Inexplicably, the FBI lab notes refer to the death as "possible manslaughter. See Churchill and Vander Wall, *The COINTELPRO Papers*, p. 293.

48. Indeed, the Bureau caused an article, headlined "FBI Denies AIM Implication that Aquash Was Informant" to appear in the March 11, 1976, edition of the *Rapid City Journal*. No one in AIM had implied that she was. Bob Robideau, a member of Northwest AIM Group, states that she was neither an informer nor suspected of being one. Rumors had been raised to that effect by FBI infiltrator/provocateur Douglass Durham nearly a year earlier. These had been checked out by AIM Security, and she had been immediately "cleared." On Durham, see Paula Giese, "Profile of an Informer," *Covert Action Information Bulletin*, No. 24, Summer 1985.

49. FBI representative James Frier was grilled by California Congressman Don Edwards on this topic during appropriation hearings in 1980. Frier's responses were deemed "less than satisfactory" by this former FBI agent turned legislator. See U.S. House of Representatives, Hearings before the Subcommittee on Civil and Constitutional Rights of the Committee of the Judiciary, First Session on FBI Authorization (1981) 97th Congress, 1st Session (Washington, D.C.: U.S. Government Printing Office, 1981), p. 666.

50. See analysis by Aquash's attorney, Bruce Ellison, and former AIM leader John Trudell in the film *Anna Mae: A Brave-Hearted Women*. For excerpts from an independent researcher's interview with Brown, see Brand, *The Life and Death of Anna Mae Aquash*, pp. 21-22.

51. See First Session on FBI Authorization (1981), p. 278. Concerning death threats, see Kevin McKiernan, "Indian Woman's Death Raises Many Troubling Questions," *Minneapolis Tribune*, May 30, 1976, especially quotations from WKLD/OC researcher Candy Hamilton. Also see Ward Churchill, "Who Killed Anna Mae," *Z Magazine*, December 1988.

52. A report titled "Law Enforcement on Pine Ridge Indian Reservation," dated June 6, 1975, calls for "massive military assault forces." A later memorandum, excerpted into a press release titled "RESMURS Press Coverage Clarification" (July 8, 1975) calls for "automatic and semi-automatic weapons" deployment among the assault forces, as well as "heavy equipment such as armored personnel carriers."

53. These events are covered well in Matthiessen, *In the Spirit of Crazy Horse*.

54. Concerning Held's prepositioning in Minneapolis, see June 27, 1975, memorandum, Gebbhart to O'Connell in Churchill and Vander Wall, *The COINTELPRO Papers*, p. 267.

55. Concerning Richard Wallace Held's involvement in the RESMURS operation from its first moments, and his eventual presence on Pine Ridge — both of which he and the Bureau have denied — see documents reproduced in ibid., pp. 268-70.

56. One result was the death of an elderly man named James Brings Yellow, who was startled into a fatal heart attack when a team of agents headed by J. Gary Adams suddenly kicked in his door on July 10, 1975. Air assaults included a raid on the property of AIM members Selo Black Crow near Wanblee, on July 8 (50 agents involved), and another on the property of AIM spiritual leader Leonard Crow Dog on September 5, 1975 (100 agents involved).

57. The Committee had issued a subpoena to FBI *agent provocateur* Douglass Durham to begin hearings as of mid-July 1975. The proceedings were called off on July 3 by a letter from committee staff member Patrick Shae to Attorney General Edward S. Levi stating in part: "[W]e will hold in abeyance any action . . . in view of the killing of the Agents at Pine Ridge, South Dakota."

58. The preliminary document was signed by Wilson on June 29, 1975. Another, improved version was signed on January 2, 1976, shortly before Wilson left office. Congress then duly consecrated the arrangement as Public Law 90-468. When the legitimacy of this measure was subsequently challenged on the basis of treaty requirements, P.L. 90-468 was amended so that surface rights might revert to the Lakotas at any time they determined by referendum to recover them (thus nearly reversing the treaty stipulation), but leaving the subsurface (i.e., mineral) rights under permanent federal ownership. See Jacquiline Huber et al., *The Gunnery Range Report* (Rapid City, S.D.: Oglala Sioux Tribe, Office of the President, 1981).

59. For analysis, see Joel D. Weisman, "About That Ambush at Wounded Knee," *Columbia Journalism Review*, September-October 1975. Also see Ward Churchill, "Renegades, Terrorists, and Revolutionaries: The Government's Propaganda War against the American Indian Movement," *Propaganda Review*, no. 4, April 1989.

60. FBI Director Kelley "corrected misimpressions" at a press conference conducted at the Century Plaza Hotel in Los Angeles on July 1, 1975, an event timed to coincide with the funeral of Williams and Coler. The Bureau's replacement story said the warrant being served on Jimmy Eagle was dated July 7, nearly two weeks after the firefight and is for the petty theft of a pair of used cowboy boots rather than "kidnapping and assault," as the Bureau originally informed the press.

61. The differences in evidentiary rulings extended by the judge presiding over the Peltier and Butler/Robideau cases account for the different outcomes of the two trials and are analyzed quite well in Messerschmidt's *The Trial of Leonard Peltier*. For the Circuit Court's opinion, see United States v. Leonard Peltier 858 F.2d 314, 335 (8th Cir. 1978), cert denied, 440 U.S. 945 (1979).

62. Judge Heaney made his remarks on the CBS program *West 57th Street* in 1989.

Part III: Terrorism and the Role of the Media

Margaret Randall

1. *I, Rigoberta Menchu*, ed. and intro. by Elisabeth Burgos-Debray; trans. Ann Wright (London: Verso Editions NLB, 1983). At the time of the Maryland Institute symposium, Menchu had not yet been awarded the 1992 Nobel Peace Prize.

2. According to Ellen Bass and Laura Davis in their comprehensive handbook on sexual abuse, *The Courage to Heal* (New York: Harper & Row, 1988), "One out of three girls and one out of seven boys are sexually abused by the time they reach the age of eighteen" (p. 20). Florence Rush, in *The Best Kept Secret: Sexual Abuse of Children* (New York: McGraw-Hill, 1980), tells us that "there seems to be a consensus . . . that the offender is overwhelmingly male (from about 80 to 90 percent), that about 80 percent of the time he is a family relative or friend of the victim and her family, that actual incidents are grossly under-reported and that the offender behavior crosses all social, economic, and racial lines" (p. 2).

3. Judith Lewis Herman, *Trauma and Recovery: The Aftermath of Violence—From Domestic Abuse to Political Terror* (New York: HarperCollins, 1992).

4. My copy of this is the old Masters of Perception Press edition, Bangor, Salinas, Sebastopol, 1970, from a time when much of Reich's work was unpublished or censored. It and his other books have since appeared commercially from a variety of publishing houses.

5. Alice Miller, *Drama of the Gifted Child* (New York: Basic Books, 1981), *For Your Own Good* (New York: Farrar, Straus & Giroux, 1983), and *Thou Shalt Not Be Aware* (New York: New American Library, 1986).

6. Miller, *Thou Shalt Not Be Aware*, p. 2.

7. Discussed in detail in Alice Miller, *Banished Knowledge* (New York: Doubleday, 1990), ch. 4, "Theories as a Protective Shield."

8. Alice Miller, *Pictures of a Childhood* (New York: Farrar, Straus & Giroux, 1986).

9. Miller, *Banished Knowledge*.

10. Alice Miller, *Breaking Down the Wall of Silence* (New York: Dutton, 1991).

11. Ibid., p. 31.

12. Many victims of sexual and other types of abuse describe "removing" themselves from the scene of torture, actually "floating above their own body as it was being abused and watching the event with a detachment that informs the rest of their lives."

13. Miller, *Breaking Down the Wall of Silence*, p. viii.

14. Michael Shelden, "Not Just Another Apocalyptian," a review of a book on Orwell by Samuel Hynes, *New York Times Book Review*, November 3, 1991.

15. Adrienne Rich, *On Lies, Secrets, and Silence* (New York: Norton, 1979), p. 187.

16. Ibid., p. 188.

17. "Rebellion," in *Rebellion: Essays 1980-1991* (Ithaca, N.Y.: Firebrand Books, 1991), pp. 22-23.

Nina Felshin, Afterword: Women and Children First— Terrorism on the Home Front

1. The impact of the William Kennedy Smith rape trial should not be underestimated.

2. "Mission Statement," Women's Action Coalition, 1992.

3. All statistics refer to the United States. "Facts on Domestic Violence," Y Care, Chicago, no date.

4. *Crime in the US: Uniform Crime Reports* (Washington, D.C.: FBI/U.S. Government Printing Office, 1987).

5. *Rape in America: A Report to the Nation* (National Center and Crime Victims Research and Treatment Center, 1992).

6. Obviously, some of these works and projects were executed after *Beyond Glory*. Deborah Small (*NHI*) was represented in *Beyond Glory* with *Atrocities Management*.

7. Although the intention is different, Alison Saar's sculpture in *Beyond Glory, Briar Patch*, 1988, resonates with Smith's work.

8. Artist's statement in *Exploring the Unknown Self: Self Portraits of Contemporary Women* (Tokyo: Tokyo Metropolitan Museum of Photography, 1991), p. 116.

9. Ibid.

10. Donna Ferrato, *Living with the Enemy* (New York: Aperture, 1991); photographs from the book were exhibited at the Eye Gallery, San Francisco, in fall 1992.

Photos from the Exhibition
Beyond Glory: Re-Presenting Terrorism

Refer to pp.287–89 for descriptions of the works corresponding to the numbers below.

285

16 17 33-40

31

3

31 51

List of Works in _Beyond Glory:_
Re-Presenting Terrorism

1 Helen Altman
Frost Queen
electric freezer with window, ice hearts,
steel basket, internal light
36 1/2" x 22" x 22"
1991
courtesy of the artist

2 Ralph Arlyck/
Timed Exposures
Current Events
film
1989
courtesy of the artist

3 Eric Avery
Face of Liberty
linocut overprint on poster
25" x 35" x 2"
1990
courtesy of the artist

4 Luis Cruz Azaceta
Latin American Victims of Dictators:
Oppression, Torture and Murder
acrylic on unstretched canvas
76 1/2" x 168"
1987
courtesy of Frumkin-Adams Gallery,
New York

5 Greg Barsamian
Putti
mechanized sculpture
8" x 18"
1990
courtesy of the artist

6 Alan Belcher
Grenade Carry-on
photographs on suitcase
dimensions variable
1988
courtesy of Brooke and Carolyn
Alexander through the Josh Baer Gallery,
New York

7 _Guns_
photographs on suitcases
dimensions variable
1988
courtesy of private collector
through the Josh Baer Gallery, New York

8 Terry Berkowitz
T/error
room-sized installation with audio,
video, and scattered debris
1992
courtesy of the artist

9 Chris Bratton/
Annie Goldson
Counterterror series
video (3 parts)
1991
courtesy of the artists

10 Nancy Burson
Big Brother
computer generated photo montage
24 1/2" x 30 1/4"
1983
courtesy of Jayne H. Baum Gallery, New York

11 Robert Byrd
Torture: The Shadow of the Beast
documentary film
1989
courtesy of the artist

12-14 Shu Lea Cheang
Until Daybreak: Korea
Produced by Han-Kyoreh
A Legacy of Violence: The Philippines
Produced by Nick DeoCampo
The Generation after Martial Law: Taiwan
Green Team Video Collective
(all 3 videos, 1990; coordinated by Shu Lea
Cheang)
courtesy of the artist

15 Mel Chin
Jilavia Prison Bed for Father Gheorghe
Calciu-Dumitreasa
steel, cotton
70" x 40" x 36"
1982
courtesy of the Frumkin-Adams Gallery,
New York

16 Lynne Cohen
Practice Range
undated
silver print
28 1/2" x 36"

17 *War Games*
silver print
undated
28 1/2" x 36"
courtesy of P.P.O.W. Gallery, New York

18 Martin Doblemeier/Journey
Communications
Grounds for Peace
documentary video
1991
courtesy of the artist

19 Willie Doherty
Same Difference
video installation
1991
20' x 20'
courtesy of the artist through the
Tom Cugliani Gallery, New York

20 Rita Duffy
Freestate General
acrylic and charcoal on paper
55" x 41" x 2"
1991
courtesy of the artist

21 *Off to War*
charcoal and acrylic on paper
55" x 41" x 2"
1991
courtesy of the artist

22 Leon Golub
Mercenaries I
acrylic on canvas
116" x 186 1/2"
1976
courtesy of the Eli Broad Family
Foundation, Santa Monica

23-26 Paul Graham
Hunger Strike Protest
1984
Unionist Posters on Tree
1985
Turf Lodge, Belfast
1984
Graffiti
1984
color photographs
30" x 40" each
courtesy of P.P.O.W. Gallery, New York

27 Gregory Green
Untitled (traces)
photo paper with 50, 000 volt electrical burn
25 3/4" x 30"
1990-91

28 *Untitled*
12 gauge shotgun shell through paper
60" x 90"
1990-91

29 *Assault*
12 saw blade floor sculpture with
electric motor
24" x 13 1/2" x 13 1/2"
1989
courtesy of the artist

30 Craig Kalpakjian
Station (bullet proof casket)
bullet resistant plexiglass
23" x 75" x 17"
1990
courtesy of the artist

31 Annette Lemieux
Hidden Tool
bronze cast in book
11 1/4" x 17 1/4" x 1 1/2" in table case
1989-90
courtesy of Brooke and Carolyn Alexander
through the Josh Baer Gallery, New York

32 Joseph Lewis and A. Tapia-Urzua
Book of Ibid
video
1991
courtesy of the artist

33-40 Mary Lum
Salvadoran Rights Abuses
Anti-Terrorist Command Post
IRA Attacks 10 Downing Street
South Africa Cracks Down
An American F-16 Fighter-Bomber...
House of Florida Family Set Afire
14 Killed in Israeli Bus Plunge
Man Accused of Murder Dies
8" x 10" each
from the *Accidents Happen* series, 1987-89,
and from the *Historical Present* series,
charcoal on paper
1990-91
courtesy of the artist

41 Daniel Martinez
Ignore Dominant Culture
four-color offset on opaline in lightbox
40" x 78" x 6"
1990
courtesy of the artist

42 Juris Padnieks, Producer and Director,
Roger James, Executive Producer
Baltic Requiem
documentary film
1991
courtesy of WETA Public Television
Station, Washington, D.C.

43 Bruce Pavlow
Design for Living
photograph, plexiglas, plywood
40"x34"x3"
1990
courtesy of the artist

44 Fred Riskin
The Assassin and the Holy Ghost
36"x18" introduction
27 11"x18" unframed photographs
with texts
20 minute ambient music tape loop
1987
courtesy of the artist with special
thanks to the Tartt Gallery,
Washington, D.C.

45 Nina Rosenblum
Through the Wire
documentary film
1990
courtesy of the artist and Daedalus
Productions, New York

46 Martha Rosler
*A Simple Case for Torture, or, How
to Sleep at Night*
video
1983
courtesy of Nina Felshin

47 Lisa Rudman
Geronimo Pratt
video
1988
courtesy of the artist

48 Alison Saar
Briar Patch
wood, wire, nails, caulk, iron, wax
9 1/2"x33"x10"
1988
courtesy of a private collector through
the Jan Baum Gallery, Los Angeles

49 Jayce Salloum and
Elia Suleiman
*Intifada: Speaking for Oneself . . .
Speaking for Others . . .*
video
1990
courtesy of the artists

50 Deborah Small
Atrocities Management
acrylic on wood and masonite
6'x5'x8'
1988
courtesy of the artist

51 Nancy Spero
Search and Destroy
wood and zinc-cut stamps and zinc-cut stamp
collage on paper, printed in color with paint
20"x156"
1977
courtesy of the Josh Baer Gallery, New York

52 T.O.D.T.
Bike Bomb
mixed media
60"x84"x51"
1987
courtesy of the Middendorf Gallery,
Washington, D.C.

53 Pat Ward Williams
Day of the Dead—Little Angels
photographs, window frame, paint, text
74"x42"x3"
1989
courtesy of the artist

54-57 Krzysztof Wodiczko
Arco de la Victoria, Madrid, Spain
1991
Monument Campanile, Venice, Italy
1986
Facade of Memorial Hall, Dayton, Ohio
1983
*Soldiers and Sailors Memorial Arch, Grand
Army Plaza, Brooklyn, NY*
1985
all-black and white photographs of
projections
16"x18" each
courtesy of the Josh Baer Gallery, New York

Film and Video in _Beyond Glory:_
Re-Presenting Terrorism

Counterterror
1991
Produced by Chris Bratton and Annie Goldson
three 30 minute segments

This three-part award-winning documentary series examines how the label "terrorism" has been used to criminalize political dissent: _Counterterrorism: The North of Ireland_ (the IRA and the British shoot-to-kill policy in Strabane County, Tyrone) and _Framing the Panthers in Black and White_ and _From Death Row: Mumia Abu Jamal._

Geronimo Pratt
1988
Lisa Rudman/PCTV
27 minutes

The former leader of the Black Panther party has been imprisoned since 1970 for a crime he did not commit. Geronimo tells his story about growing up in the segregated South, serving two tours in Vietnam, how the FBI framed him, and how he views the current situation of black people.

Current Events
Ralph Arlyck
55 minutes

Unspeakable things occur daily in the world, but for most of us they are just momentary interference on the screens of our personal lives. Distant people and terrible events break the surface, thrash around for a few days, and then disappear, as if that other reality were only a dream. How should we bridge the gap between concern and action, between What Is and What Ought to Be? Arlyck's film is a sensitive yet humorous, disturbing yet inspiring, examination of life in a cocoon of relative comfort.

The Book of Ibid
1990
Joseph Lewis and A. Tapia-Urzua
5 ½ minutes

This 5 ½ minute exploding barrage of images and voice questions the polarity of race, class, gender, friendship, and politics.

Through the Wire
1990
Nina Rosenblum
narrated by Susan Sarandon
77 minutes

This award-winning documentary provides a penetrating look at the personal stories of three female prisoners who received lengthy sentences for non-violent, politically motivated crimes. In the controversial high-security prison unit in Lexington, Kentucky, the prisoners were held in isolation for two years, kept under twenty-four-hour surveillance and were sexually humiliated in daily strip searches.

Baltic Requiem
produced and directed by Juris Padnieks for public television station WETA, Washington, D.C.
executive producer: Roger James, Central Independent Television
narrated by Hedrick Smith
87 minutes

An astonishingly beautiful film centered around the Lithuanian Song Festival where over thirty choirs sing songs banned since the Nazis invaded their land. The power and commitment of the struggle of the Baltic States in seeking their recent independence from the Soviet Union could never have been more beautifully witnessed. Our special thanks to WETA for such a wondrous achievement.

Grounds for Peace

1991

produced by Martin Doblemeier/Journey Communications

57 minutes

Grounds for Peace highlights the Corrymeela Community's struggle for peace in Northern Ireland, where peacemaking is a dangerous business. Shown are the efforts of Corrymeela to bring together Catholics and Protestants, with hopefulness for the future.

Until Daybreak: Korea

produced by Shu Lea Cheang

curated by Hye Jung Park

60 minutes

As video camcorders became more widely distributed in Asia, video makers have become activists toward social and political change. This tape features South Koreans' decade-long street insurrections from the point of view of students, farmers, and workers who have stood in the front line for the Reunification movement against economic exploitation and militarism.

The Generation after Martial Law: Taiwan

produced by Shu Lea Cheang

curated by Ching Jan Lee

60 minutes

Alternative media makers have joined farmers, workers and students to press for social and political change after thirty-eight years of martial law was lifted in 1987.

A Legacy of Violence: The Philippines
produced by Shu Lea Cheang
curated by Nick Deocampo
60 minutes

In a weekly comic show, "Sic O'Clock News," a Ms. Aquino appears at "D Wayt Haus" where a genial Mr. Bush twists her arm for continued military bases. In addition, an emotional melodrama uses double exposures and several juxtapositions to address the current military repression.

Torture: The Shadow of the Beast
1989
produced by Robert Byrd
56 minutes

This film shows how the systematic use of torture controls and enforces behavior, maintaining fear and distrust in Third World countries.

Intifada: Speaking for Oneself . . . Speaking for Others . . .
Jayce Salloum and Elia Suleiman
45 minutes

Taking snippets from feature films (*Exodus, Lawrence of Arabia, Black Sunday*, etc.) and network news, Suleiman and Salloum have constructed an oddly wry narrative mimicking the history of Mideast politics. The storehouse of misconstrued ideas about Arab culture is shown in all its cinematic splendor.

A Simple Case for Torture, or, How to Sleep at Night
1983
a videotape by Martha Rosler
62 minutes

Rosler rescues semiotics from its ivory tower with a work that is a complex manipulation of newspaper clippings, magazine articles, and paperback texts. She builds a frightening case against media manipulation of information on terrorism and torture, which cloaks the involvement of American business and government in human rights violations around the world.

Symposium Participants:

Maurice Berger
Cultural historian and art critic. He has taught and lectured extensively and has written for numerous publications including *Art in America*, *Artforum*, and *The Village Voice*. He is the author of two books, *Labyrinths: Robert Morris, Minimalism, And the 1960s,* Harper & Row, 1989, and *How Art Becomes History,* Harper Collins, 1992.

Chris Bratton and Annie Goldson
Independent video producers and media educators. Chris is currently teaching at the Art Institute of Chicago, and Annie is a Lecturer in Video Production and Cultural Studies at Brown University's Center for Modern Culture and Media.

David J. Brown
Artist and curator who has been Director of Exhibitions at the Maryland Institute, College of Art since 1989.

Ward Churchill
Associate Professor of Communications, rostered in American Indian Studies, Center for Studies of Ethnicity and Race in America, University of Colorado, author of scores of publications including *Critical Issues in Native North America, Volume II*, edited, International Work Group on Indigenous Affairs Document No. 68, Copenhagen, 1991, and *The American Indian Movement: A Socio-Political History*, Twayne Publishers, 1992.

The Honorable Ramsey Clark
U.S. Attorney General from 1967 to 1969.

Alexander Cockburn
Journalist, editor, and author who writes "Beat the Devil," a column for *The Nation*. His articles have also appeared in the *Wall Street Journal*, *Village Voice*, *Atlantic Monthly*, *Harper's,* and *New York Review*, to name a few.

Edward S. Herman
Professor of Finance, Wharton School, University of Pennsylvania, author of numerous articles and books including *The Terrorism Industry: The Experts and Institutions That Shape Our View of Terror* (with Gerry Sullivan), Pantheon Books, 1990.

Robert Merrill
Chair of the Language and Literature Department at the Maryland Institute and author of four books including *Ethics/Aesthetics: Postmodern Positions* and *Sir Thomas Malory and the Cultural Crisis of the Late Middle Ages*.

Michael Parenti
Scholar, lecturer, and author of articles and books including *Make-Believe Media: The Politics of Entertainment*, St. Martin's Press, and *Ethnic and Political Attitudes*, Arno Press.

Margaret Randall
Writer, photographer, political activist, and author of over sixty books including *Gathering Rage: The Failure of 20th Century Revolution to Develop a Feminist Agenda*, Monthly Review Press, 1992; *Dancing With the Doe*, West End Press, 1992; and *Santino's Daughters Revisited*, Rutgers University Press (forthcoming, 1994). Ms. Randall lived in Mexico, Cuba, and Nicaragua for twenty-three years and won a five-year court battle with the U.S. Immigration and Naturalization Service to remain in the United States in August 1989.

Randall Robinson
Director of TRANSAFRICA, an organization based in the United States to support the development of African nations and to promote an understanding of the problems Africa is having with Americans.

Angela Sanbrano
Executive Director of Citizens in Support of the Peoples of El Salvador, Washington, D.C. (CISPES).

William Schaap
Co-editor, *Covert Action Information Bulletin*, managing director, Sheridan Square Press, Director for the Institute for Media Analysis, Inc., and managing editor of *Lies Of Our Times*.